AF478840

Women *Picturing* Women

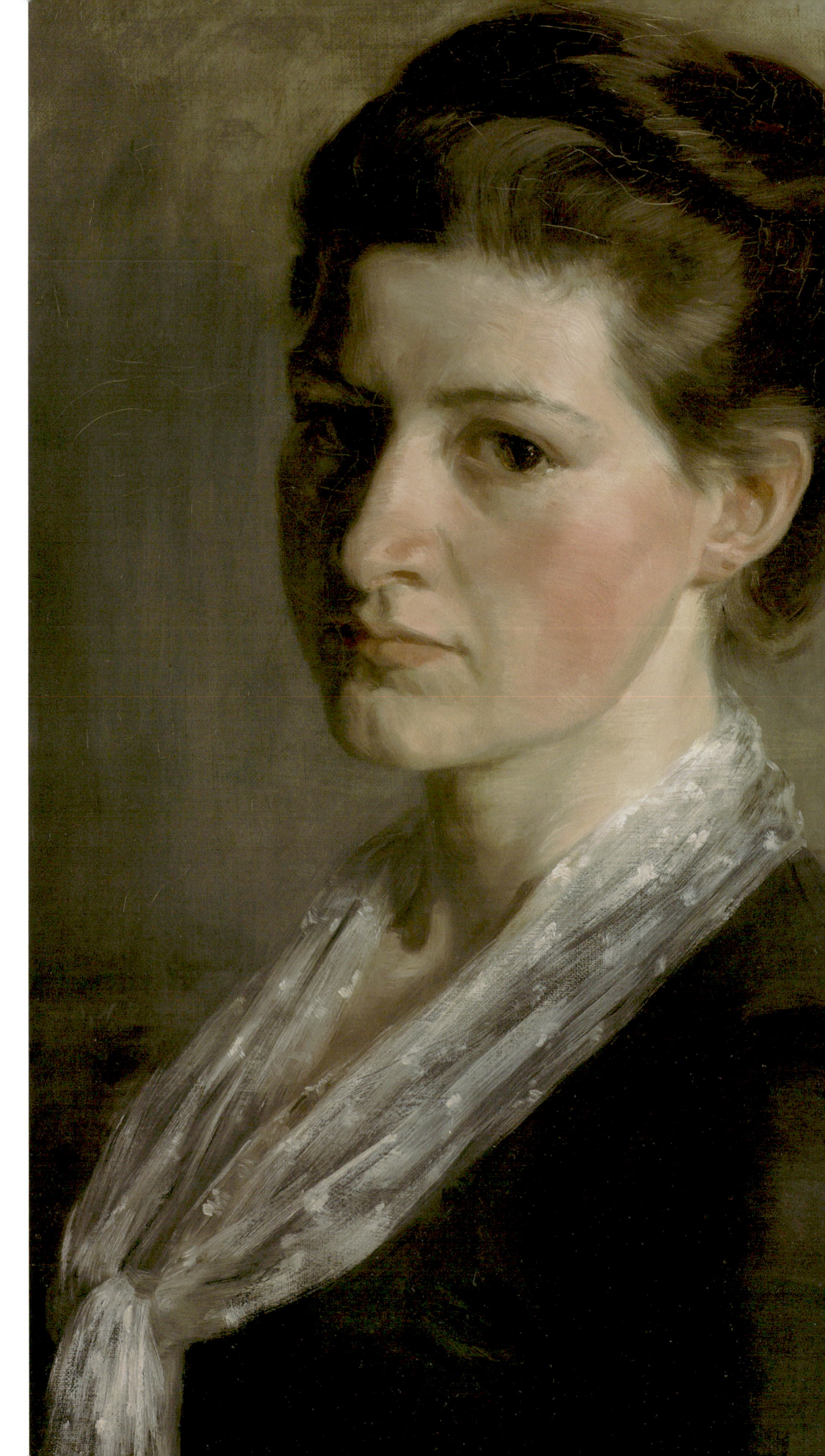

Women *Picturing* Women

From Personal Spaces to Public Ventures

Patricia Phagan

FRANCES LEHMAN LOEB ART CENTER
VASSAR COLLEGE | POUGHKEEPSIE, NEW YORK

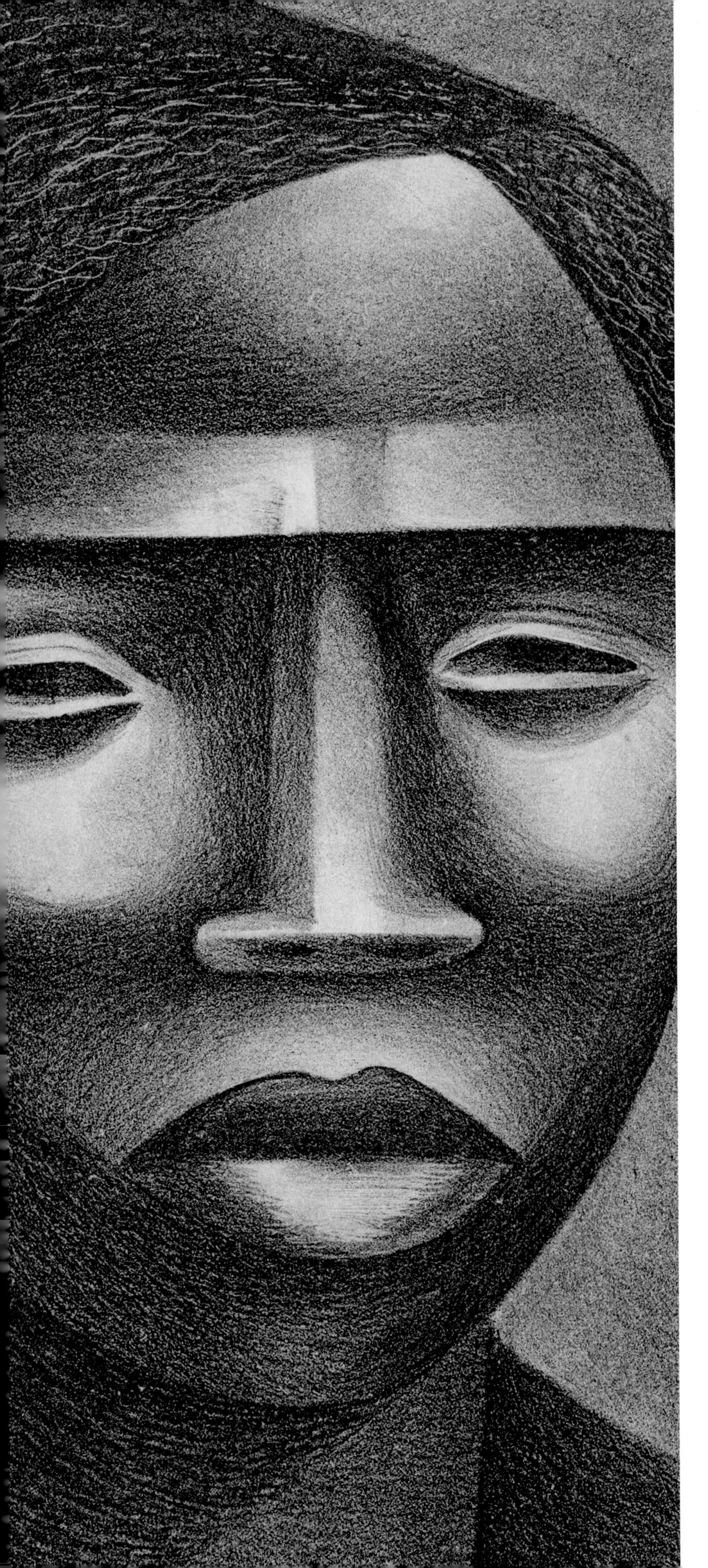

Contents

Director's Foreword

In the April 1, 1877, issue of *Vassar Miscellany*, the student news-paper, it was announced that the Observatory had been temporarily converted for a "few days into a sculptor's studio, with Miss Emma Brigham as the artist [and] Prof. [Maria] Mitchell as the subject." It was Vassar College's first commission of a female artist to portray a contemporary female figure, paid for by students in the senior astronomy class. Mitchell, one of nine faculty members hired to teach at the newly established institution, was already highly praised as the first woman elected Fellow of the American Academy of Arts and Sciences in 1848. Brigham, class of 1877 (1855–1881), who had just started to make a name for herself as a gifted artist, continued to work diligently. She eventually wrote to Mitchell in early 1878 that one prominent sculptor "considers [the commission] the finest bust I have done" and requested additional sittings in her Brooklyn studio. The relationship between the artist and her subject was clearly very close, as the same lengthy letter went into considerable detail about the circumstances surrounding the younger woman's engagement. She added, "I will be very pleased to see you in the sitters [*sic*] chair again, for I have a great deal to talk to you about."[1] The modeling sessions served as opportunities for conversations between them. Later that year, a plaster version of the bust was subsequently exhibited on Class Day in the parlor in Main Building, and—after additional

fundraising—a metal cast was made in 1896 and installed the following year on the facade of the Observatory, where it remains to this day (see page 8).

In the ensuing years, the work of an increasing number of women artists was exhibited in various College buildings and discussed in print, including paintings by Lilly Martin Spencer, Cecilia Beaux, and Mary Cassatt, all of whom are discussed in the following text. The subjects are not always identified in the early references, but in the case of Spencer the *Vassar Miscellany* of June 1, 1880, noted that the large female allegorical subject of "Truth Unveiling Falsehood" (1869, unlocated) on view in the Art Gallery had previously been "placed in the Woman's [*sic*] Pavilion at the Centennial Exhibition . . . in Philadelphia," established in 1876 to display women's contributions to arts, sciences, education, and industry.

Perhaps the most well-publicized example of a female painter depicting a female subject within the first sixty years of the College's establishment is *The Great Wonder: A Vision of the Apocalypse* by Violet Oakley (1874–1961). The painting, which has been on view continuously in Alumnae House since its completion in 1924, was a memorial to the painter's sister (see page 9). Hester Caldwell Oakley Ward (1871–1905) was a member of the class of 1891, and the painting was commissioned by one of her roommates. The central panel of the colossal triptych depicts, in

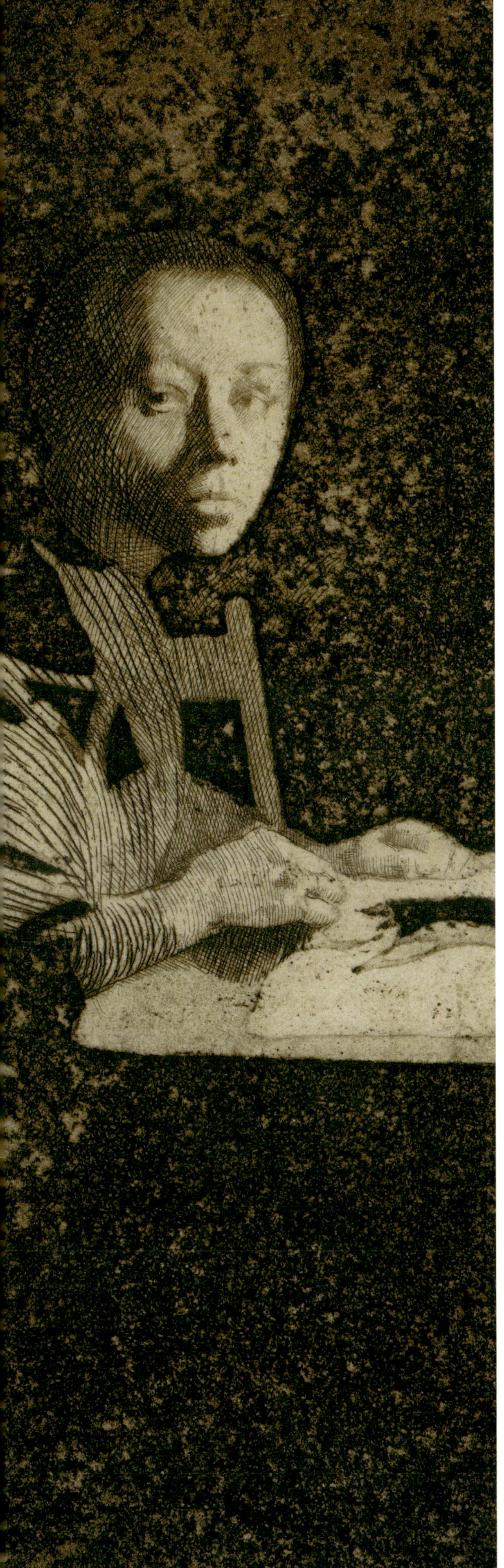

the words of the artist, "The Ideal Woman," who, in the words of the book of Revelation, is "clothed with the sun, and the moon under her feet, and upon her head a crown of twelve stars."[2] Many surviving drawings, watercolors, and other documents record the undertaking, which functioned as the centerpiece for an elaborate interior design project. The space was dedicated with a sumptuous medieval pageant orchestrated by Oakley to commemorate the opening of the building.

The aforementioned campus artworks serve to highlight both the private and public spheres discussed at length in this volume. These commissions honor the personal esteem for specific individuals—documented in letters along with the publication of detailed accounts—yet are visible for everyone to admire. In the case of Emma Brigham's bust of Maria Mitchell, it was the first sculpture to be displayed conspicuously (and more than a century before a bronze cast of the College's founder was finally installed outdoors), and still holds a special place in Vassar's history. Created nearly fifty years later, the so-called Living Room in Alumnae House, the elegant setting and objects designed and executed by Violet Oakley, endures as an environment for reflection and contemplation. Further examples of art by women in the Loeb's collection, along with their historical contexts and in-depth biographical details of the artists, are explored extensively and expertly in the following pages.

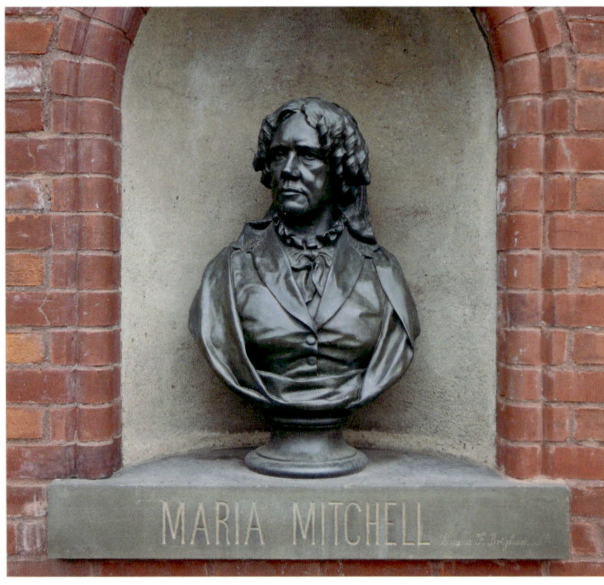

Emma F. Brigham, *Maria Mitchell*, 1877–78, cast in 1896. Coated zinc. Maria Mitchell Observatory, Vassar College

Perhaps not surprisingly, many of the drawings, prints, sculptures, and photographs selected for this exhibition were added during the years that Linda Nochlin, class of 1951, taught at Vassar College, from 1952 to 1980. During those years, the Vassar College Art Gallery presented more historical and contemporary women-centered exhibitions than ever before. Nochlin's innovative teaching and scholarship, including the publication a half century ago of her seminal article "Why Have There Been No Great Women Artists?," formed the basis of a new feminist art history.

I want to acknowledge the tireless efforts of Patricia Phagan, the Philip and Lynn Straus Curator of Prints and Drawings, who is responsible for the success of this project from conception to the final installation. During my short tenure at Vassar College, I have come to count on her supreme professionalism, profound expertise, and sharp intellect. *Women Picturing Women* is evidence of her considerable knowledge of the Loeb's collection of works produced in different media in Europe and America over the course of four centuries. A number of the works featured in the exhibition were either donated or acquired during her twenty-one-year career at the Loeb, reflecting careful donor stewardship and a keen eye.

Finally, I want to express my sincere appreciation to the many contributors who years ago established the Friends of the Frances Lehman Loeb Art Center Exhibition Fund, which has supported the entire project. It was the donors' preference that the majority of the income be applied regularly to a single, significant initiative, and I can think of no better allocation to celebrate both the strength of the Loeb's collections and the scholarship of one of its highly regarded curators.

T. BARTON THURBER
The Anne Hendricks Bass Director

NOTES

1. Nantucket Maria Mitchell Association, box 11, folder 3, January 21, 1878.

2. Queene Ferry Coonley, "Our Alumnae Home," *Vassar Quarterly* 8, no. 3 (1 May 1923): 108–9.

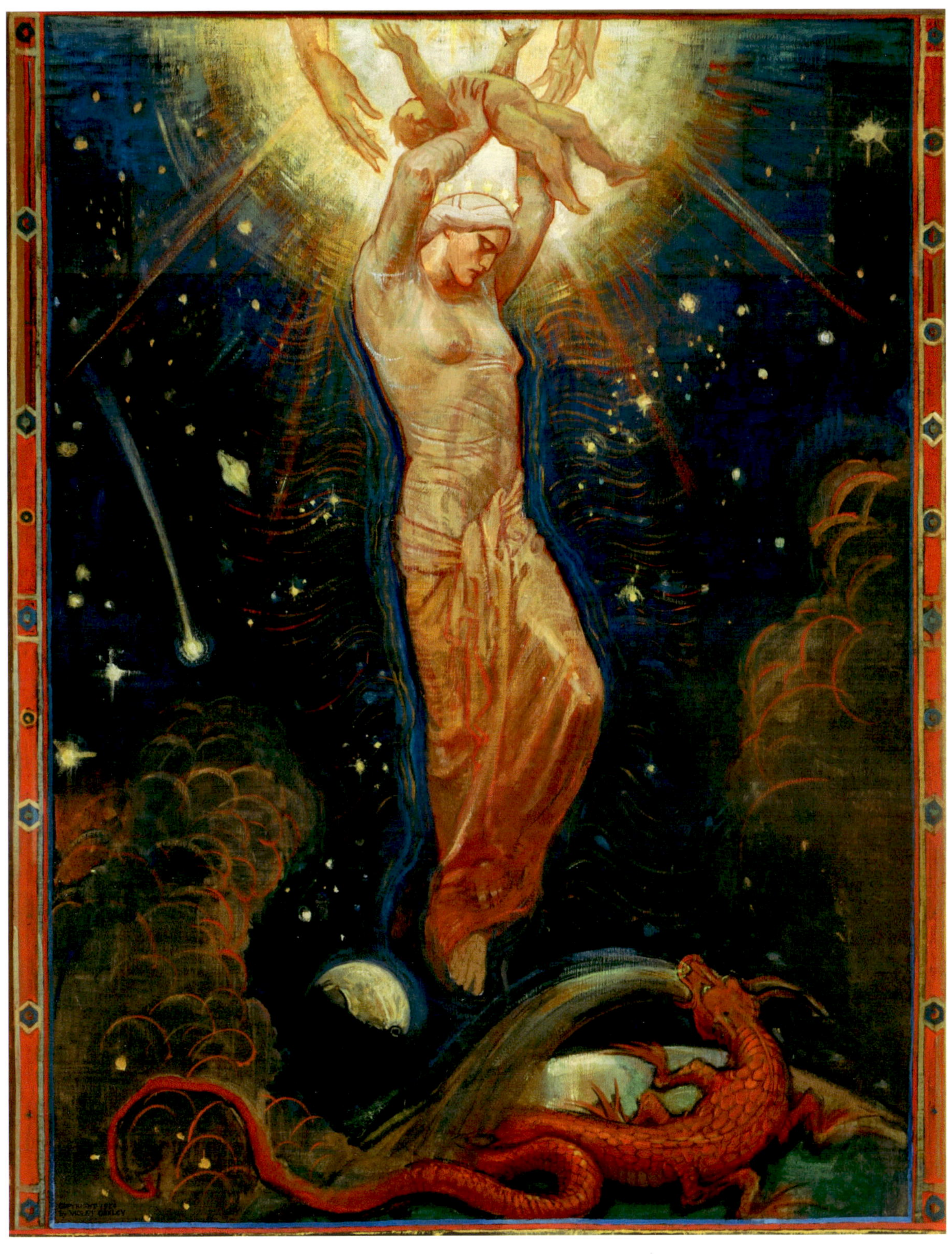

Violet Oakley, *The Great Wonder: A Vision of the Apocalypse*, 1924. Seven-paneled triptych (center panel). Alumnae House, Vassar College

Acknowledgments

The idea for *Women Picturing Women* was prompted when I learned from a colleague that the experiences of women is a thriving research topic among historians. Why not carry this idea into the art museum and look at works of art by women representing women? What experiences could be gleaned? For the exhibition, I sought to explore themes that rose to the surface and ask why an artist would choose this subject, and why, in particular, a woman would choose it. Further, is there a special, unique circumstance that ties the female artist to her female subject or not? And what relationship did these women artists and their subjects have with the world around them?

That colleague, Vassar professor of history Miriam Cohen, deserves my profound thanks. I am also indebted to numerous others. At the Loeb, Director Bart Thurber gave unstinting encouragement and support, as did Deputy Director and Curator Mary-Kay Lombino and Sheryl McMahan, Francine Brown, Joann Potter, Karen Casey Hines, Eleanor White, Margaret Vetare, Delaney Cabellero, and Elizabeth Nogrady, as well as my student assistants Anna Molloy, Breanna Piercy, Emily Lesorogol, and Pindyck Fellow Gillian Redstone. Staff in the Office of Communications, especially Alison Hendrie and Tamar Thibodeau, and Vassar Library, especially Ronald Patkus and Dean Rogers in Special Collections, were always gracious and helpful. Graphic designer Diane Gottardi used her perceptive and nuanced eye to create beautiful exhibition signage. I also owe sincere gratitude to the staff at Williamstown Art Conservation Center, in particular Rebecca Johnston, paper conservator, and Karen Parrino, Brook Prestowitz, and Montserrat Le Mense.

At Lucia | Marquand, we give our deep thanks to Adrian Lucia and Ed Marquand and their talented staff, including Ryan Polich, Melissa Duffes, Kim Kent, Leah Finger, and Kestrel Rundle. I must also point out the intelligent catalogue design by Meghann Ney and award her with my keen thanks. Gina Broze, rights specialist, and Susan Higman Larsen, esteemed editor, were both essential to this project, and I am appreciative of their discerning skills and good humor. Equally, I am grateful for the adjustments and insights of the anonymous peer reviewer who read the following text in this volume.

The works of art in the exhibition would not be in the collection at the Loeb without the donors who gave them, some of whom were the artists themselves—namely, Elizabeth Coffin, class of 1870; Doris Lee; Dorothy Meigs Eidlitz, class of 1914; and Rosalie McKenna, class of 1940—or Vassar alumnae/i. Of those earlier donors, we are indebted to Mary S. Bedell, class of 1873; Mary Thaw Thompson, class of 1877; Elizabeth Gillmer Packard, class of 1894; Louise Woodruff Johnston, class of 1922; Marion Davis Cale, class of 1929; Suzette Morton Davidson, class of 1934; June Bingham Birge, class of 1940; Frances Jones Brooks, class of

1940; Barbara Rodie Shultz, class of 1942; and Dorothy Seiberling Steinberg, class of 1943.

Of later donors, we heartily thank Susan and Steven Hirsch, class of 1971; Alicia Craig Faxon, class of 1952; Mary Coxe Schlosser, class of 1951; and Michael and Joyce Axelrod, class of 1961. I am beholden to Patsy Denton Corbett, granddaughter of Elba Huffman Bouslog, and to an anonymous donor who gave the albumen photograph by Florence Cushing. The estate of Sylvia Sleigh donated the painting by Sleigh a few years ago, and several donors contributed funds for the lithograph by Elizabeth Catlett, and to all of them I am obliged.

I feel privileged to have had art historian Linda Nochlin, class of 1951, as a professor at CUNY Graduate Center many years ago. She was a stimulating teacher, and her rigorous, philosophical approach to art history and advice on word craft were deeply influential. It is fitting that we dedicate this volume to her memory on the fiftieth anniversary of her famous 1971 article, "Why Have There Been No Great Women Artists?"

Lastly, we are grateful to the many contributors to the Friends of the Frances Lehman Loeb Art Center Exhibition Fund.

PATRICIA PHAGAN
The Philip and Lynn Straus
Curator of Prints and Drawings

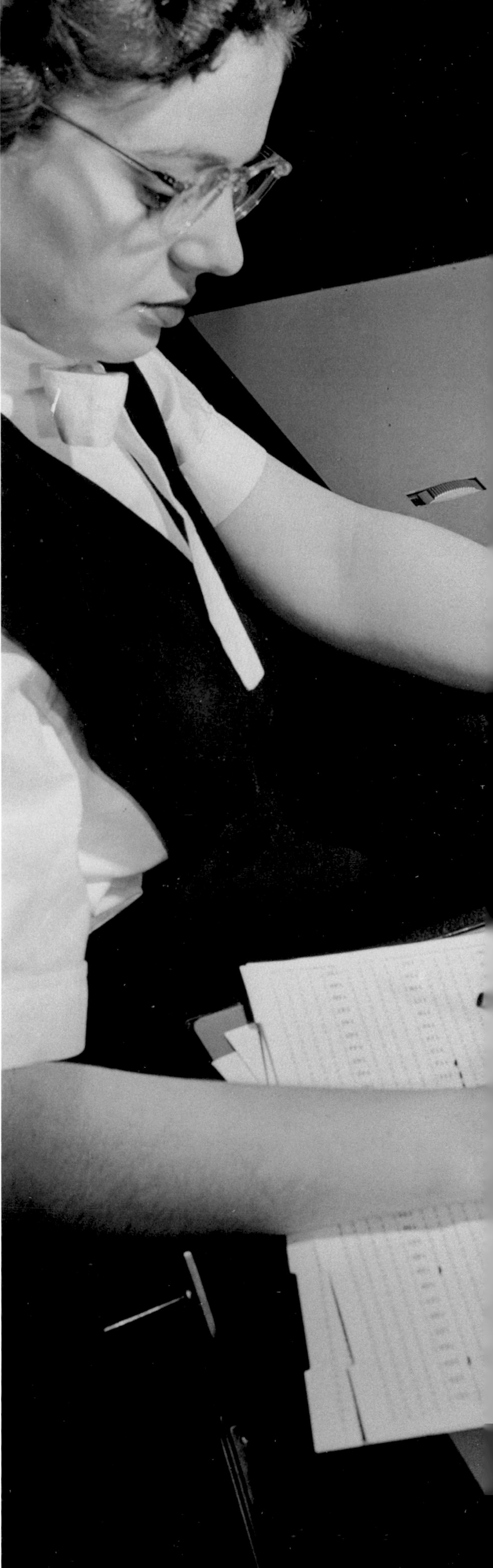

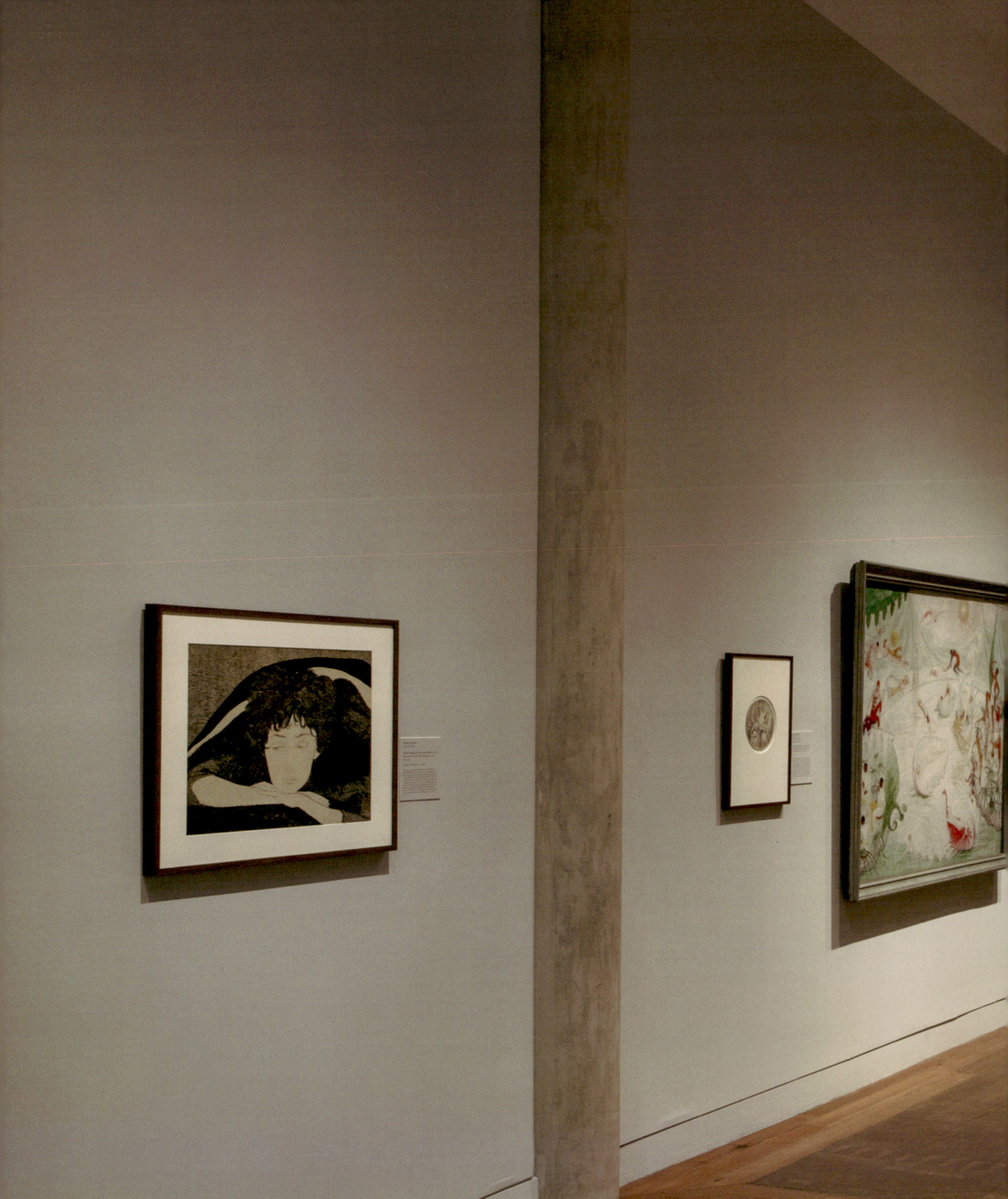

Women *Picturing* Women

From Personal Spaces to Public Ventures

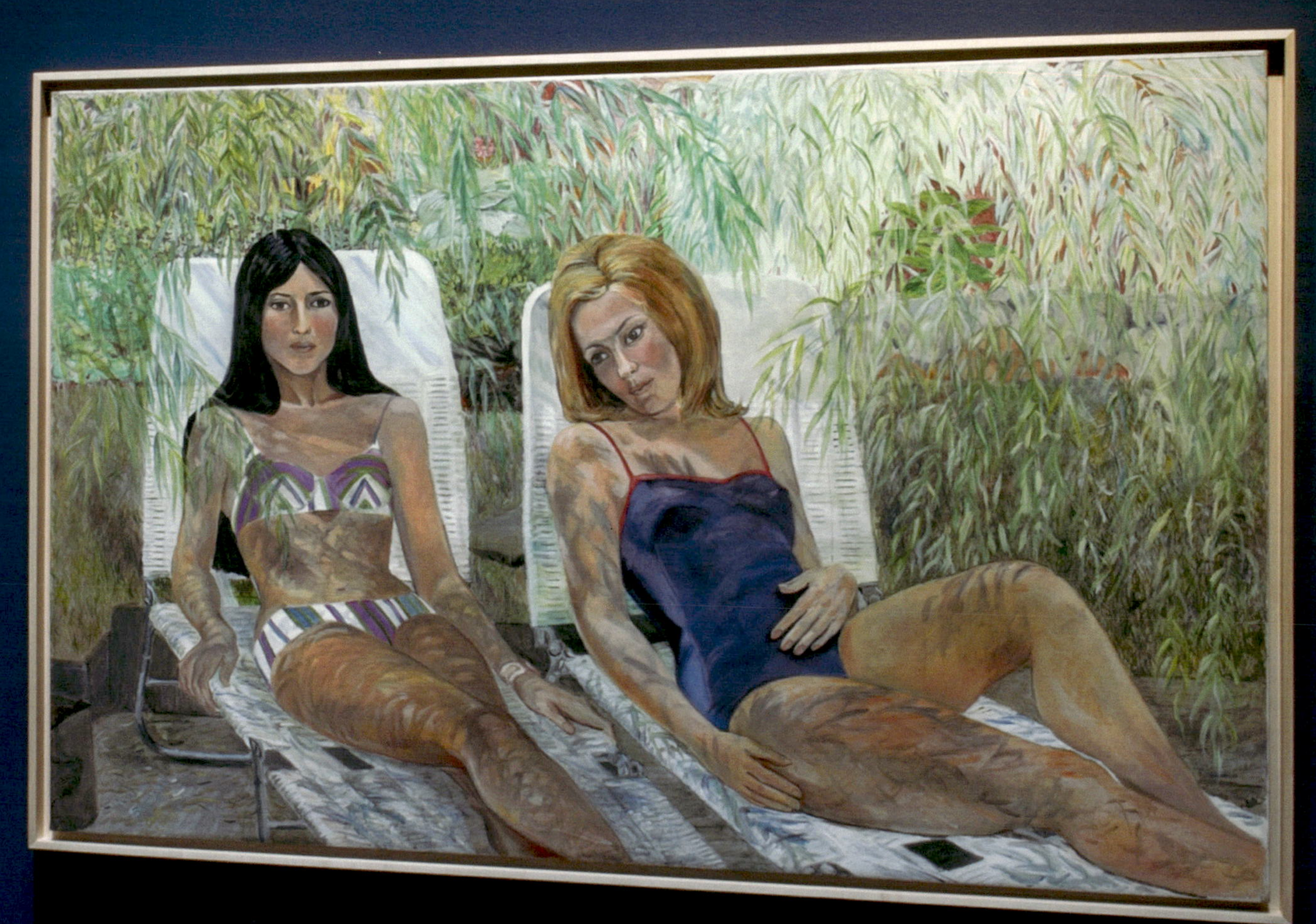

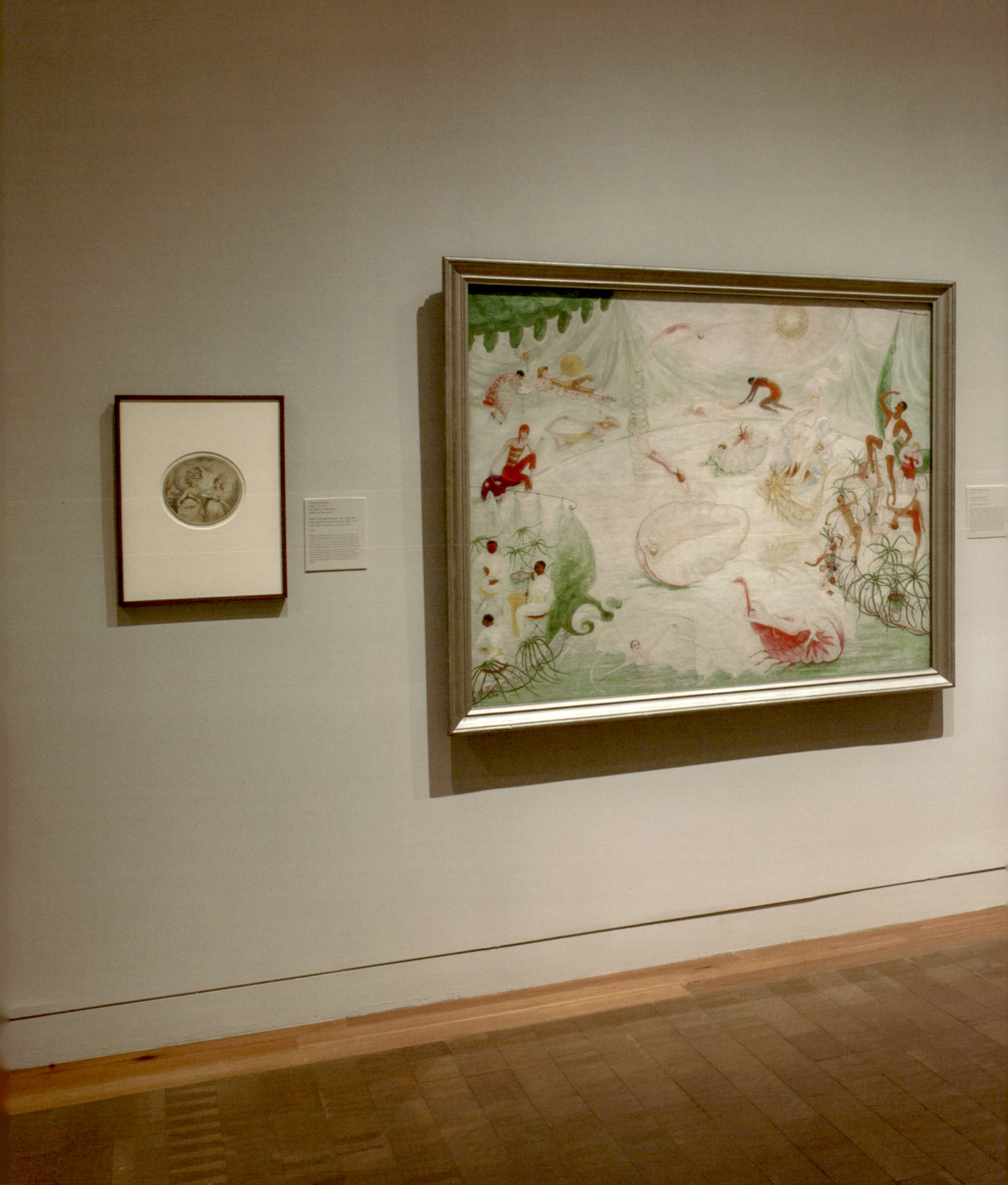

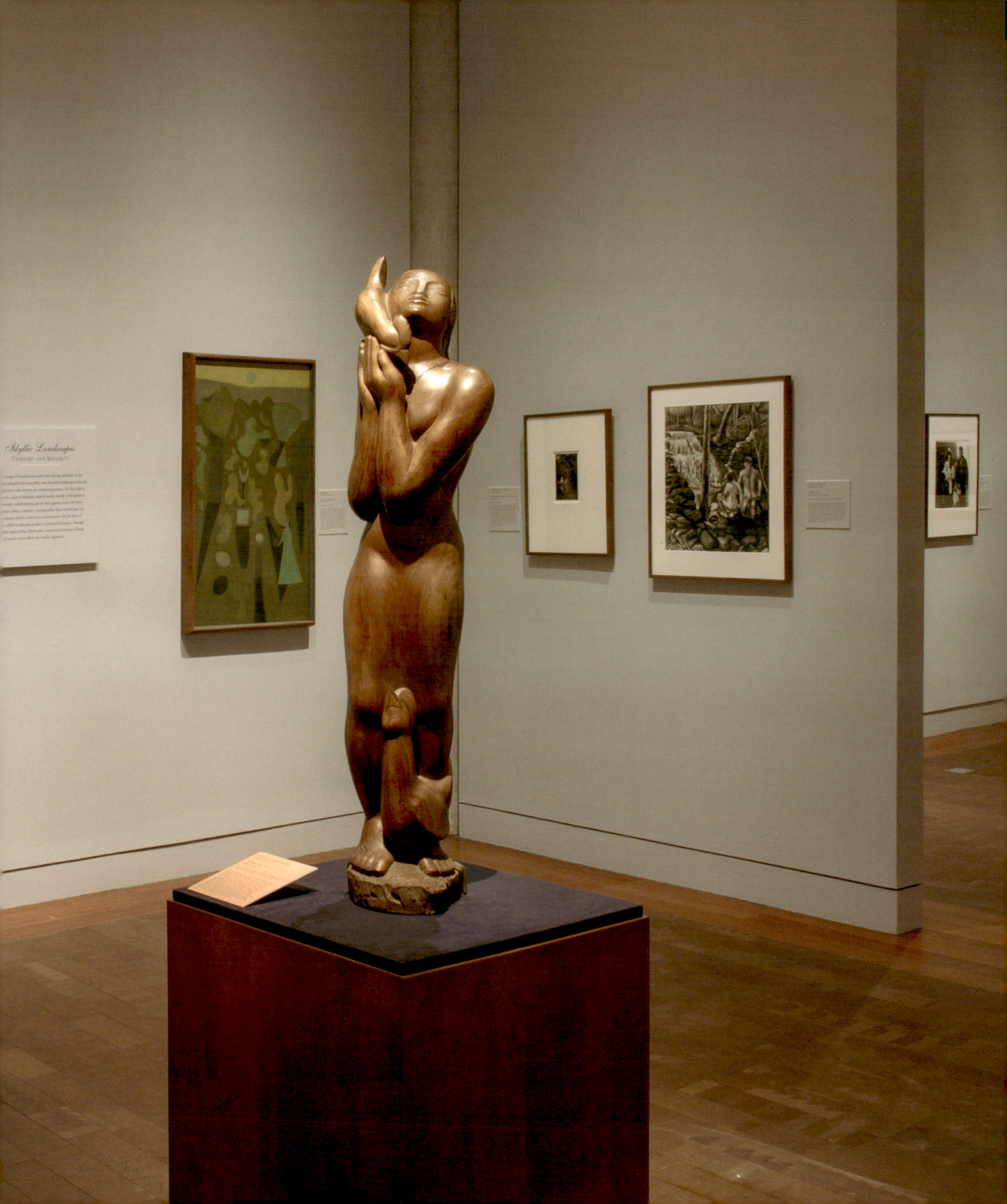

Documentary Photographs
INTO THE STREETS

Photography catapulted a number of women artists into the cities, towns, and countryside in the twentieth century, where they exerted their profound and critical presence. The documentary tradition fostered an influx of new images for women artists, including moments at work or scenes in the street. Their photographs share with painters in the exhibition including Alice Neel that urge to go out into the streets for subject matter. Such was the legacy of Ashcan School leader Robert Henri and his teachings at art schools in Philadelphia and New York in the early twentieth century.

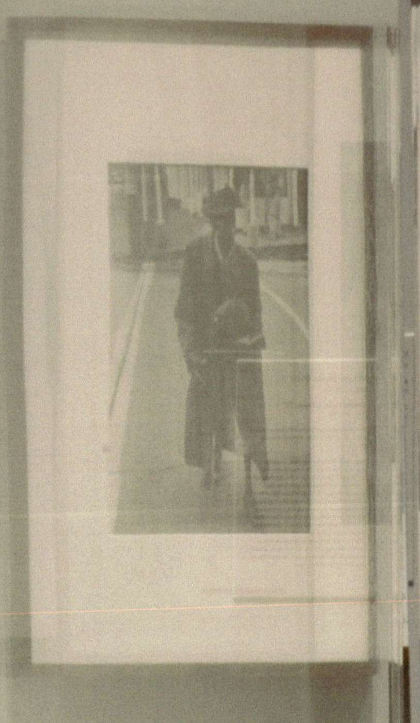

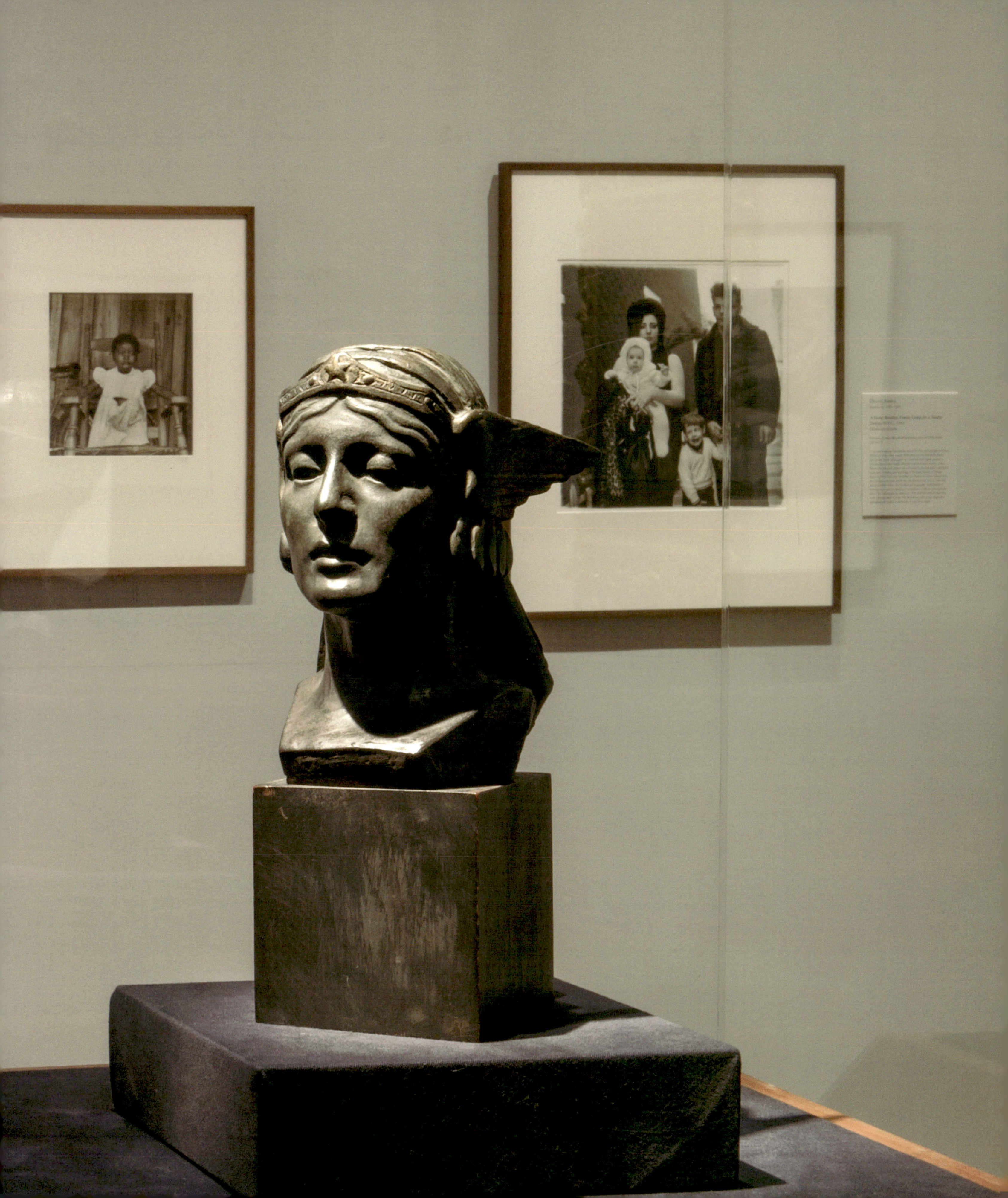

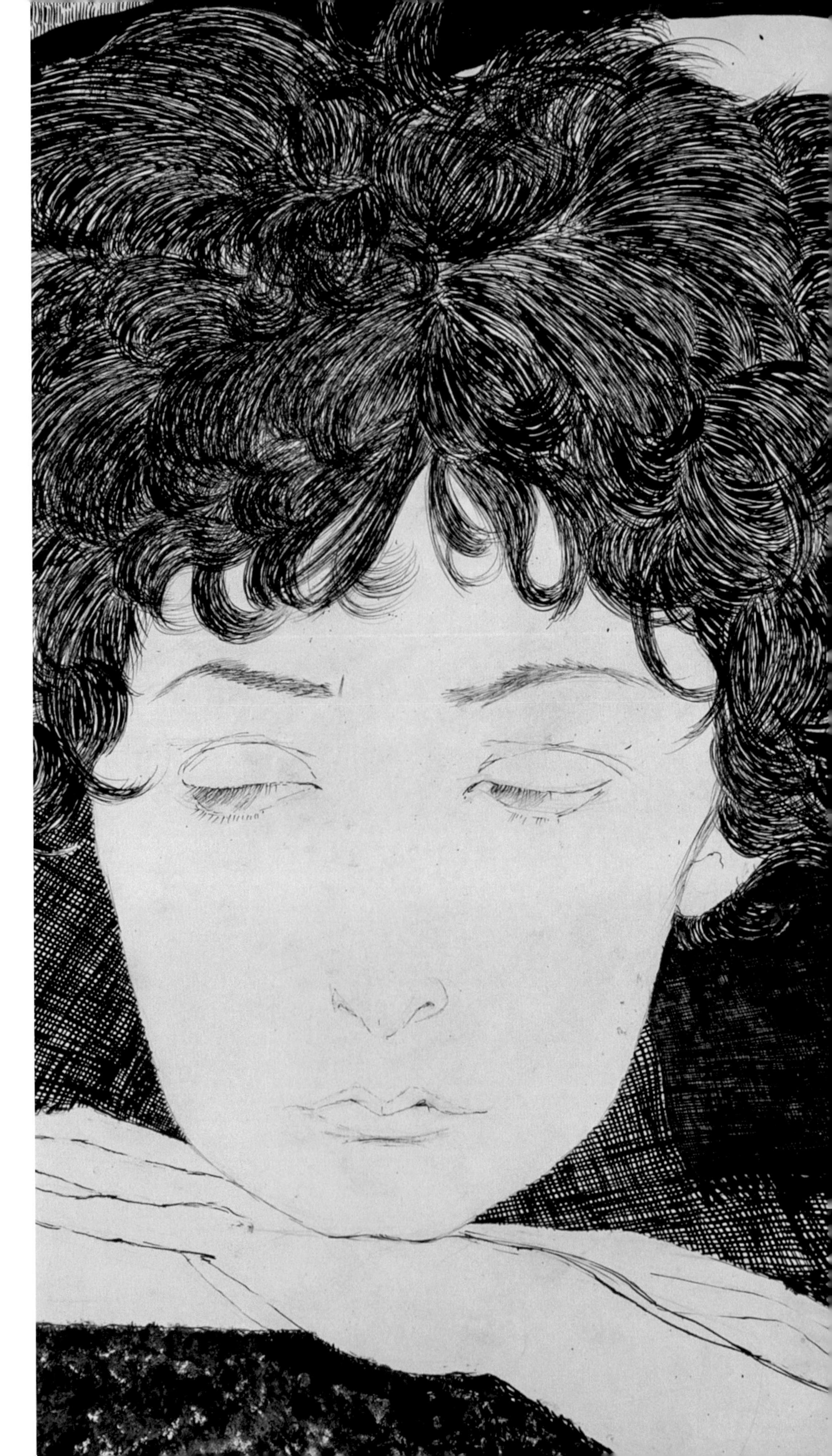

Introduction

From the seventeenth century to the 1960s, female artists often conveyed the idea of an intimate or sheltered enclosure, such as a room or a garden, in their works. Others presented the artist venturing into a public place, such as a street or office, with her camera, or into the intellectual world of religion, classicism, or social critique. *Women Picturing Women* explores these spaces, arenas, and personal and public worlds in the collection of the Frances Lehman Loeb Art Center.

Organized by subject, the exhibition examines thirty-nine works of art by women. Portraits and domestic locales—"spaces of femininity," as Griselda Pollock calls them—appear often.[1] Women chose portraits and domestic scenes overwhelmingly as subjects, as reflected in this informal survey. Given the traditional roles and education of women and girls, home-centered scenes and situations, including views of mothers and children, proliferated in works from the nineteenth century onward, when most of the works in this exhibition were made.[2] Most of the portraits feature the artist herself, or friends, family members, and other favored models. Several writers have suggested that women seem to be peculiarly well equipped to excel in the genre. An obituarist for Angelica Kauffman explained, in 1807, women's great skill at portraits: "for they have received from Nature a susceptibility to seize and express every trait of the countenance, and every peculiar gesture. It is a gift with which, as the weapon

of the weaker sex, Nature has evidently provided them."[3] The feminist art historian Linda Nochlin, Vassar class of 1951, begged to differ:

> In the field of portraiture, women have been particularly active, both in the past and today. This hardly seems accidental: women have, after all, been encouraged, if not coerced, into making responsiveness to the moods, attentiveness to the character traits (and not always the most attractive ones) of others into a lifetime's occupation.[4]

Many of the women in these portraits fill the pictorial space, making them seem assertive and confident, even larger than life. Their direct gazes involve us in a kind of superficial intimacy and telegraph an emotional vulnerability. Others appear more distant, with eyes cast downward or to the side, their modest, deflecting, and unchallenging attitudes befitting traditional social expectations of women.

Idyllic landscapes, mostly of the here and now, also appear, from the late eighteenth century on. Unexpectedly, these landscapes are almost always tied to a domestic environment. Together with the domestic scenes and portraits, these views project a sense of intimacy and an overwhelming sense of privacy that is more often connected to the home, garden, or studio than the public aspects that inform them.

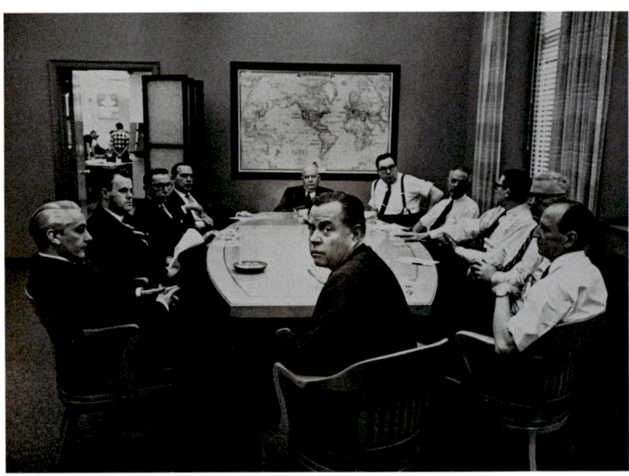

Figure 1. Rosalie Thorne McKenna, *New York Times, Men Around Conference Table*. Gelatin silver print. 7 × 9⅜ in. (17.8 × 23.8 cm). Frances Lehman Loeb Art Center, Vassar College, Gift of the Artist, 1987.53.121

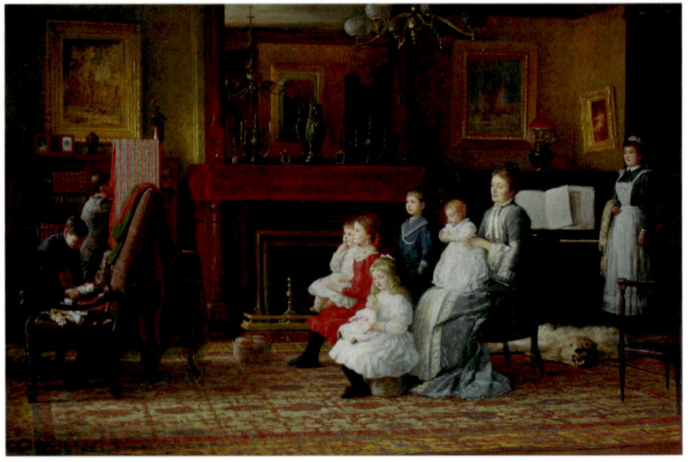

Figure 2. William H. Lippincott, *A Private Rehearsal*, 1896. Oil on canvas. 21⅞ × 32⅛ in. (55.6 × 81.6 cm). Frances Lehman Loeb Art Center, Vassar College, Museum Purchase, 1896.1

In contrast, the more intellectual works and photographs present pathways into relatively unstable public discourse or social situations. Opportunities for documenting social conditions and fraught events, and for opposing what they saw as inequities between the wealthy and the working classes, brought female artists into the public sphere. The participation of female artists in the more worldly, public aspects of artistic expression expanded greatly in the twentieth century, with an influx of photographic images representing moments at work and in the streets, along with the occasional social or political critique.

In the end, however, all the works in the exhibition can be described as falling into the two very broad areas of public and private spaces, or spheres, as one would say in the parlance of the eighteenth and nineteenth centuries. "Public" invariably meant the world of men, business, science, art, and politics, as pictured in a mid-twentieth-century view of a *New York Times* conference room by Rosalie McKenna (fig. 1), while "private" denoted the world of the home, children, and devoted wife, as in an 1890s scene of an upper-middle-class home and family at leisure by American artist William H. Lippincott (fig. 2).

While I tend to concentrate as an art historian on the crossings of politics and art, I was not aware of the themes of private and public spaces as major interests for feminist art histori-

ans. Their challenges, especially those by Temma Balducci and Heather Belnap Jensen, to reexamine women's relations to the public sphere expanded my looking and thinking, and ultimately in this exhibition I explore both the public and private sides of these works, which range over a period of 350 years.[5]

Consequently, the idea of "space" means several things in this exhibition. It indicates that three-dimensional mirage of pictorial space within a portrait, landscape, domestic scene, intellectual-based work, or documentary photograph, and how the woman inside the frame navigates that space, whether by looking out at the viewer or walking along a street. It takes into consideration the "background" of a work. Is it a nondescript, neutral place or a definite image that calls for interpretation? For instance, some portraits have a plain, shaded background, while the watercolor by Hilda Belcher gives us a make-believe facade of a wall with just the barest hint of the domestic setting (cat. 4), and the painting by Sylvia Sleigh presents her friends beneath the acid-colored fronds of weeping willows (cat. 11).

With the idyllic landscapes, the "pleasant" factor of the background is a given. Women imagining harmonious episodes in the outdoors propelled the peaceful, easy, even fanciful landscapes that are featured in the exhibition, with women as their central characters. The English amateur artist Miss Bennett gives us hints of a serene Italianate setting (cat. 12), and the English schoolgirl

Eliza Phipps wants us to see the edge of a manicured garden and the peacock she added for the finishing touch (cat. 13). Meanwhile, Florine Stettheimer throws back the curtain on a wild party straddling the indoors and outdoors (cat. 16), and Doris Lee floats us high above a flat, green, somnolent world simulating a garden at night (cat. 18).

The domestic images present a background of rooms, from a grand British manor by Miss Cornwallis (cat. 19), a humble American log cabin by Lilly Martin Spencer (cat. 20), and a color-saturated sixties bathroom by Joan Brown (cat. 24). In contrast, the backdrops of scenes featuring mother and child are non-descript or limited, such as the one by Alice Neel (cat. 22). Her watercolor confronts us with bare, wintry trees; at the time, the artist's baby was ill and Neel was experiencing great poverty.

Other works share an interest in religion, classical mythology, and social or political ideas. The backgrounds of these works are sometimes neutral, though Maria Cosway and Caroline Watson place us in a modest bedroom (cat. 27), Margaret Burroughs creates an effusive ocean scene (cat. 32), and Marion Greenwood presents a view of a capitalist atop a skyscraper (cat. 31). With the photographs, Rosalie McKenna confronts us with a hard, concrete crosswalk in downtown Jackson (cat. 37), and Edith Tudor-Hart shows us apartment buildings masked by full, feathery trees (cat. 34). Other works reflect the legacy of the highly influential Ashcan School and its leader Robert Henri, who took everyday life as their subject, in the early twentieth century.

In a larger way, "space" also reflects the artist's interior life, meaning her private world in the studio and home, and her own thoughts. This personal world is palpable in the paintings and poems of Stettheimer, for example. The term can also encompass the artist's public world, including her engagement with art schools; participation in exhibitions; circulation of prints; and immersion in political, social, cultural, or intellectual arenas. This outside world can be viewed perhaps most intensely with Kauffman, who was a successful entrepreneur. Opportunities for academic training and exhibiting pushed female artists into the public sphere of men and left them exposed to criticism. In the nineteenth century, some questioned whether women would actually use their schooling or abandon it for marriage.

Biography plays an important role in understanding these artists, with glimpses of their interior thoughts and intentions gleaned from letters, journals, and other autobiographical material. If a sitter or subject is a personality of the era, her biography also connects with the larger world of the royal court, salons, or high society. Fashion also links the artist and her sitter to a larger social world of trends, cultural notions, and markers of social status.

In addition, printmaking, which in general allows for wide circulation of images, catapults the prints in the exhibition

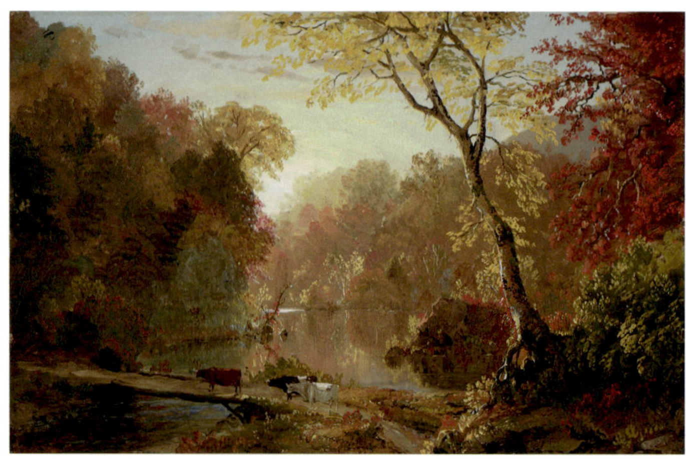

Figure 3. Frederic Church, *Autumn in North America*, ca. 1856. Oil on board. 11¼ × 17 in. (28.6 × 43.2 cm). Frances Lehman Loeb Art Center, Vassar College, Gift of Matthew Vassar, 1864.1.16

beyond the private studio of the artist or the family workshop into the public arena of an international world of publishers, print-shops, and other distributors. The several prints in the exhibition have this "added" layer of making works accessible to a larger, wider audience.

Private spaces are usually important to the public settings of these works, too. In other words, these two environmental circumstances—the private and the public—overlap. Organized roughly chronologically within each subject, the works in the exhibition are examined through private and public lenses to focus on the circumstances of the artist, her training, and the content of the work. The exhibition ends just before the 1970s, when the women's movement cast a brilliant light upon art made by women, both historical and contemporary, accompanied by new scholarship that has expanded greatly over the years.

The initial foray into the Loeb's collection database uncovered about three hundred images of women and girls by female artists, whereas there were thousands of these works made by men. Though Vassar College was established as a women's college in 1861 and became coeducational in 1969, its art collection has never been based wholly on works made by women. Rather, the collection began as an assemblage of mostly British and American drawings and prints of an antiquarian, topographical, and architectural nature, as well as Hudson River School oil studies, such

as Frederic Church's *Autumn in North America* (fig. 3). Few works by women were included. After Matthew Vassar's founding gift in 1864, donations to the museum followed, with Old Master prints, works by artists in Alfred Stieglitz's circle, and examples of American mid-century modernism, among others. Many Vassar women graduates facilitated gifts or donated works and funds. Art by women of color began entering the collection in the 1970s through purchase and gifts.

The twentieth century saw a steady focus on collecting and exhibiting art by women. At mid-century, gallery director Agnes Rindge Claflin aimed to present contemporary art, including art by women.[6] This initiative was supported by the revelatory courses taught in the art department by Nochlin, after she learned of the "women's liberation movement," as she put it, in the late 1960s.[7] Her first feminist art history course, "The Image of Women in the 19th and 20th Centuries," announced in late 1969, proved groundbreaking for her subsequent work and for the field of art history.[8] Several historical and contemporary female-centered exhibitions ensued at Vassar College Art Gallery.

Though art museums are trying to make up for lost ground on many fronts, life situations for women fundamentally differed from those of men for a long time, and they still do. It goes without stating that marrying, having children, and tending the home have been broad societal norms for women, though that was less the case in 2019, when slightly fewer than one-third of American women were never married.[9]

During the Italian Renaissance and Baroque periods, females of the middle and upper classes were given an education centered around the domestic arts, especially needlework and spinning, supplemented by reading literature and devotional texts. One English mother, Elizabeth Joceline, wrote that on behalf of her forthcoming baby, if it were a girl, "I desire her bringing up may bee learning the Bible, as my sisters doe, good housewifery, writing, and good works: other learning a woman needs not."[10] The main seat of learning for women was the convent, with its rich history of scholarship. Education for women outside the church was promoted by elite proto-feminists like Marie de Gournay (1565–1645) and Anna Maria van Schurman (1607–1678), the Dutch writer and humanist whom Magdalena de Passe (cat. 1) mentored in engraving. In early sixteenth-century England, the statesman Sir Thomas More (1478–1535) educated his daughters alongside their brother so that they would be informed companions for their future husbands.[11]

In the eighteenth century in England, seminaries and boarding schools for girls became more numerous, though their value was questioned, and their offerings later in the century did not satisfy early feminist Mary Wollstonecraft (1759–1797), who desired more substantial teaching and challenging subjects.

Rather, middle-class girls were overwhelmingly educated at home with a regimented curriculum that could include the social sciences, physical sciences, literature, fine arts, and letter writing, in contrast with the classical curriculum at boys' schools.[12] At the royal court or within more well-to-do families, girls might receive more advanced study with private instruction.

In nineteenth-century Europe, middle- and upper-class girls and young women would attend boarding schools, though debates still raged about whether advanced study was practical.[13] In the United States, similar questions were raised at the end of the eighteenth century on the necessity for more challenging material in girls' education. At the same time, wealthy American families educated their daughters at home in French, drawing, music, and literature, so that they would be capable of teaching their own children those subjects, but they also received instruction in needlework and other domestic arts. Academies and seminaries akin to high schools for young women were also formed, growing into more substantial educational institutions, including women's colleges.[14]

For centuries, taking care of the home was the top concern for most women, as relayed by an old Italian saying, "A girl should be taught to sew and not to read, unless one wishes to make a nun of her."[15] Indeed, needlework played an outsized role in women's education and accomplishments, and the exhibition

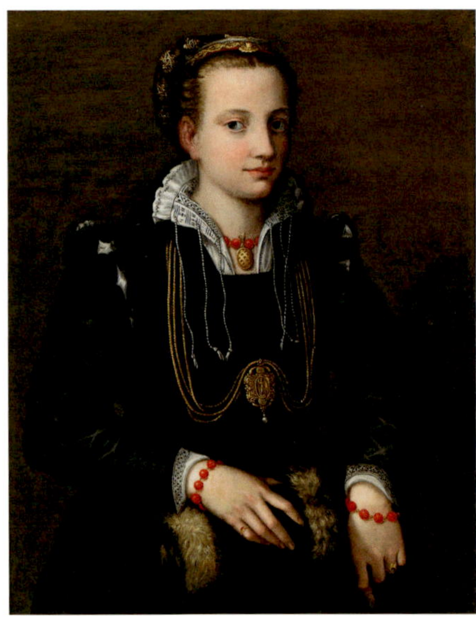

Figure 4. Sofonisba Anguissola, *The Artist's Sister Minerva Anguissola*, ca. 1564. Oil on canvas. 33½ × 26 in. (85.1 × 66 cm). Layton Art Collection Inc., Gift of the family of Mrs. Frederick Vogel Jr., at the Milwaukee Art Museum, L1952.1

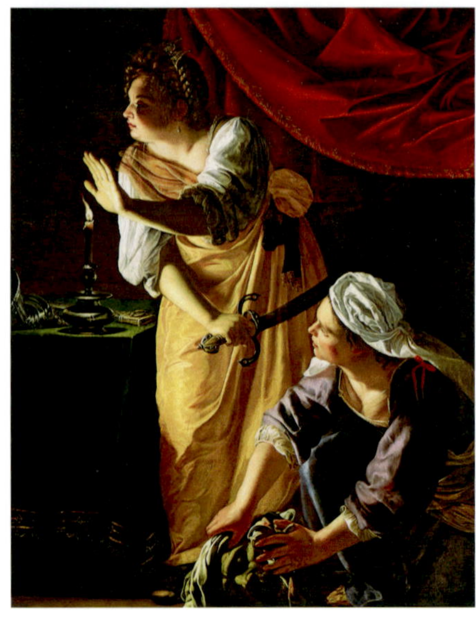

Figure 5. Artemisia Gentileschi, *Judith and Her Maidservant with the Head of Holofernes*, between 1623 and 1625. Oil on canvas. 73¹¹⁄₁₆ × 55⅞ in. (187.2 × 142 cm). Detroit Institute of Arts, Gift of Mr. Leslie H. Green, 52.253

includes two samplers (cats. 13 and 14). They are reminders of the role needlework—rather than academic education—played in women's lives, from biblical times through to the mid-nineteenth century, as scholar Betty Ring has so eloquently written.[16]

Early on, however, several women of the Italian Renaissance and Baroque periods managed to pursue painting and printmaking, including portraits and the history paintings that Kauffman would do much to introduce in London 200 years later. The first major woman artist of the Italian Renaissance, Sofonisba Anguissola (1532–1625), painted an elegant portrait of her sister Minerva in about 1564 (fig. 4), which shows her skills at portraiture and the rendering of the rich textures of delicate lace, silky fur, and fine metallic jewelry. A noblewoman, Anguissola was encouraged by her Cremonese father to pursue art, and she studied with two local masters, reportedly receiving encouragement from Michelangelo as well. So renowned was her reputation as an artist that she painted at the court of Philip II in Madrid for about ten years.[17]

Artemisia Gentileschi (1593–1652/53), a painter's daughter born in Rome, decades later centered the grand, theatrical Caravaggesque style of painting which her father knew so well onto largely female mythological and biblical subjects such as Judith and Holofernes (fig. 5). Artemisia's father, Orazio Gentileschi (1563–1639) trained her, in what would become a common occurrence among female artists in this exhibition.[18] She and Kauffman

and other women artists were restricted from drawing the male nude, but they took advantage of rendering the female form and female subjects in their paintings.

In the salon culture of the seventeenth and eighteenth centuries, creative women and their works came to the public's attention. This was especially the case in Paris, where Elisabeth Sophie Chéron excelled in portraiture and poetry, attracting a large following, and later in London, Maria Cosway was urged by her artist husband to establish her own soirées. However, the salon, or soirée—that combustible mix of creative people—made an impression on the lives of women artists and appears to have been almost essential to Stettheimer's life in early twentieth-century New York.

The idea of separate "public and domestic domains," or spheres, entered into British culture in the mid-to-late eighteenth century and altered general attitudes toward the proper place for women. This trend spread to the United States. Conduct books promoting the domestic woman, especially after she married and had children, replaced earlier writings admiring women with wide-ranging scholarly interests and accomplishments.[19] Ambition that was not tied to domestic or virtuous themes seems to have grown suspect for most middle- and upper-class women, and this new attitude held great sway through the nineteenth century. Serving others was uppermost, though some saw the value of personal pursuits for the unmarried woman. Vassar College's second president, John Howard Raymond, spoke on the subject on Founder's Day in 1870, as relayed by a student Elba Huffman (later Bouslog),

> Then he talked of the privileges women ought to have. While their sphere was home—this he does not deny—(nor do we)—if any love literature or art better than married life, that the women should be free to choose. "Who," he asked, "is to say it was wrong for Florence Nightingale, Miss Martineau, and Maria Mitchell to do so?"[20]

As Bouslog cheerily and somewhat tongue-in-cheek confided in a letter to her mother in 1870, "My idea of heaven is an atmosphere of study and research, with plenty of books and a whole eternity to read!—Probably just a species of intoxication, all this, for which women have no more need than for a binomial theorem."[21] Societal pressures and traditions toward choosing home and motherhood rather than an artist's financially difficult life grew to be a heavy, values-laden weight upon middle- and upper-class women for a long time. As late as 1893 the World's Columbian Exposition in Chicago boasted of numerous displays at the Woman's Building that built upon this "cult of domesticity," though financial necessity could trump those considerations, as Lilly Martin Spencer and Jessie Tarbox Beals both thrived and

had open-minded husbands who shared in household or work responsibilities.[22] Even as a girl growing up in a Jewish family in New York in the 1920s and 1930s, however, Miriam Schapiro felt confused about the absence of great women artists in the books she was reading:

> I made up my mind very early that I was going to be an artist. I never read about a woman artist of the stature of Velázquez or Vermeer. That proved to be the basis of another confusing message to me. Who was I supposed to be? I was obviously in a woman's body with a man's concerns.[23]

A leading feminist artist in the 1970s, Schapiro was set on revolutionizing the way female artists thought about themselves. She lived not only with her parents growing up in New York from the 1920s to early 1940s but also with her aunt and maternal grandmother:

> During this early period of my life, I had conflicting messages from the wonderful women in my life. On the one hand, they wished to see the line move towards glory and fortune and they could fantasize me as a girl-child grown to a woman, achieving all this—so they encouraged me to be an artist. However, their fantasies had

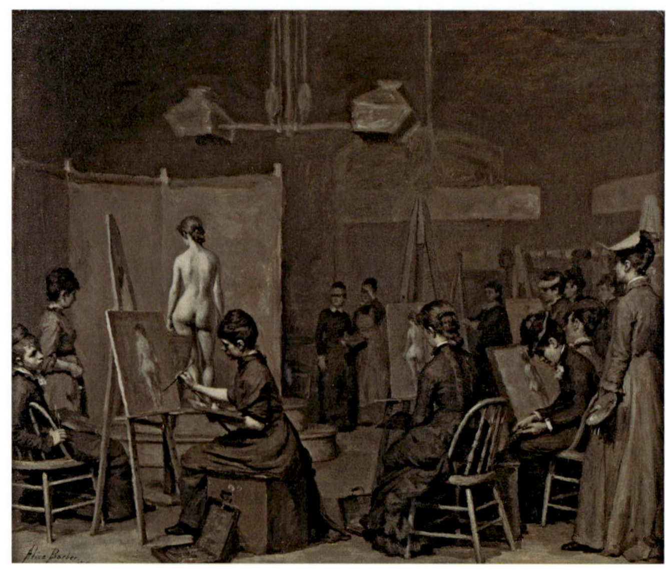

Figure 6. Alice Barber Stephens, *The Women's Life Class*, ca. 1879. Oil on cardboard (grisaille). 12 × 14 in. (30.5 × 35.6 cm). Pennsylvania Academy of the Fine Arts, Gift of the artist, 1879.2

limitations. Socially speaking, it was all right to go so far and no farther. One should get a husband to provide. Now how could both dreams come true? A thread which ran through their thinking was that a woman moves from her mother's womb to her husband's womb.[24]

Schapiro and Judy Chicago came together in the 1970s at the California Institute of the Arts to educate women about the possibilities of making their own original art, an innovative idea given the history of restrictions from major art schools that American and European women had experienced in the past. These restrictions remained in place until the mid-nineteenth to early twentieth century. For instance, from its founding in the late eighteenth century until the 1890s, women could not attend life classes at the Royal Academy of Arts in London.[25] In Paris, women could not attend the École des Beaux-Arts until 1897, whereas men learned to draw from antique casts and the male anatomy, and drawing from the nude model was part of the entrance exam. Women could train privately with École faculty or attend private institutions, such as the Académie Julian, founded in 1868.[26] Women could also copy paintings at the Louvre, and many did this for a living. Some women in France, however, formed a separate public organization, the Union des Femmes Peintres et Sculpteurs, in 1881, which provided opportunities to exhibit their work, though many members chose to maintain female themes rendered in conservative artistic styles.[27]

The National Academy of Design in New York, founded in 1826, was patterned after the Royal Academy in London. In its art school, male students drew from plaster casts of the antique and live models. Women were allowed to have their own life class beginning in 1871.[28] They could attend the student-funded Art Students League in New York as soon as 1875, when it was founded, and be elected to its governing system, but in the early decades women could only draw and paint from the nude female, not male, model, after completing coursework in drawing from plaster casts.[29]

In Philadelphia, the Pennsylvania Academy of the Fine Arts, founded in 1805, instituted drawing from casts and the model beginning in 1810, but only for men. However, women could attend life classes by 1868 (fig. 6).[30] By the 1880s, the realist painter Thomas Eakins (1844–1916) emphasized anatomy and drawing from the nude model at the school, and caused controversy by removing the loincloth from a male model in a drawing class attended by female students.[31]

The number of women studying art multiplied in the nineteenth century, though it would take a while before the number of female professional artists increased significantly. They were among the generations of women in the second half of the

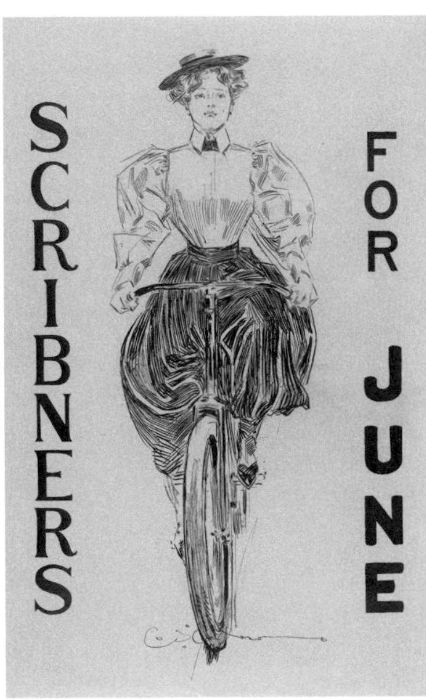

Figure 7. Charles Dana Gibson, *Scribner's for June*, 1895. Zinc engraving. 22⅛ × 14¹⁄₁₆ in. (56.2 × 35.7 cm). Library of Congress, Washington, D.C., 004.00.00

century who would venture into male professions and sports, challenging gender roles and becoming associated with the New Woman, personified in the illustrations of Charles Dana Gibson (1867–1944) (fig. 7). Even their clothes were suspect, as Minnie Bourke, the mother of Margaret Bourke-White, noted on the back of an 1890s photograph of herself on a bicycle. Noting the shirtwaist she was wearing—an off-the-rack blouse inspired by men's shirts—Minnie wrote, "advanced" and "not quite nice."[32] With these women going to college, venturing into the professional world of art, and developing a public record, in the future more information may be obtained in documenting and telling the stories of their lives and art, and private family sources and public archives may also be made available. However, we are still in the developmental stage of research, with many artists emerging from obscurity only recently.

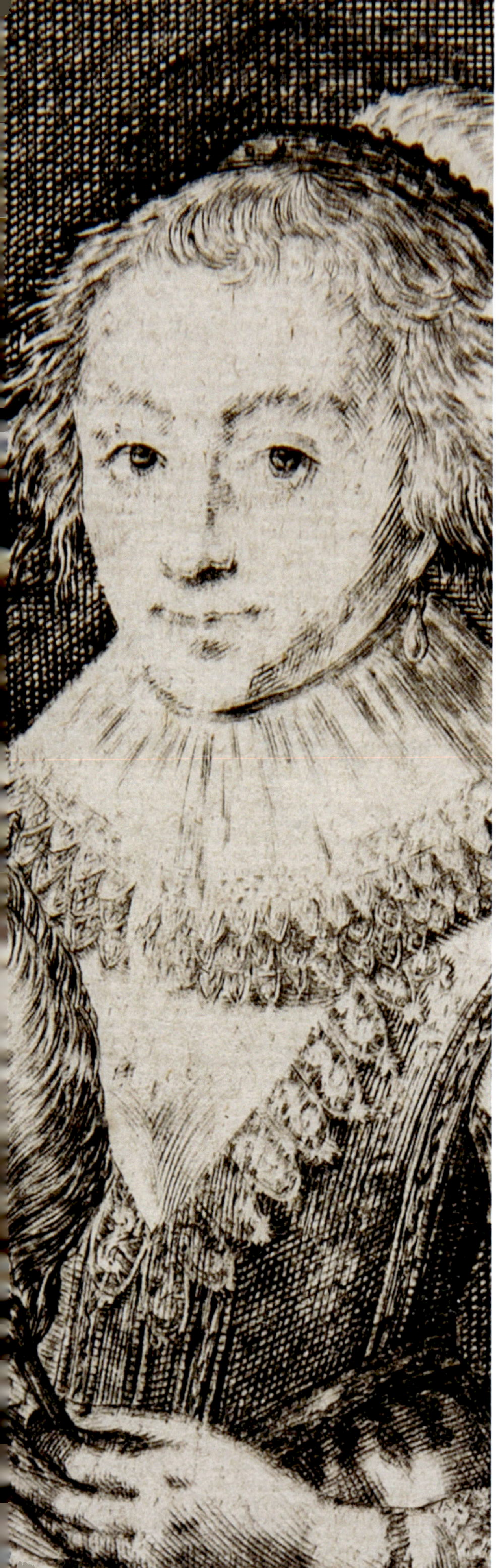

Portraits
Intimate Appraisals

A 1968 statement by painter Sylvia Sleigh reveals why she looked to familiar faces:

> *The sitters are my friends, because the act of painting someone is very intimate, a personal relationship.*[33]

Linda Nochlin noted that making a portrait was reciprocal:

> *. . . if the artist watches, judges the sitter, the sitter is privileged, by the portrait relation, to watch and judge back.*[34]

MAGDALENA DE PASSE

Katherine Manners, once one of the best-known aristocrats in England, is the subject of a small portrait engraving from about 1620–23 (cat. 1). She occupies most of the sheet and looks directly out at the viewer from a dark, neutral background that heightens her bright youthful face, falling lace ruff, and fashionable ostrich fan. A three-line caption is written below. Magdalena de Passe (1600–1638), who made the portrait, belonged to a family of Dutch printmakers then based in Utrecht.

In the family workshop, Magdalena, her father and mentor Crispijn de Passe (1564–1637), and brothers Crispijn the Younger

(1594–1670), Simon (1595–1647), and Willem (1597/98–1636/37), created more than 14,000 individual works and dozens of books, including *Hortus floridus* (Book of Flowers) by Crispijn the Younger (fig. 8).[35] The portrait was the most executed subject among professional engravers in early seventeenth-century Jacobean London (from 1603 to 1625), and the De Passe family was an important source of these prints.[36]

Magdalena de Passe was active as a printmaker by 1614, as evident by two signed works, and she probably continued her practice until her marriage in 1634. She died four years later. De Passe might be best known for her innovative set of sleep caps, printed with engravings, for which she was granted a privilege, or early copyright.[37] For single-sheet prints and series, she engraved allegorical, biblical, landscape, and mythological subjects mostly after her father and Dutch, German, and Flemish artists, such as Roelandt Saverij. Many of those works take women as subjects or central figures, however, with themes such as the Annunciation, Christ and the woman of Canaan, Anna the prophet, Latona, the Sibyls, and the nymph Salmacis.[38] She engraved a few portraits of women, but it seems that most portraits she made were in conjunction with her brother Willem for *Heroologia Anglica*, a folio-size book of sixty-five engravings of English royals, aristocrats, clergymen, and others of distinguished rank, dedicated

to James I that appeared in 1620.[39] The designs for those prints were furnished by bookseller Henry Holland, who had written the Latin text.[40]

With this experience collaborating with her brother, De Passe would have been well suited to making the portrait of Katherine Manners. The plate could have been given to her brother Willem, who had arrived in London by 1621.[41] He worked for Thomas Jenner, the London publisher of Willem's sports-border engraving that surrounds some impressions of the portrait (fig. 9).[42] It has been suggested that Magdalena used a print of Manners by Francis Delarum (1590–1627) as her model, but her print's exact origin is unclear.[43]

The spirited engraving of the Midlands noblewoman features "the lively portraicture," as inscribed in print below the image, of Marchioness Katherine Manners (ca. 1603–1649), the daughter of Francis Manners, sixth Earl of Rutland, of Belvoir Castle in Leicestershire. De Passe pictured the wealthy heiress after she had married the court favorite of James I, George Villiers, Marquis of Buckingham, in 1620, and before he had become the Duke of Buckingham in 1623. Her father was opposed to their marriage, and the king was opposed to his court favorite marrying a Catholic bride, though the couple finally wed with the Marchioness renouncing Catholicism for Protestantism.[44]

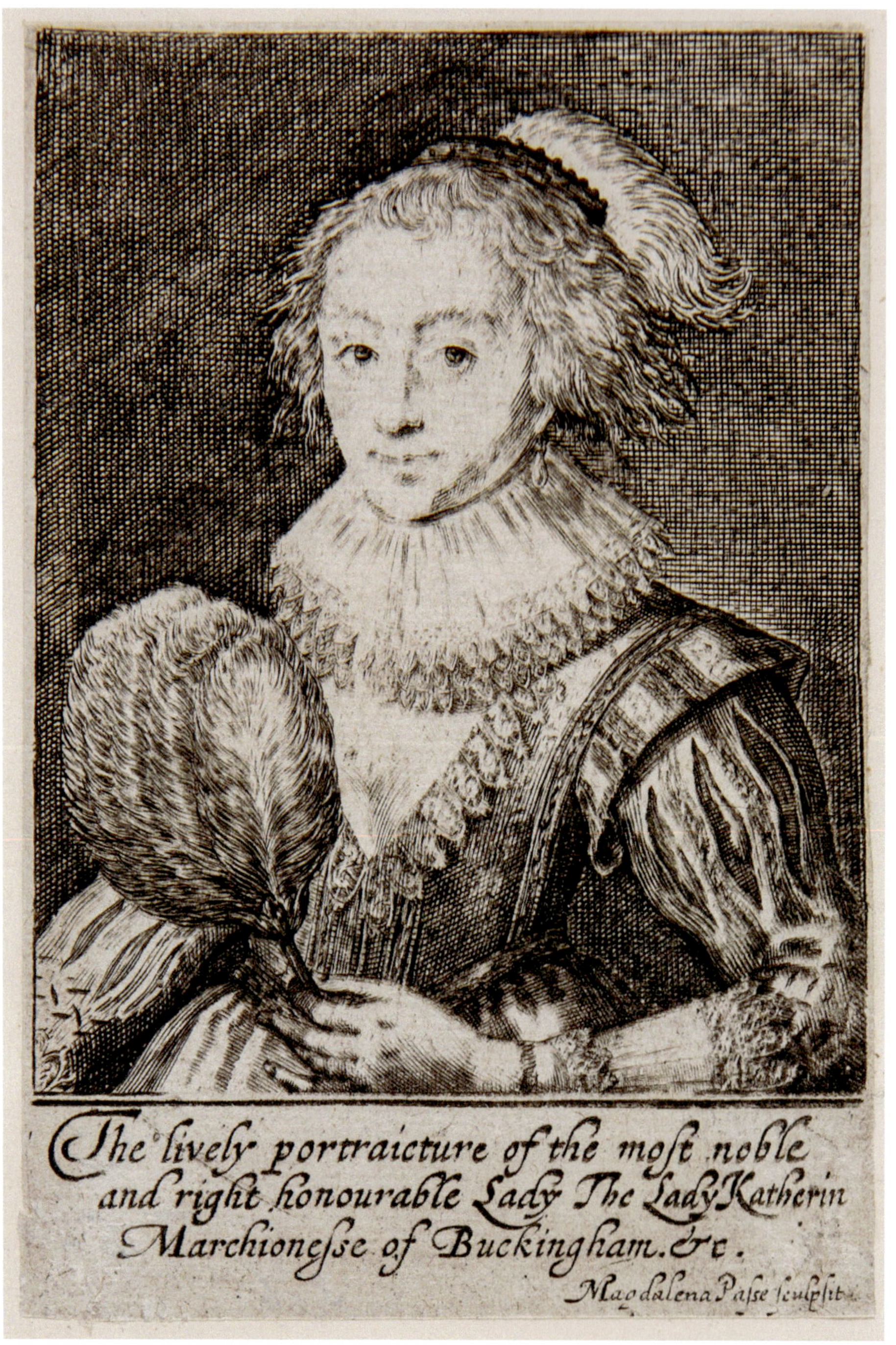

Cat. 1 **Magdalena de Passe**

The lively portraicture of the most noble and right honourable
Lady The Lady Katherin Marchionesse of Buckingham. &c.

Engraving, ca. 1620–23
Gift of Mrs. William Reed Thompson (Mary Thaw, class of 1877)
Reproduced oversize

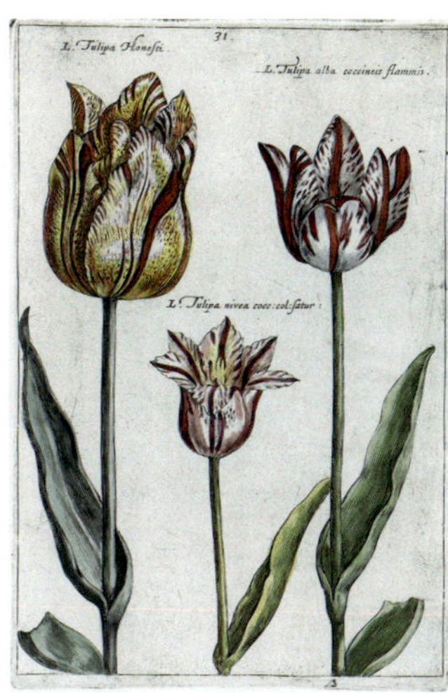

Figure 8. Crispijn de Passe the Younger, *Broad-leaved Tulips*, plate 31 from *Hortus floridus* (Book of Flowers), 1614. Hand-colored engraving on cream laid paper. 10⅜ × 6¾ in. (26.4 × 17.2 cm). Frances Lehman Loeb Art Center, Vassar College, Purchase, Betsy Mudge Wilson, class of 1956, Memorial Fund, 1987.44.2

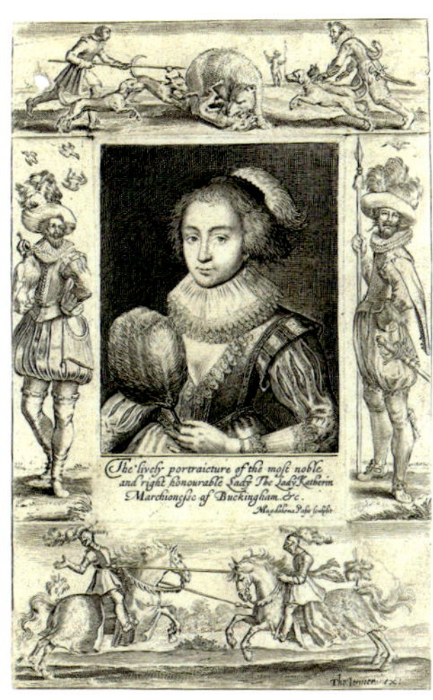

Figure 9. Magdalena de Passe and Willem de Passe, published by Thomas Jenner, "*The lively portraicture of the most noble and right honourable Lady The Lady Katherin Marchionesse of Buckingham &c.,*" ca. 1618–1623. Engraving. Portrait: 4¾ × 3¹⁄₁₆ in. (12 × 7.8 cm); overall: 8³⁄₁₆ × 5⅛ in. (20.8 × 13.1 cm). British Museum, Bequeathed by Clayton Mordaunt Cracherode 1799, P,1.279

De Passe shows the sitter with hair gathered in back, tendrils about her face, against a dark background of crosshatchings. Prominent patches above the head and fan, made by rubbing the lines on the plate with a burnisher, may indicate that this is an early impression for which the artist was still making adjustments. With pride, it seems, the marchioness holds the fan, a fashionable article favored by noblewomen and royals after the era of Henry VIII (r. 1509–1547) and especially during the later years of the reign of Elizabeth I (r. 1558–1603).[45]

The approximate dating for the portrait and the bold, country-life themes in Willem's sports border—bear hunting, a tournament, a falconer, a halberdier—suggest symbols of estate life and privilege. In 1622, George Villiers acquired the royal residence New Hall, a mansion and estate in Essex developed by Henry VIII.[46] The stately residence near Boreham, Chelmsford, now only partially surviving, was nestled amid 200 acres of parkland, with abundant woods and stags, as the marquis wrote in a letter to James I after returning from a trip to Spain.[47]

Magdalena de Passe gained fame during her life and afterwards for the delicacy of her engraved line. In *Biographical History of England from Egbert the Great to the Revolution*, first published in 1769, the author James Granger praised her as "ingenious" and recalled her print of Katherine as one of her "principal works."[48] She made the likeness in a medium meant for public distribution,

and there are several extant impressions of this print. Horace Walpole noted of the "very scarce" impression in his collection that "It is slightly finished, but very free."[49] Given these descriptions and high praise, perhaps this is why imperfect impressions from the portrait plate have survived, such as our impression, which appears to still show the burnishing that the artist used to adjust her composition. It also shows doubling of lines, perhaps caused by the paper undergoing too much pressure when printed, or shifting when printed, an effect which can be seen in at least one other extant impression.[50] Her lauded print career, with her portraits of aristocrats and engravings after prominent artists, seems to have ended when she got married, as there are no recorded prints by her after that time.[51]

ELISABETH SOPHIE CHÉRON

A lively salon culture flowered in seventeenth-century Paris, enjoyed by female artists, poets, and writers. Madeleine de Scudéry (1607–1701) often attended the salon of Elisabeth Sophie Chéron (1648–1711) on the rue de Grenelle.[52] Chéron would have had a ready audience for portrait commissions,[53] and a biographer wrote that patrons flocked to her studio, especially women in the arts. By contemporary accounts, her portraits were in high demand. Most have stayed with the sitters' families, while the engraved portraits after them only furthered the fame of those depicted.[54]

German artist Johann Georg Wille (1715–1808) gathered the design for his print of Scudéry after Chéron (cat. 2) through the publisher. His work is a three-quarter-view etching and engraving of the French writer, published in Paris in 1739, a few years after he had arrived there as a young man.[55] A middle-aged Scudéry meets the viewer's gaze. She is attired in the fashion of a hundred years earlier, her pearl brooch and ringlets in the court mode of the 1640s, all in a simple oval frame. Her name is inscribed in ink on the base below.[56] The Loeb impression is an unrecorded proof, before the letters were engraved onto the plate.[57] The completed print includes the writer's name and records her death date in 1701 at the age of ninety-five. Perhaps the original design by Chéron was made about that time as a tribute to her friend, though it has not been located.[58] The print was published by Michel Odieuvre

(1687–1756), who was in the midst of an engraved-portrait project on the French kings when he hired Wille. So began Wille's lengthy portrait work for the publisher, who furnished him with portrait drawings, as noted by the engraver in his memoirs.[59] How the publisher would have acquired the design by Chéron is unknown.

A painter, poet, and printmaker, Chéron was a prominent figure in French cultural circles. She was admitted as a member of the Académie Royale by the age of twenty-one for her portrait paintings. As a biographer noted, portraiture was the fashion in France in the seventeenth century.[60] A prolific and successful miniature portraitist in watercolors, pastel, and enamel, as well as a history and landscape painter, Chéron was the daughter and student of Henri Chéron, a portrait miniaturist, engraver, and painter of enamels.[61] Her portraits were much admired in her day according to a sympathetic writer, who singled out the ones after nature and the likenesses of contemporary women that she incorporated into her history paintings.[62]

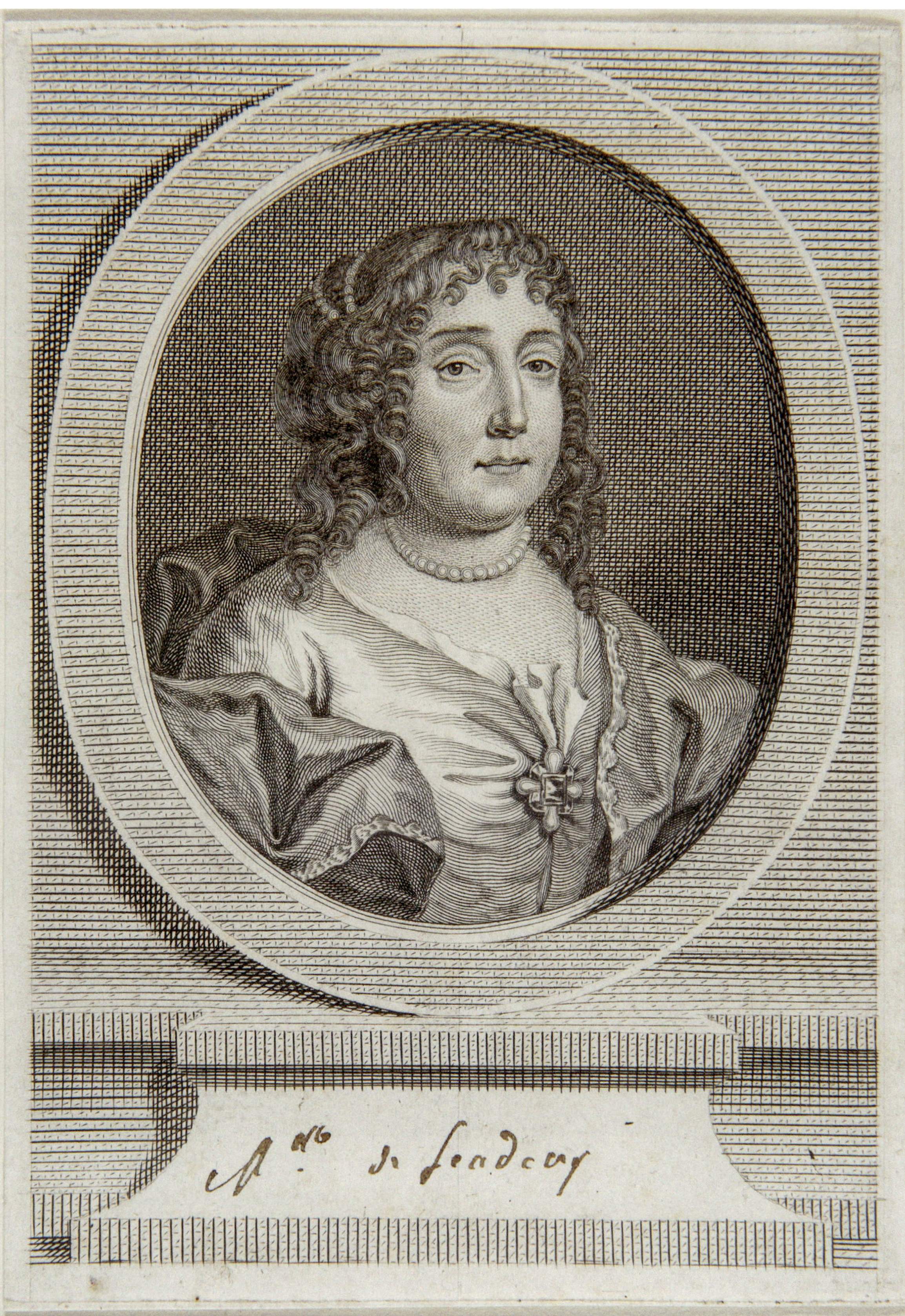

M.lle de Scudery

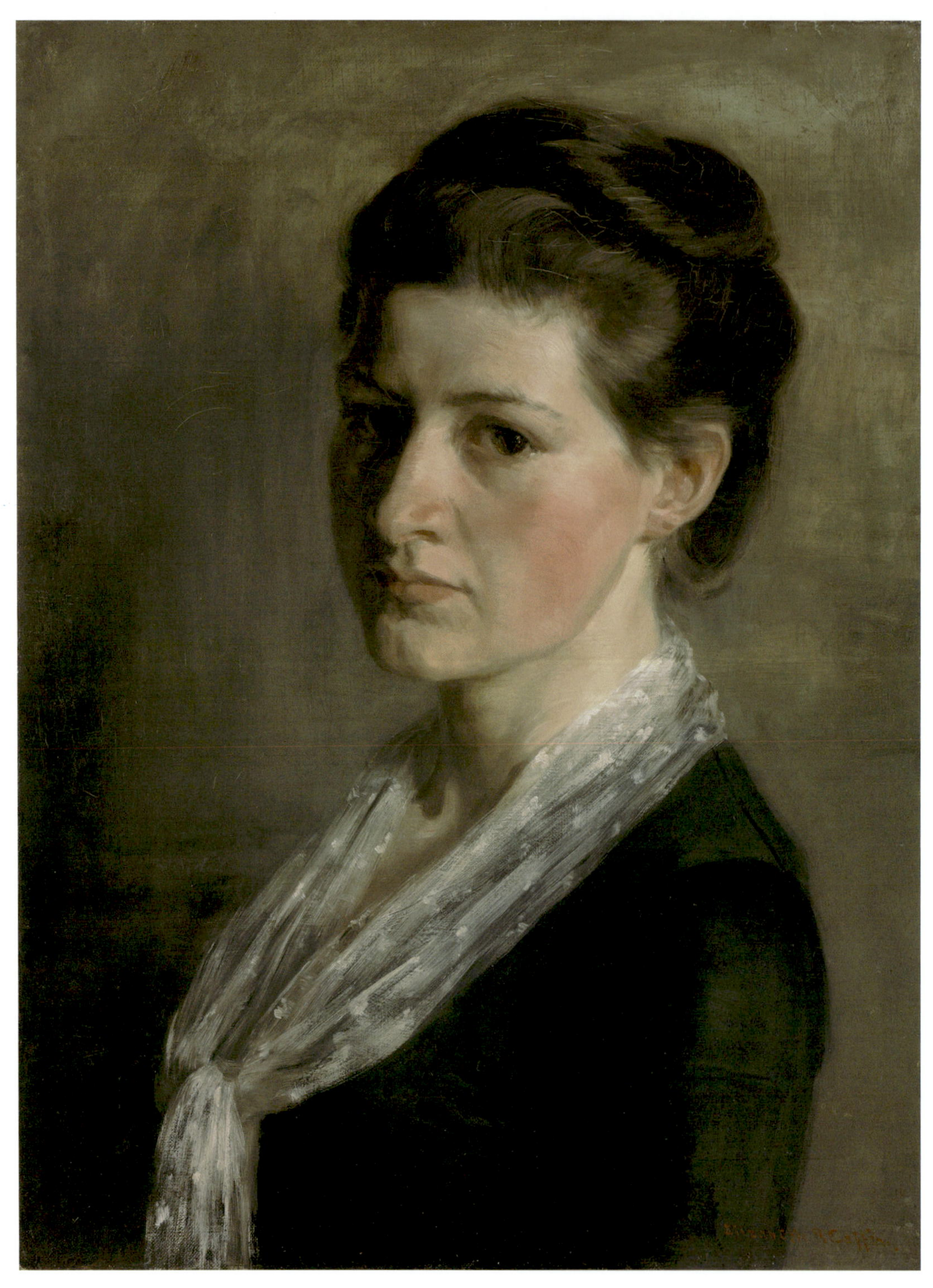

Cat. 3   **Elizabeth Rebecca Coffin**
Study of a Head

Oil on canvas, ca. 1893
Gift of the artist, class of 1870

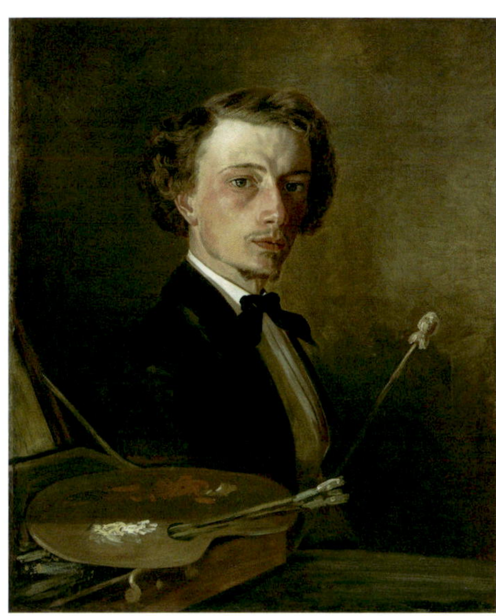

Figure 10. Henry Van Ingen, *Self-Portrait*. Oil on canvas. 24³⁄₁₆ × 20¹⁄₁₆ in. (61.4 × 51 cm). Frances Lehman Loeb Art Center, Vassar College, Gift of Ruth M. Keeney, class of 1905, 1960.8

ELIZABETH REBECCA COFFIN

The sitter in *Study of a Head* (cat. 3) peers out in a kind of daring close-up. In three-quarter view, her portrait crowds the space like a bust within a medallion. She wears a diaphanous white scarf over a tight-fitting dark dress or blouse. Her face is youthful, with pronounced lips and a firm, cleft chin above an exposed neck. Her hair is styled like that of a Gibson Girl, the late nineteenth-century advertising icon that promoted the spunky spirit and casual fashions of the young, independent New Woman. The painting was made by the late nineteenth- and early twentieth-century American painter Elizabeth Rebecca Coffin (1850–1930), who was the subject of her first in-depth study only twenty years ago.[63] Physically, the sitter strongly resembles the painter in Coffin's *Artist and Model in the Studio* of ca. 1890.[64]

Coffin studied painting with the Dutch artist Henry Van Ingen (fig. 10), as well as art history and art theory, at Vassar. She also spent much time copying in the college's art gallery.[65] Born in Brooklyn, she received a Quaker education in lower Manhattan. Her rich cultural and religious background instilled in her a belief in equal education for the sexes. Coffin was urged to apply to the college by her aunt, the noted astronomer and Vassar professor Maria Mitchell,[66] and she enrolled at the age of fifteen. She was president of her class, graduating in 1870. In an address to the alumnae in 1895, she thanked Vassar for "the gift of a liberal education," and added that the "burning question of our youth, 'Can woman take and use a college education?' was settled so long ago."[67]

After graduating from college, Coffin entered the Academy of Fine Arts in the Hague in the Netherlands, staying almost three years. There she was allowed to study anatomy, the antique, perspective, and the history of architecture in the "boys classes," as she recalled. In fact, she "received six prizes, four of these medals in competition with the boys."[68] She also took private lessons for about half a year with Johan Philip Koelman, the director of the academy, who was the brother-in-law of Van Ingen. Koelman's canvases of idealized city and country scenes, and sheets of portrait drawings, show a tight, highly polished style. In 1876, she returned to Vassar to earn a master's, or second, degree in art.

Coffin became a professional artist, teaching in Brooklyn and exhibiting and traveling frequently. She never married. She gained attention from reviewers and earned awards, including (rather disparagingly) the "Norman W. Dodge prize for the best picture by a woman" at the National Academy of Design in New York in the spring exhibition in 1892.[69] She also trained at the Brooklyn Art Guild, which she co-founded, studying there with Thomas Eakins, as well as the Art Students League. She did further studies at the Pennsylvania Academy of the Fine Arts with several artists, including Eakins again, from 1883. Starting that decade she would spend summers in Nantucket, and in 1897 she bought property on the island. After a trip to Egypt in 1898, the artist injected brighter colors into her works, and from then on gave much of her attention to reviving the Coffin School of manual training for local students in Nantucket.[70]

Coffin exhibited from 1884 to 1895, according to her artist statement for her exhibition at Vassar in 1920.[71] The style of the Loeb work suggests a date of about 1893, the year a reviewer for an exhibition at the Brooklyn Art Association may have pointed out the painting. As noted by Margaret Moore Booker, the critic observed, "Another of Miss Coffin's canvases was the head of a girl, whose close black waist gave excellent opportunities for painting the whiteness of the throat and the rich colored auburn hair."[72] The actual circumstances around the making of *Study of a Head* remain elusive. Coffin gave it directly to the art department, but the date and year of the gift are not documented.

HILDA BELCHER

In 1907, American illustrator, cartoonist, and painter Hilda Belcher (1881–1963) exhibited *The Checkered Dress (Portrait of O'Keeffe)* at the New York Water Color Club to great acclaim (cat. 4). The work won Belcher membership into the Club, and was reproduced and discussed with praise in an exhibition review in the *International Studio* in January 1908.[73] The sheet features a young woman in a striking checked dress seated in a large chair against a bare wall. A footstool and rug lend a hint of domesticity. Belcher's sitter is plain and wears a narrow-waisted but billowy gingham dress with no corset. Her eyes glance to our left, and a stray wisp escapes from her up-to-date hairstyle. The rendering shows Belcher's awareness of the New Woman, the independent, college-educated, ambitious, sports-loving young single woman. Belcher did not marry. Her mother, Martha Wood Belcher (1844–1930), a landscape painter who contributed significantly to the family income, was her role model.

Belcher constructed this work from three sources. She used her memory of the sitting pose and dress of a Mrs. Hagan, while the face was that of her friend, the young art student Georgia O'Keeffe. (Belcher and O'Keeffe roomed together at the Little Eva boarding house in New York.) She looked to her imagination for the hairstyle and the sparse setting, according to a letter she sent her mother in November 1907. She considered the composition "faked," and wrote about the attention it was attracting in the

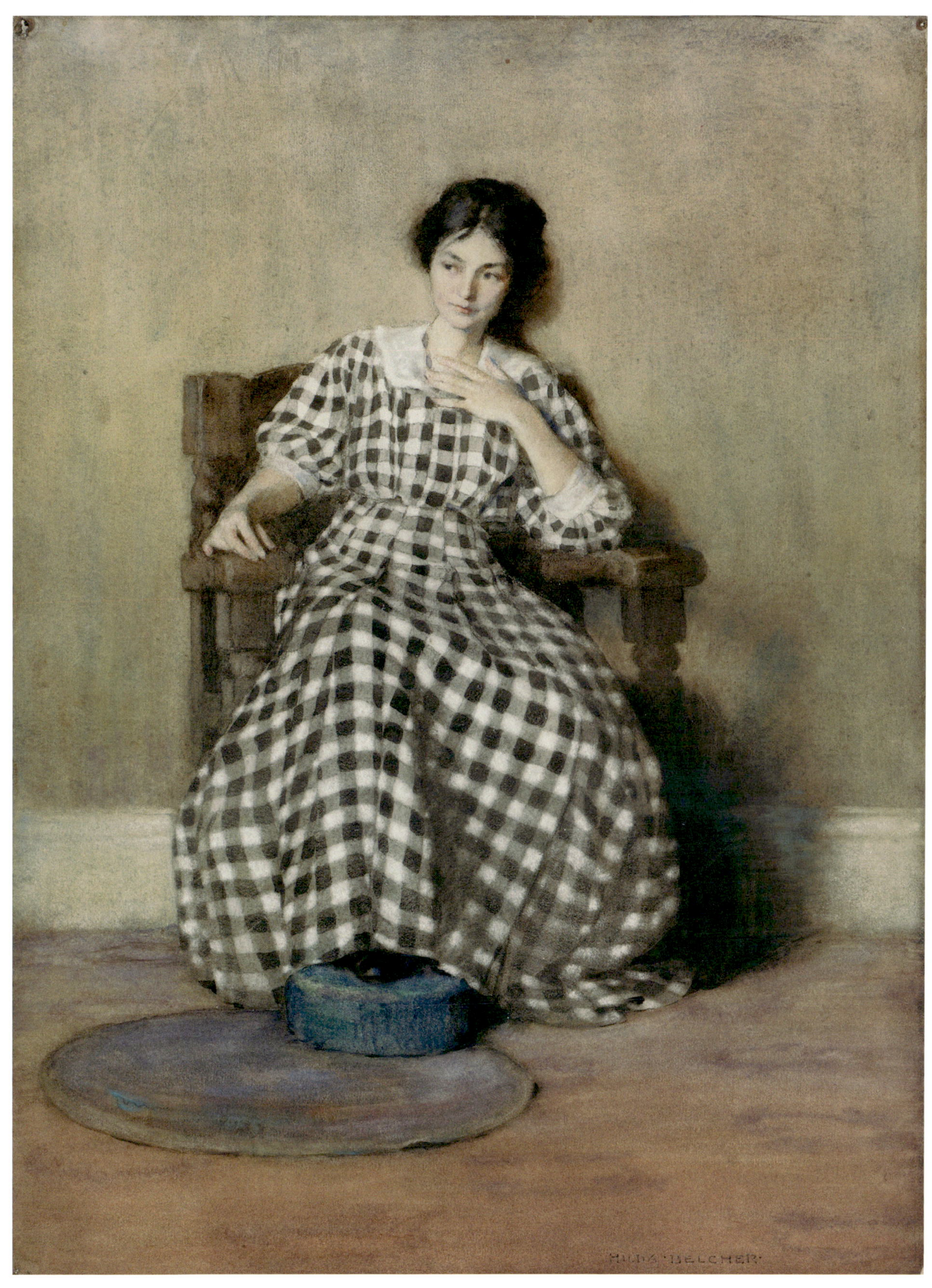

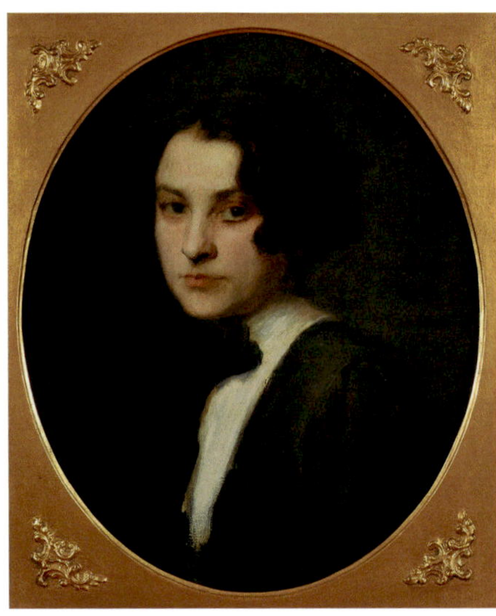

Figure 11. Eugene Speicher, *Portrait of Georgia O'Keeffe*, 1908. Oil on canvas. Oval: 22½ × 17½ in. (57.2 × 44.5 cm); frame: 29¼ × 25¼ in. (74.3 × 64.1 cm). The Art Students League of New York, Permanent Collection

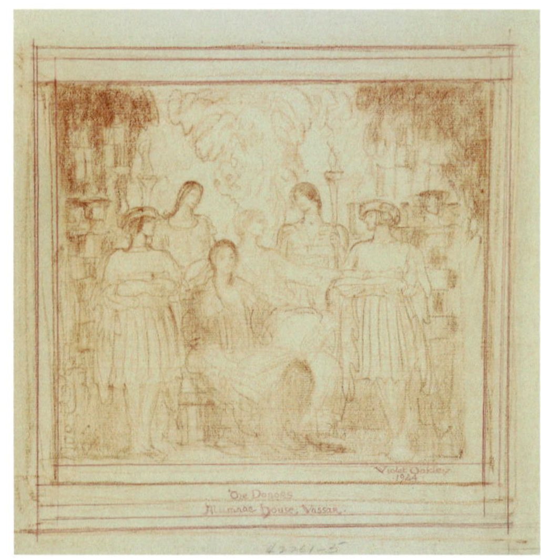

Figure 12. Violet Oakley, *Composition Study for "The Donors,"* 1924. Red chalk and red-colored pencil on beige laid paper. 16⅝ × 14¾ in. (42.2 × 37.5 cm). Frances Lehman Loeb Art Center, Vassar College, Gift of the Violet Oakley Memorial Foundation, 1983.29.11

papers and at the exhibition, where it was "hung splendidly, the center of a group of smaller, slighter sketches."[74]

This Vermont and New York artist participated in the public art worlds of the time with her magazine illustrations and cartoons, her paintings in prestigious exhibitions, and her training at a leading New York art school. From 1901 to 1904 Belcher attended the New York School of Art with American Impressionist painter William Merritt Chase and Robert Henri, the leader of the Ashcan School.[75] Her watercolor, with its controlled, contemplative air and subdued chromatic range, favors Chase's paintings of about the same period.[76] At the time, in 1907–8, the Wisconsin-born O'Keeffe was studying with Chase and others at the Art Students League in New York, where she was often a model (fig. 11).

VIOLET OAKLEY

In this drawing from 1924 (cat. 5), two young women are absorbed in a quiet moment. The artist sketched them to help document the donors of Alumnae House, a newly constructed, prominent building at Vassar. The two sitters, Blanchette Hooker (1909–1992, on the left) and her older sister Helen Hooker (1905–1993, on the right), emerge from stop-and-start lines of grainy red chalk transcribing their smart styles and youthful faces, with the blank, fiber-speckled paper serving as the background. The teenagers were daughters of Blanche Ferry Hooker (Vassar, class

of 1894), a donor of the American Tudor–style building. (Her sister, Queene Ferry Coonley, Vassar, class of 1896, was the other donor.) The two young sisters pose as torchbearers in one of several preparatory studies for *The Donors*, a painting by Oakley commemorating the funders of Alumnae House (fig. 12).[77] The completed painting is on view in the building, which was dedicated in 1924.

A rare female artist amid the leading American beaux-arts muralists in the early twentieth century, Violet Oakley (1874–1961) made this stylized drawing with traces of the Art Nouveau style found in her earlier illustrations. Of the sitters, Blanchette developed into a major American art collector and patron after she graduated from Vassar in 1931 and married John D. Rockefeller III. Helen became a portrait sculptor and art patron, and formed a modern art collection in Ireland with her first husband, Irish writer Ernie O'Malley. She later married Richard Roelofs.[78]

In the pageantry-filled dedication ceremony for the building and its living room, painted and decorated by Oakley in Trecento fashion, torchbearers lit the fireplace and candles that were placed in front of a closed triptych by Oakley called *The Great Wonder*.[79] A Christian Scientist, she rendered a radiant "spiritual ideal" from the Book of Revelation for its center panel with its imagery of a "woman clothed with the sun" (see page 9). Here, the triumphant figure lifts up a baby who is destined to rule all

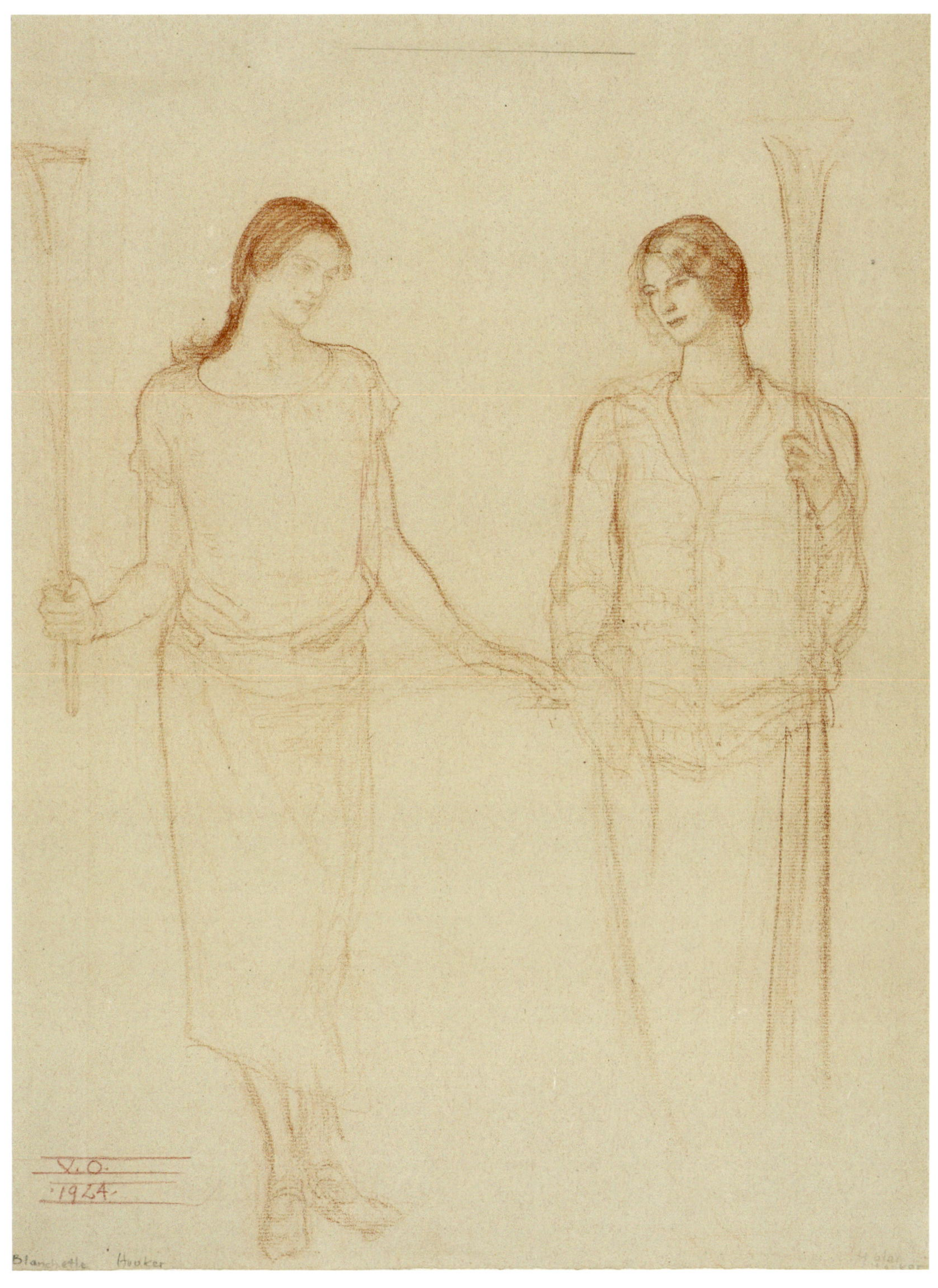

Cat. 5   **Violet Oakley**

Blanchette Hooker and Helen Hooker as Torchbearers

Red chalk with traces of graphite, 1924
Gift of the Violet Oakley Memorial Foundation

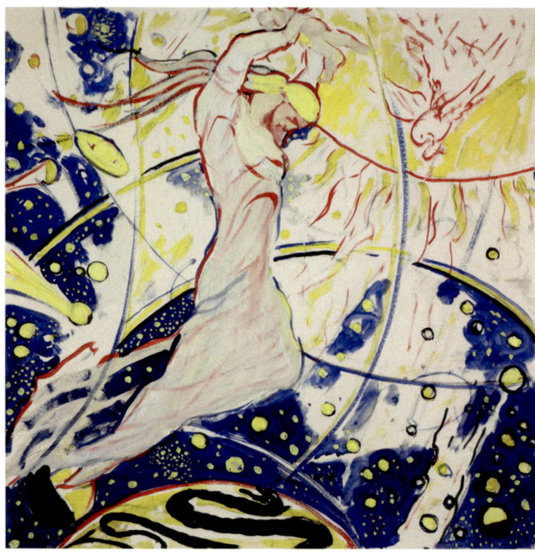

Figure 13. Violet Oakley, *The Woman Clothed with the Sun*, ca. 1916. Gouache over charcoal and graphite on board. 31⅞ × 27¹¹⁄₁₆ in. (81 × 70.3 cm). Frances Lehman Loeb Art Center, Vassar College, Gift of the Violet Oakley Memorial Foundation, 1983.29.10

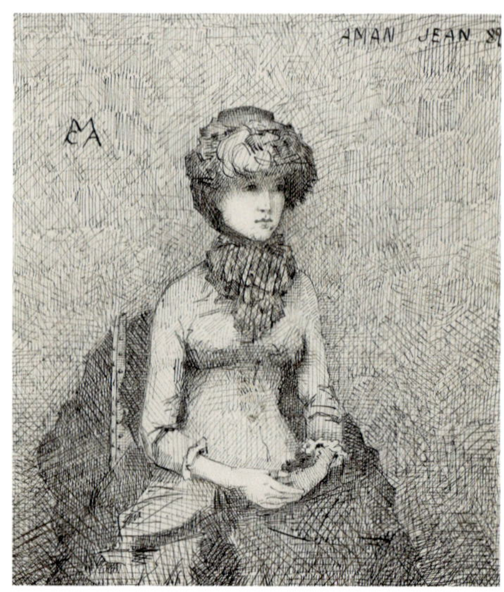

Figure 14. Edmond François Aman-Jean, *Portrait of a Seated Woman*, 1889. Pen and black ink on ivory wove paper. 7¾ × 6½ in. (19.7 × 16.5 cm). Frances Lehman Loeb Art Center, Vassar College, Purchase, Betsy Mudge Wilson, class of 1956, Memorial Fund, 1971.39

nations, as pictured in a study on the theme (fig. 13).[80] Its religious symbology is heavily indebted to Mary Baker Eddy's *Science and Health with Key to the Scriptures*.[81] Louise Lawrence Meigs, a roommate of Oakley's sister Hester at Vassar, funded the triptych. She and the class of 1891 joined Oakley in dedicating the triptych to Hester, who had died.[82] The artist had tried to recreate an Old World Trecento atmosphere with the entire room at Alumnae House, with the beamed ceiling painted with stencils, the antique furniture and silver candlesticks brought in from Europe, and the gold-framed triptych installed on the end wall like an altarpiece. She hoped the young women of the college would commune with it.[83]

Oakley led the highly focused life of a serious, independent, and unmarried female artist. A New Woman, this New Jersey–born muralist had several single artist-aunts and artist-cousins as precedents, and she would live in a colony of women artists and friends.[84] She trained at the Art Students League in New York during 1892–95. Oakley had wanted to attend Vassar like her sister Hester, but because she had asthma her family thought she would be unable to withstand the challenges of college life. She also ventured to Paris, studying in 1895 at the private art school Académie Montparnasse with Edmond Aman-Jean (fig. 14), and to Philadelphia, training at the Pennsylvania Academy of the Fine Arts with portraitist Cecilia Beaux. At Drexel

Institute, in 1896–97, she studied with illustrator Howard Pyle, who championed her mural and stained-glass designs. By the 1900s, however, he was averse to allowing women into his illustration classes.[85]

Idea-driven on a grand scale, Oakley turned from book and magazine illustration to mural-making full-time, designing and executing Italian Renaissance–inspired historical murals for state and county government buildings in Pennsylvania and Ohio. She also painted a number of World War II public altarpieces.[86] At the same time, Oakley created more than one thousand preparatory studies for portrait commissions, and rendered portrait sketches and paintings of her close women friends.[87] She would employ these portrait-making skills when producing preparatory studies for paintings such as *The Donors*.

KÄTHE KOLLWITZ

In *Self-Portrait at the Table*, from about 1893 (cat. 6), the German artist Käthe Kollwitz (1867–1945) documented herself, presumably by looking in a mirror. The faint glow of the oil lamp barely lights her face, her hands, and the tabletop.[88] Though she wrapped herself in a private moment, she used a centuries-old medium made for multiple distribution, for an audience, whether small and elite or expanded and popular. At the time she was just learning to etch, but she would eventually make

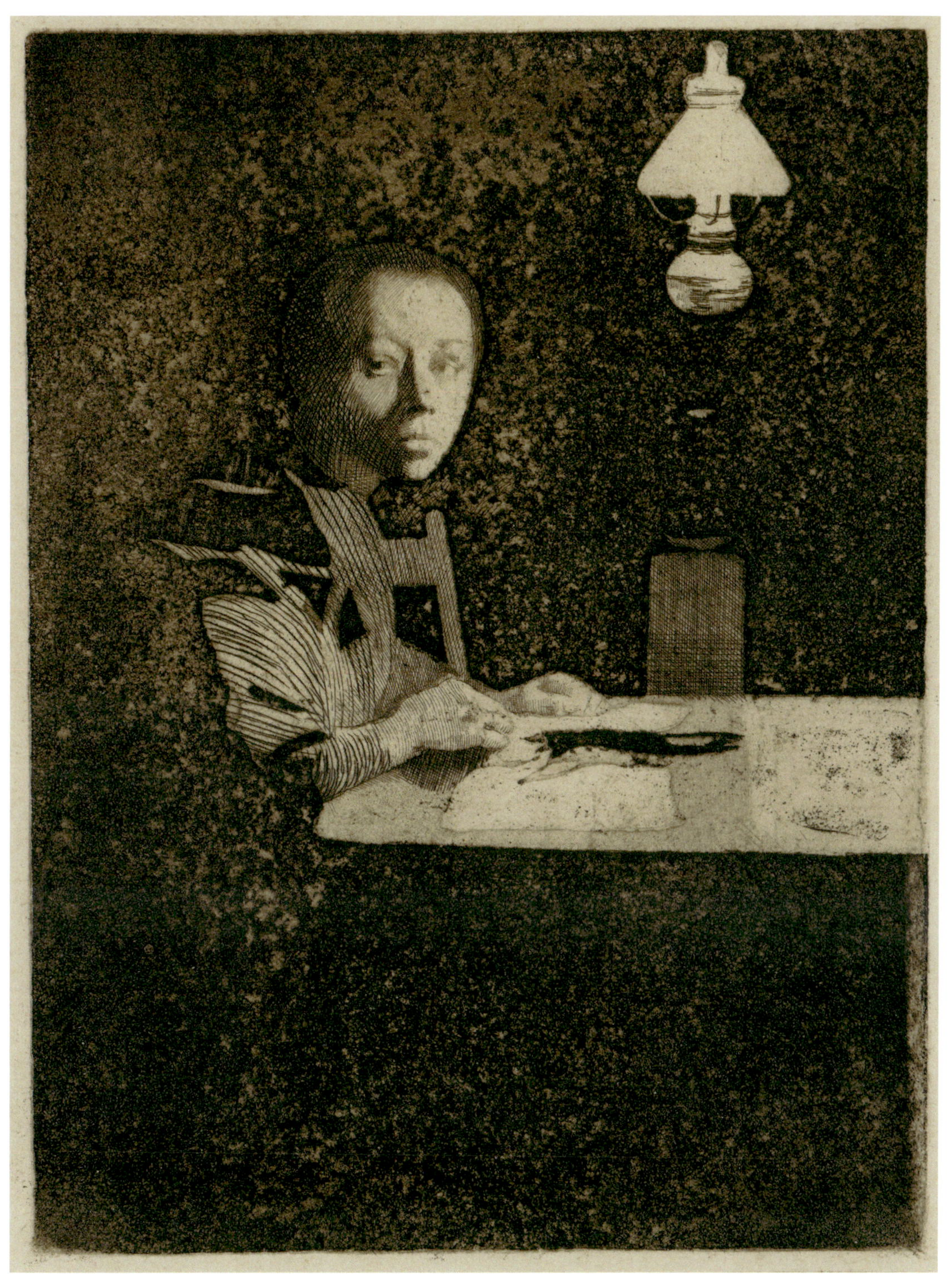

Cat. 6 **Käthe Kollwitz**

Self-Portrait at the Table

Etching and aquatint, ca. 1893
Gift of Emily Brown
Reproduced oversize

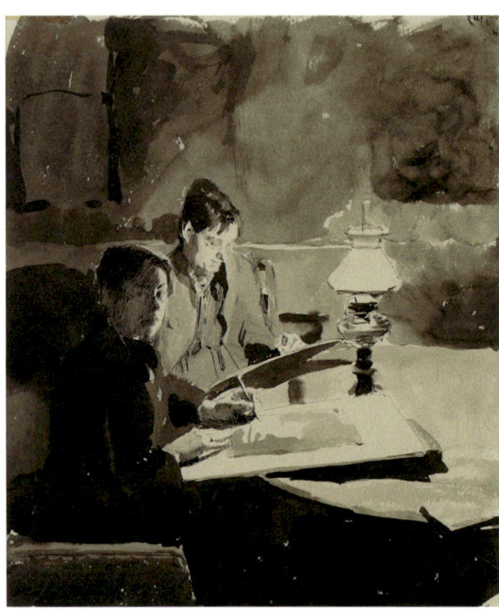

Figure 15. Käthe Kollwitz, *Self-Portrait with Fellow Student*, 1889. Pen and ink with brush and wash. 11⅝ × 10⅝ in. (29.5 × 27 cm). Private collection, courtesy of Galerie St. Etienne, New York

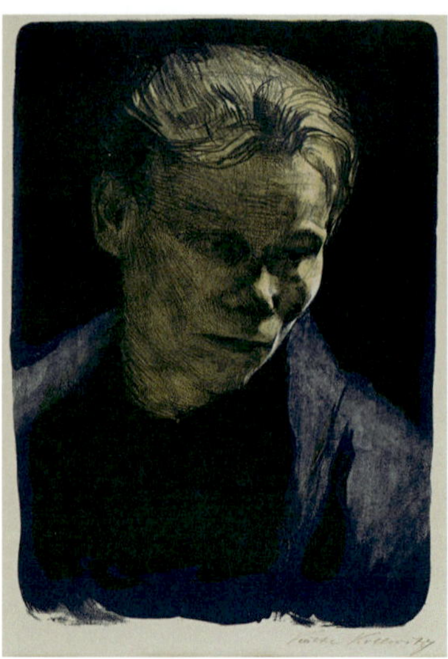

Figure 16. Käthe Kollwitz, *Working Woman with Blue Shawl*, 1903. Color lithograph on cream wove paper. 22⅜ × 17⅞ in. (56.8 × 45.4 cm). Frances Lehman Loeb Art Center, Vassar College, Gift of Lynn G. Straus, class of 1946, 2013.25.1

almost three hundred prints, going from the privacy of her own thoughts to the busy worlds of publishers and printers.

By the time this print was made, Kollwitz had already drawn several images of herself, and they telegraph a theme that would stay with her throughout her life: a series of self-conscious records in printmaking, drawing, and sculpture of her posed face, many of which gravitate toward nighttime and chiaroscuro effects. Even as an art student in Munich, in 1888–89, the young Käthe Schmidt had drawn herself and another female pupil working at their drawing boards, brilliantly lit by a table lamp (fig. 15). She was exploring her sympathies toward socialism and issues regarding the independence of women. Kollwitz attended a speech in Munich by the influential Marxist August Bebel and read his book signaling women's equality with men, *Die Frau und der Sozialismus*.[89]

Kollwitz did not train at an officially sanctioned, government-run academy of art. Rather, she attended one of the separate art schools that had been established for women in Munich, Berlin, and Karlsruhe.[90] In Munich she took private evening sessions and also went to classes at the art school for women with portrait painter Ludwig Herterich. She also spent some time in the mid-1880s in Berlin studying at the Zeichen- und Malschule of the Verein der Berliner Künstlerinnen, another art school tailored to women. After returning to Königsberg, her hometown in Prussia,

in 1890, her first art instructor, Rudolph Mauer, taught her how to put ground on an etching plate and what kind of acid to use to make a print. She was thus equipped to study the technique in her small Berlin apartment. Prints were avidly collected, and etching, she noted, was a practical alternative to painting, though she emphasized in a letter that she worked long and hard by herself to learn the process.[91]

Kollwitz executed the plate for this early print when she lived in an industrial area of Berlin called Prenzlauer Berg, where her physician husband Karl, a social democrat, had opened a clinic for disadvantaged tailors and their families in 1891 (fig. 16). The isolated shapes and somewhat disjointed outcome of the self-portrait design, coming early in her prints, stems from her lack of experience with aquatint, evident here in the too deeply bitten, shadowy tonal areas in the background that seem to cast her silhouette as a jigsaw puzzle of independent shapes. The technically complicated plate (for a beginner) and her bright lamp-lit image against pitch-black darkness announce her ambitions as a serious artist; however, it also raises the question of how she might have been aware of *Under the Lamp*, an aquatint and etching by Mary Cassatt from about 1882 (fig. 17). Kollwitz's self-portrait bears a striking similarity in subject matter and chiaroscuro treatment with Cassatt's mother and sister mending and reading by lamp in their Paris apartment. The nighttime labor in Kollwitz's etching,

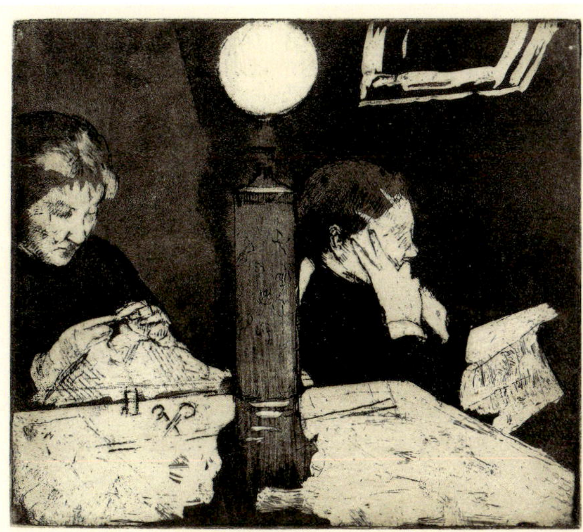

Figure 17. Mary Cassatt, *Under the Lamp*, ca. 1882. Soft-ground etching and aquatint in black on cream wove paper. 9⁵⁄₁₆ × 12⁵⁄₈ in. (23.7 × 32.1 cm). Art Institute of Chicago, Albert H. Wolf Memorial Collection, 1938.33

moreover, suggests a busy time for the artist, who, having given birth to her first son in 1892, would have had little free time for her art. She wrote, however, "My husband did everything possible so that I would have time to work."[92]

Kollwitz was not born into a family of artists, but they did have deep social democratic roots and intellectual interests within the Königsberg community, in what is now Kaliningrad, Russia. Kollwitz had received much encouragement for being an artist from her father, in an era when the independence of women, prompted, in part, by Bebel's writings, was an issue of passionate public interest. As suggested by her many renderings of mothers, widows, and other females, Kollwitz's concern for women and their well-being remained constant throughout her life and work.

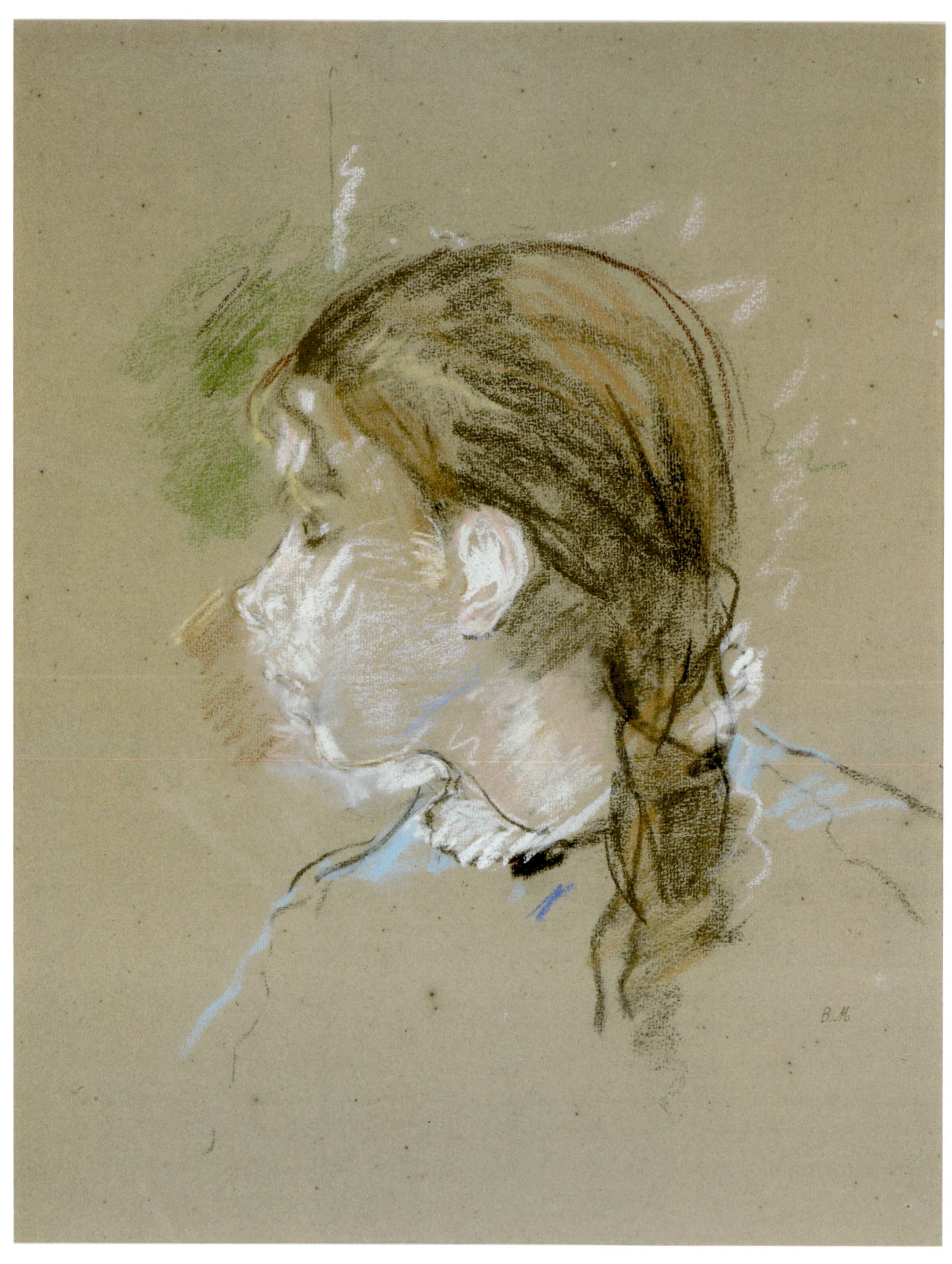

Cat. 7   **Berthe Morisot**

Profile Portrait of Paule Gobillard

Pastel, 1886
Gift of Jane Crowley Koven in memory of her daughter Constance
Henriette Koven Stransky, class of 1960

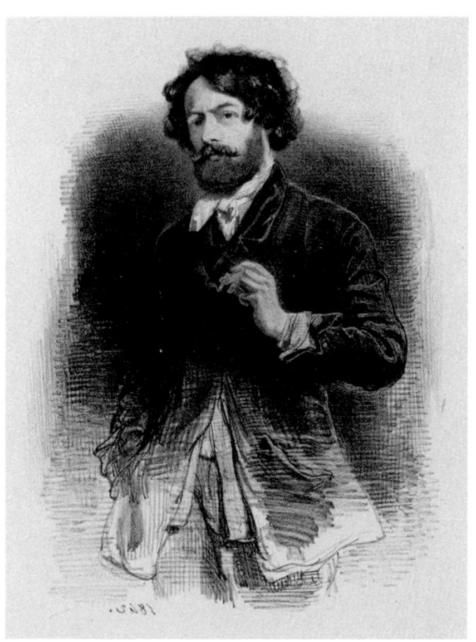

Figure 18. Paul Gavarni, *Self-Portrait*, 1842. Lithograph. 8⅞ × 6⅛ in. (22.5 × 15.6 cm). Frances Lehman Loeb Art Center, Vassar College, Purchase, Betsy Mudge Wilson, class of 1956, Memorial Fund, 1975.21

BERTHE MORISOT

In 1886, the French Impressionist painter Berthe Morisot (1841–1895) masked a profile portrait of her niece and student Paule Gobillard (1867–1946) with strokes of brilliant white pastel, insinuating a shower of dazzling outdoor light (cat. 7). Morisot used her niece as a subject in a series of portraits that year.[93] The Impressionists were noted for capturing modern life through portraiture, and many paintings and works on paper record their families and their circles of fellow artists and writers. Morisot, exhibiting with the French Impressionists from the start, in 1874, would paint canvases and draw pastels of girls and women from her immediate and extended family, and portraits of neighbors and friends in her own and others' intimate, well-appointed homes and gardens.[94]

The liberated sketching and nervous, slashing whites in Morisot's drawing transmit her modern concerns with sensuous light, fugitive color, and atmospheric, momentary effects with suggestions of energy and action. The indeterminate hints of outdoors—those patches and smudges of lime green—and brilliant splashes of white also suggest a plein-air setting, a hallmark of Impressionist practice and familiar to her from her studies with the Barbizon painter Camille Corot in about 1860.[95] Yet, the supple, dark outlines she used underneath her coat of pastel remind us of her early lessons in precision and the importance of line. Both of these were working guideposts, perhaps driven in part

by her private lessons in 1857–59 with Joseph-Benoît Guichard (1806–1880), who introduced her to plein-air work.

Though there were state-sponsored design schools open to young women, in the mid-nineteenth century it was de rigueur for French girls and young women of the upper classes to learn how to draw through private instruction.[96] An academic history and portrait painter trained at the Écoles des Beaux-Arts in Lyons and in Paris, Guichard possessed a close, tight draftsmanship and strong color sense, rooted in his training with Ingres and his admiration of Delacroix. He taught Morisot and her sister Edma the importance of line by instructing them to study the satirical lithographs by Paul Gavarni in the newspaper (fig. 18), and he taught them the significance of color by having them copy the Old Masters in the Louvre, a practice the sisters continued for at least ten years.[97]

Morisot, whose family claimed indirect descent from the eighteenth-century painter Fragonard, dared to become a professional artist. She showed a seriousness toward her early lessons that drove Guichard to caution her mother that she and her sister Edma would become "painters, not minor amateur talents. Do you really understand what that means? In the world of the *grande bourgeoisie* in which you move, it would be a revolution, I would even say a catastrophe."[98]

In her own way, Morisot kept undermining social expectations, and she passed on these art lessons to a later generation of

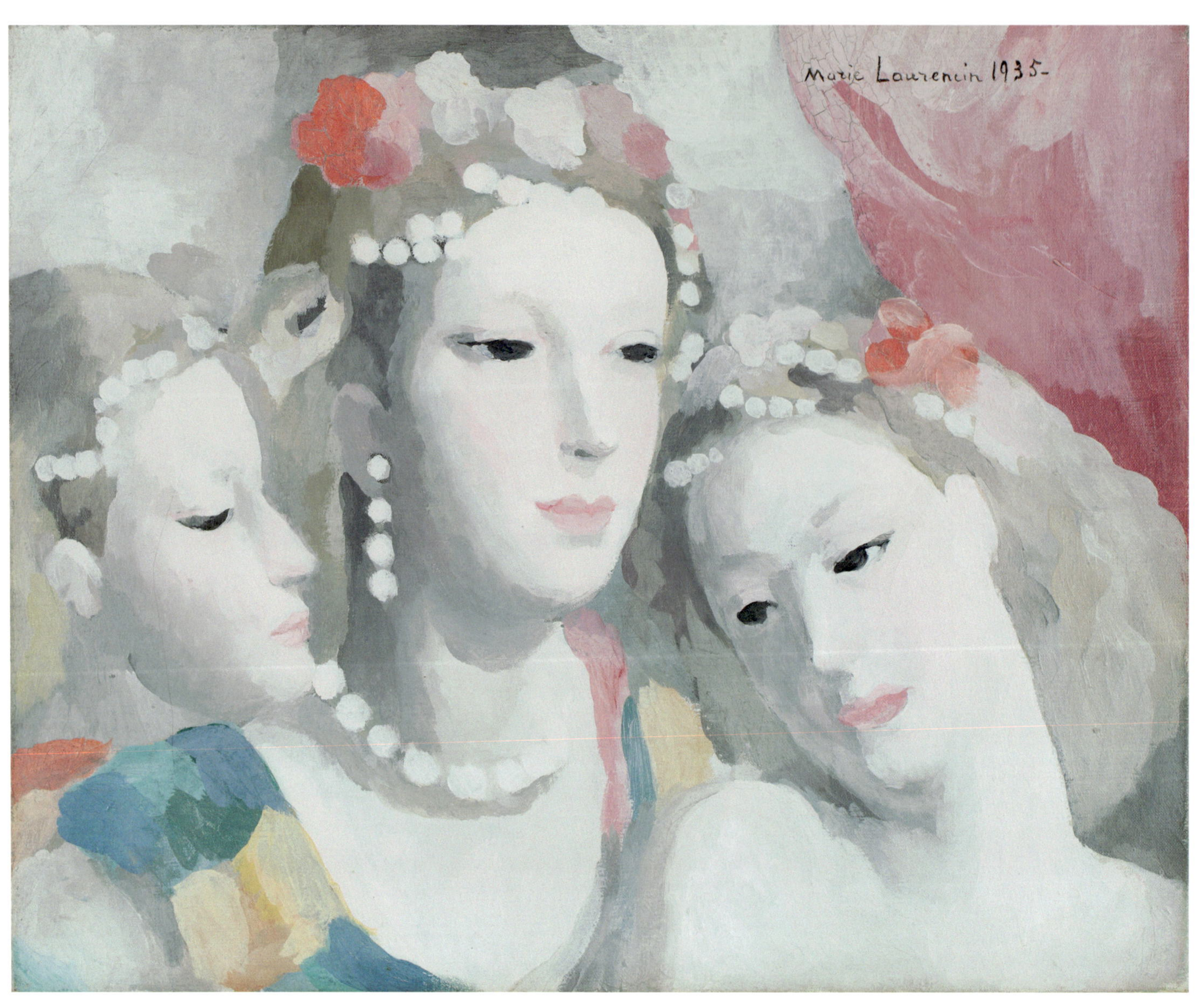

Cat. 8   **Marie Laurencin**

Three Women

Oil on canvas, 1935
Bequest of June Bingham Birge, class of 1940

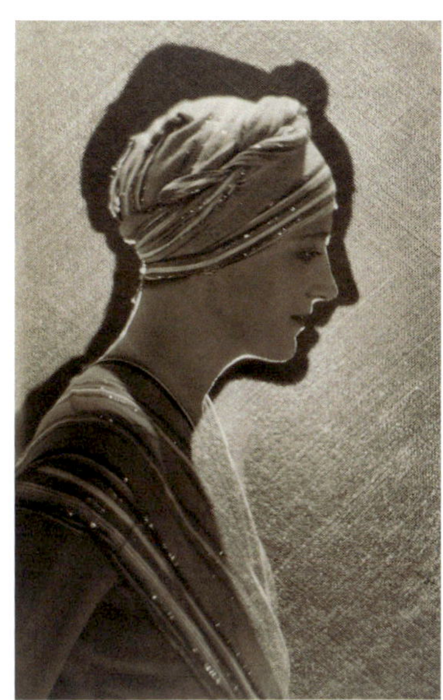

Figure 19. Adolf de Meyer, *Portrait of Daisy Fellowes*, ca. 1924. Vintage gelatin silver print. 6 × 9 in. (15.2 × 22.9 cm). Frances Lehman Loeb Art Center, Vassar College, Purchase, Friends of the Vassar College Art Gallery Fund, 1986.38.2

female artists. In 1886, she was teaching her niece how to paint and offering encouragement, writing in a letter from the Isle of Jersey to her young protégée, "Do anything to practice precision, drawing, and tonal exactitude."[99]

MARIE LAURENCIN

In 1935 the Parisian modernist Marie Laurencin (1883–1956) painted *Three Women* (cat. 8), an oil she brushed in her trademark gray, white, rose, lemon, and Mediterranean blue, representing a trio of exotic, closely placed young women with black, opaque eyes. She frequently painted portraits of stylized, attractive young women such as these, often in reverie among animals in idealized corners of nature.

In general, however, the women projected by Laurencin are self-conscious and on display. Here, they look away from the viewer. They wear fashionable strings of pearls in their hair like headbands, suggesting 1920s chic, perhaps best personified in the international socialite Daisy Fellowes (fig. 19). The muted palette brings to mind the stylish gray and pink, Egyptian-inspired woman's bedroom designed by André Groult for the Exposition Internationale des Arts Décoratifs et Industriels Modernes in Paris in 1925, to which Laurencin contributed paintings.[100]

Early influential critics considered Laurencin to be one of the most "feminine" of female artists because of her subjects, which were nearly all delicate renderings of women involved in feminine pleasures and pursuits. She was said to have created an idyllic "child-woman, slender and delicate," a description that reflects years of debate in France over the idea of a "feminine" art. She may have even encouraged this reading of her work.[101] However, while the young women in this reverie could be interpreted as delicate objects of desire, their white-powdered faces and coal-black eyes act as public fronts, masking their thoughts or true natures. Because we cannot look "into" their eyes, they appear unknowable and untamable. As Elizabeth Louise Kahn surmised from the writings of the artist, Laurencin combined the personal and the public as a strategy.[102] The artist's close friend Armand Lowengard recalled that Laurencin preferred "the artificial" and "fabrications—dolls, phantoms, beings that cannot possibly be brought to life."[103]

An artist with Cubist roots in the Bateau-Lavoir circle of artists around poet Guillaume Apollinaire, Laurencin had become successful and internationally known as a prolific, high-society French portrait painter and designer by the 1930s, and her paintings were widely collected.[104] Early on she had studied porcelain painting and drawing at a teachers school in Sèvres and drawing under Madeleine Lemaire (1845–1928), a painter of flowers and leisure-filled scenes of women, at the city-administered art school in Paris.[105] She then trained in painting at the private

Académie Humbert in Paris in 1903–4, where she met Georges Braque and Francis Picabia. By the 1930s she had relaxed her flattened, arabesque visual language and worked with a more sculptural, malleable reshaping of forms, a stylistic departure that can be seen here and in the works of many European and American artists between the two world wars.

Whether Laurencin was being strategic or more ambiguous with her feminine images, she was a modernist who championed femininity, exhibiting in the 1930s at a recently formed collective, the Société des Femmes Artistes Modernes, whose founder sought modern "School of Paris" female artists for membership, while self-conscious women's themes, including self-portraiture, proliferated in members' works.[106] She was also teaching female art students, from 1932 to 1935, at the Académie of the Sixteenth Arrondissement.[107]

ELIZABETH CATLETT

The face of *Negro Woman* (cat. 9) insists on our attention. Executing it in 1945, the African American sculptor and printmaker Elizabeth Catlett (1915–2012) magnified this Black female image so markedly that she confronts us in a powerful lithographic portrayal. Whether imagined by the artist or posed, Catlett's woman is unadorned. Her textured hair is short, her lips are full, and her dark eyes look out narrowly from an egg-shaped face set against a blank background. Her distilled ovoid and angular features project an almost palpable three-dimensionality and visual language recalling African sculptural masks, especially those from Gabon.

The boldness of Catlett's print telegraphs her profound interest in the identity and strength of African American women. She won a Julius Rosenwald Fund Fellowship and renewal award for 1945–46, which allowed her to work on a sequence of images of Black women called "The Negro Woman."[108] She made the Loeb lithograph during 1945, and for her fellowship in 1946 she traveled to Mexico to continue the project.[109]

The assertiveness that is projected so well in this print also transmits the artist's individual resolve, after a personal and public journey to develop her art that was fueled by recognition of her talent but also the obstacles of prejudice and racism. Her maternal grandmother was enslaved. Catlett grew up in Washington, D.C. She had applied to the Carnegie Institute of Technology in

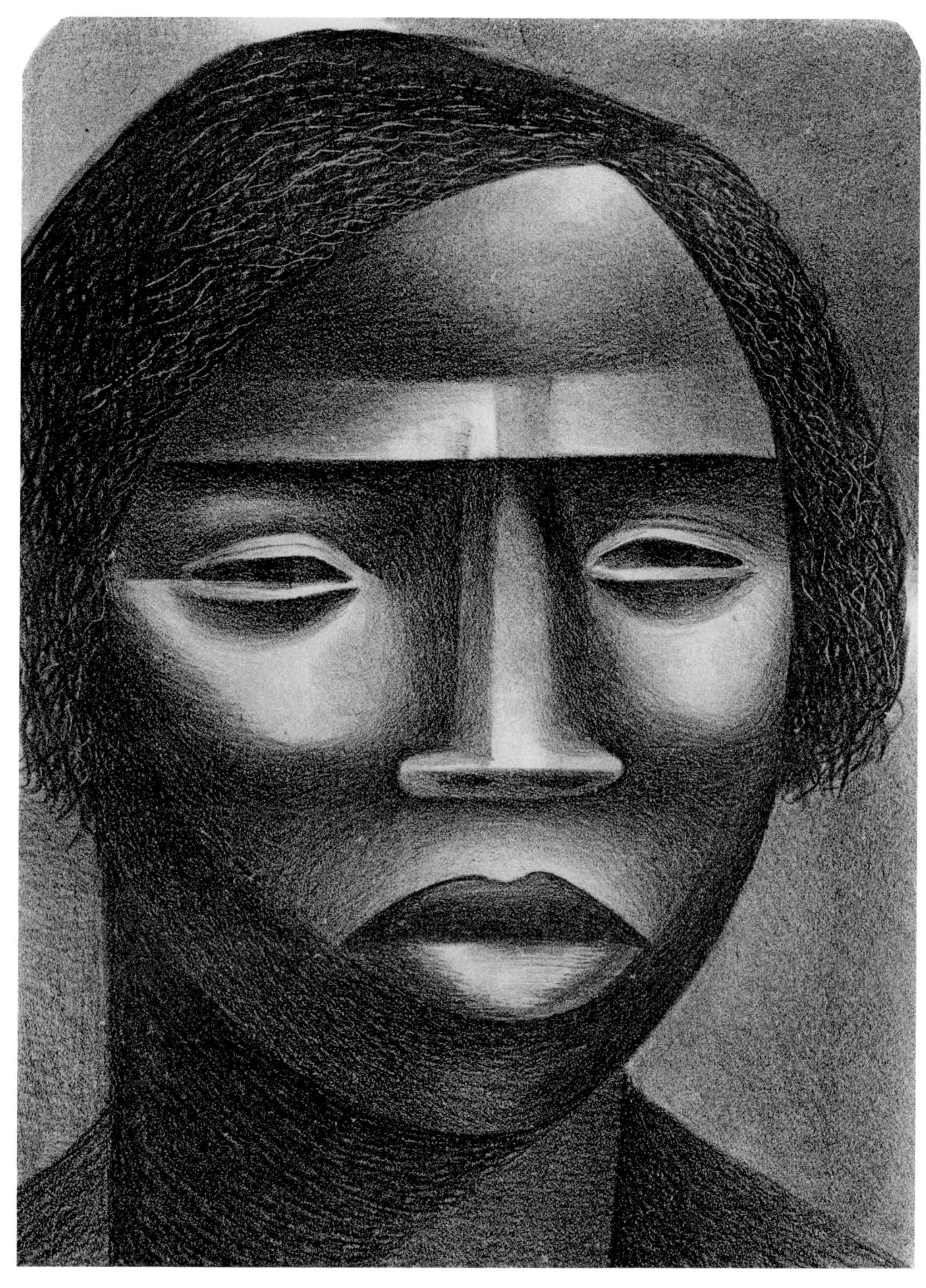

Cat. 9 **Elizabeth Catlett**
Negro Woman

Lithograph, 1945
Purchase with funds given by Arthur A. Anderson,
Edward J. Guarino, Marcia Widenor, Africana Studies,
and various donors

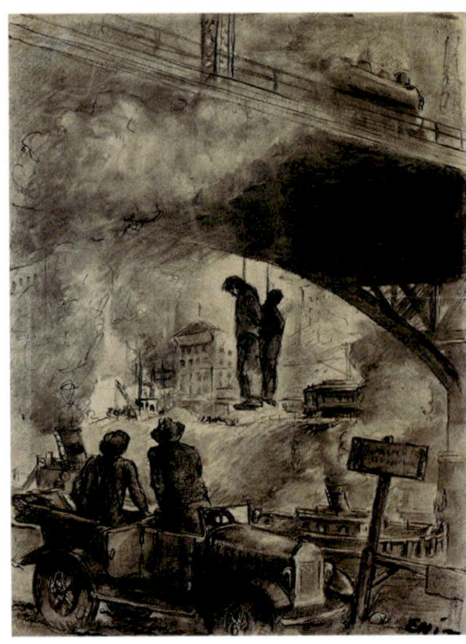

Figure 20. Fred Ellis, *Lynching under the Bridge*, ca. 1915. Charcoal, brush and black ink, wash, graphite, and gouache on beige paper. 17 × 12⅜ in. (43.2 × 31.4 cm). Frances Lehman Loeb Art Center, Vassar College, Gift of Susan and Steven Hirsch, class of 1971, 2003.43.4

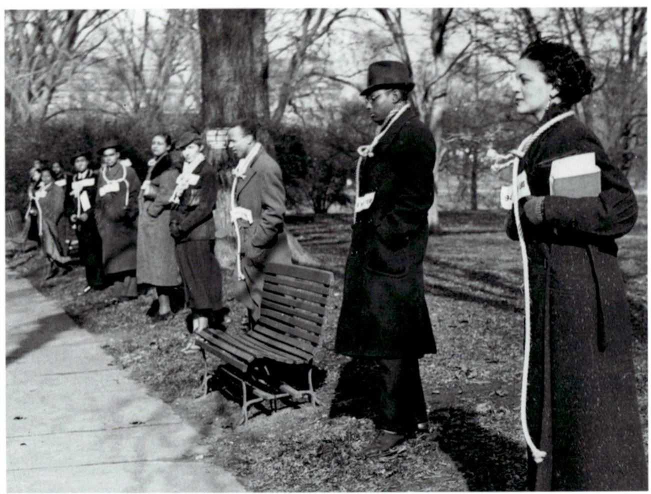

Figure 21. *Anti-Lynching Protest*, 1934. Students from Howard University picket National Crime Conference over the refusal of conference leaders to acknowledge lynching as a national crime, Washington, D.C. Photograph, December 1934. The Granger Collection, Granger Historical Picture Archive

Pittsburgh to study art but was turned down for racial reasons.[110] She went instead to Howard University, the historically black university in the nation's capital, from which she graduated in 1935, taking art classes with James Wells, James Porter, and Loïs Mailou Jones, and majoring in painting.[111]

While living in Washington, Catlett joined protests at the U.S. Supreme Court against the lynching of Black men.[112] Lynching had increased in the United States in the first half of the twentieth century and was documented in photographs. Socially concerned artists protested the practice in paintings, prints, political cartoons, sculpture, and drawings, including one in charcoal by the *Masses* illustrator Fred Ellis (fig. 20).[113] Howard University students were active in demonstrations demanding anti-lynching legislation, and in December 1934 a wire service photographed several of them wearing nooses and protesting against the National Crime Conference when its leader failed to consider lynching a national crime (fig. 21). At the State University of Iowa, where Catlett's painting instructor, the American regionalist Grant Wood, championed her sculpture and encouraged her to focus on familiar subjects, she was almost denied an M.F.A. in sculpture in 1940 by the head of the art department.

During World War II, while teaching art at the George Washington Carver School in Harlem, where local working-class Afri-can Americans attended programs, Catlett concluded from the audience's devotion and attention that she "wanted to do art that black people would relate to."[114] The decade of the 1940s was a turning point for her in finding and developing those primary subjects, and printmaking played a crucial role in her work. In the early 1940s, when prints were a key part of the national conversation to democratize art and employ artists, Catlett made the medium into a channel for delivering her own thoughts and views to a large audience. In the summer of 1941 she worked in lithography in Chicago at the South Side Community Art Center, a Works Projects Administration–sponsored arts center co-founded by artist Margaret Taylor Goss Burroughs (see cat. 32), with whom she roomed.[115] Granting Black artists access to new opportunities, the community art center was one of several locations across the country with printmaking facilities or workshops overseen by the graphic arts division of the WPA's Federal Art Project.[116] The South Side Community Art Center's artists encouraged activist art and bettering the lives of African Americans during a harsh social period of Jim Crow laws and lynching. These painters, sculptors, and printmakers helped shape the movement during the Great Depression and for decades afterwards to make art for everyday people and weaponize it in the struggle for equality, workers' rights, and social justice.

In 1942, Catlett and her new artist-husband, Charles White, moved to New York City, where she studied lithography at the Art Students League in 1944 with the social realist and art-activist printmaker Harry Sternberg. With Sternberg, known for his vital worker-themed lithographs, she found even more fertile ground in which to further her knowledge of techniques and develop a body of socially conscious prints.[117] In Mexico she would become associated with the Taller de Gráfica Popular (People's Graphic Arts Workshop) and made prints in keeping with the popular social tenets of the collective, namely, to identify with the working class of Mexico and create art that would reveal social ills and rally around improved conditions. She would spend much of the rest of her life in Mexico, becoming a joint citizen and making a body of prints and sculptures devoted to her social ideals.

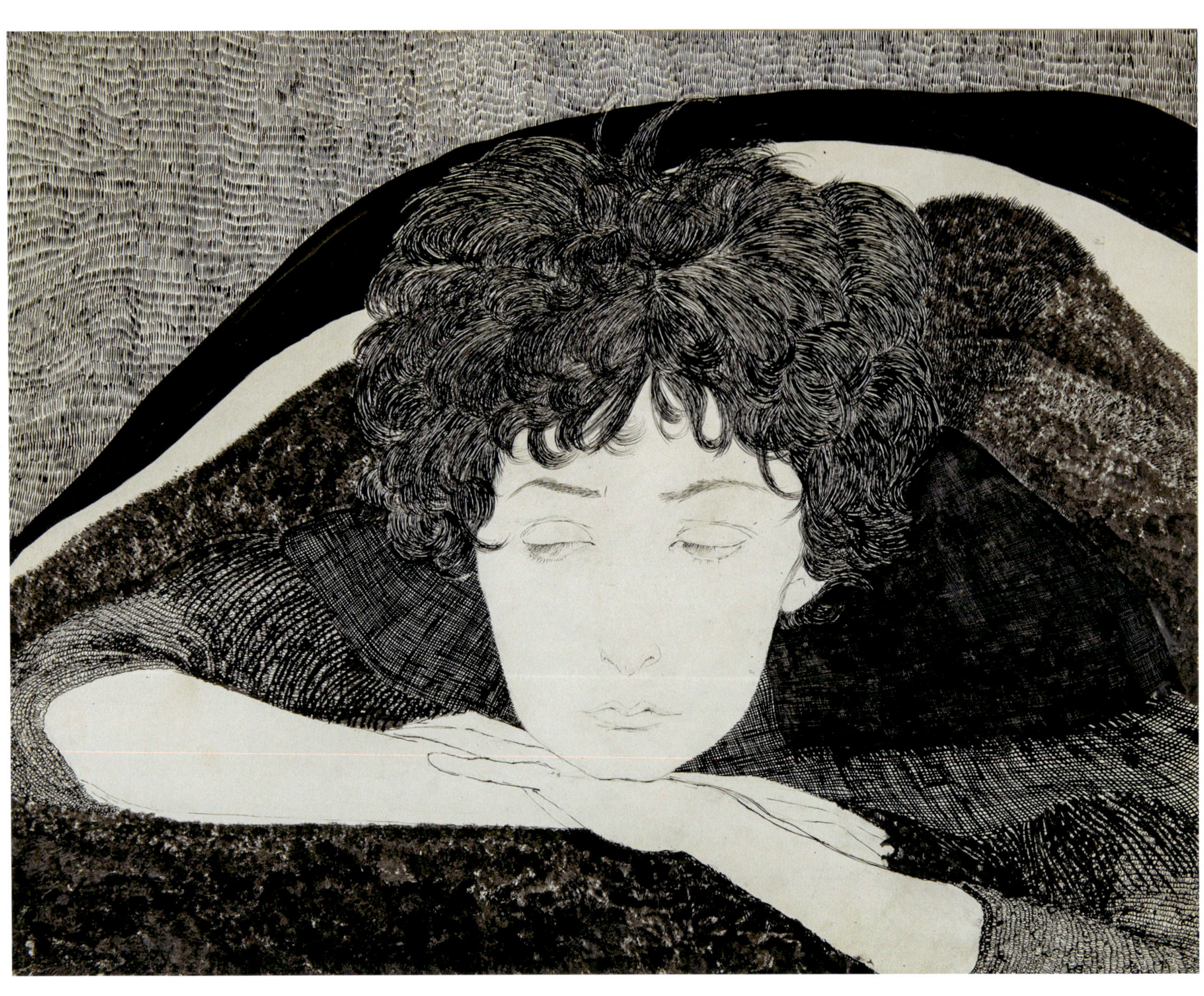

Cat. 10 **Titina Maselli**

Woman Resting Her Head on Her Hands

Pen and ink, brush and wash, and graphite, ca. 1955
Gift of Mrs. R. Kirk Askew, Jr.

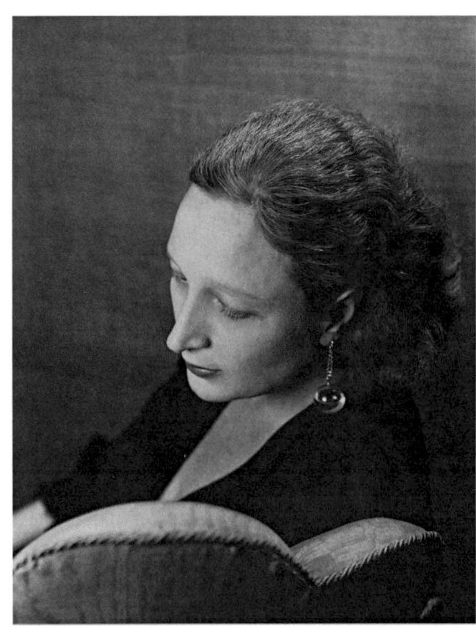

Figure 22. George Platt Lynes, *Constance Atwood Askew*, ca. 1932. Gelatin silver print. 9⅜ × 7¹⁄₁₆ in. (23.8 × 17.9 cm). Frances Lehman Loeb Art Center, Vassar College, Gift of Agnes Rindge Claflin, 1977.22.26

TITINA MASELLI

Looking down and away, the sitter in Titina Maselli's drawing (cat. 10) rests close to the viewer, outlines of her head and hands visible among layers of blankets and strands of hair. This private moment appears rare among Maselli's publicly accessible work, which is limited.[118] Her face and hair compare favorably with images of the artist, suggesting this may be a self-portrait.[119]

Born in Rome, Maselli (1924–2005) painted as a young girl, encouraged by her parents and family friends.[120] She moved to New York in 1952 and showed at Durlacher Brothers shortly thereafter, with solo exhibitions of paintings in 1953 and 1955.[121] Writing in the *New York Times*, Howard Devree observed that "Her color is quite a match for the masculine vigor of her compositions and well suited to the industrial subjects she has chosen."[122] In the 1950s and 1960s, Maselli used flat poster-like colors, minimalist images from nature and pop culture, and suggestions of a pulsating artificial light to create brilliantly painted, large, patterned abstractions that are quite antithetical to this small, quiet drawing. Many of her paintings are night scenes or cityscapes, and combine both realism and abstraction.[123]

Durlacher's director, R. Kirk Askew, dealt in Old Master paintings and drawings, as well as work by the Surrealists. He and his wife Constance Atwood Askew (fig. 22) were well known for holding salons in the 1930s at their home in New York. Those gatherings attracted established and emerging artists, musicians, actors, and intellectuals, including Agnes Rindge of the art department at Vassar, composer and critic Virgil Thomson, and art dealer Julien Levy.[124]

Records for the artist at the Durlacher Brothers gallery cover only the years 1953 to 1957.[125] The gallery lent an exhibition of Maselli's paintings to Vassar College Art Gallery during March of 1955. The show received an enthusiastic review in the student newspaper, in which junior Sylvia May Stern, class of 1956, noted the artist's camera-like vision and vibrant urban subjects.[126] Through the years the Askews gave Old Master works and numerous works on paper and paintings to the Vassar art collection from their circle of artists, including Peter Blume, Eugene Berman, Kurt Seligmann, and Pavel Tchelitchew. Constance Askew gave the drawing by Maselli to Vassar in 1983, long after her husband's death in 1974.

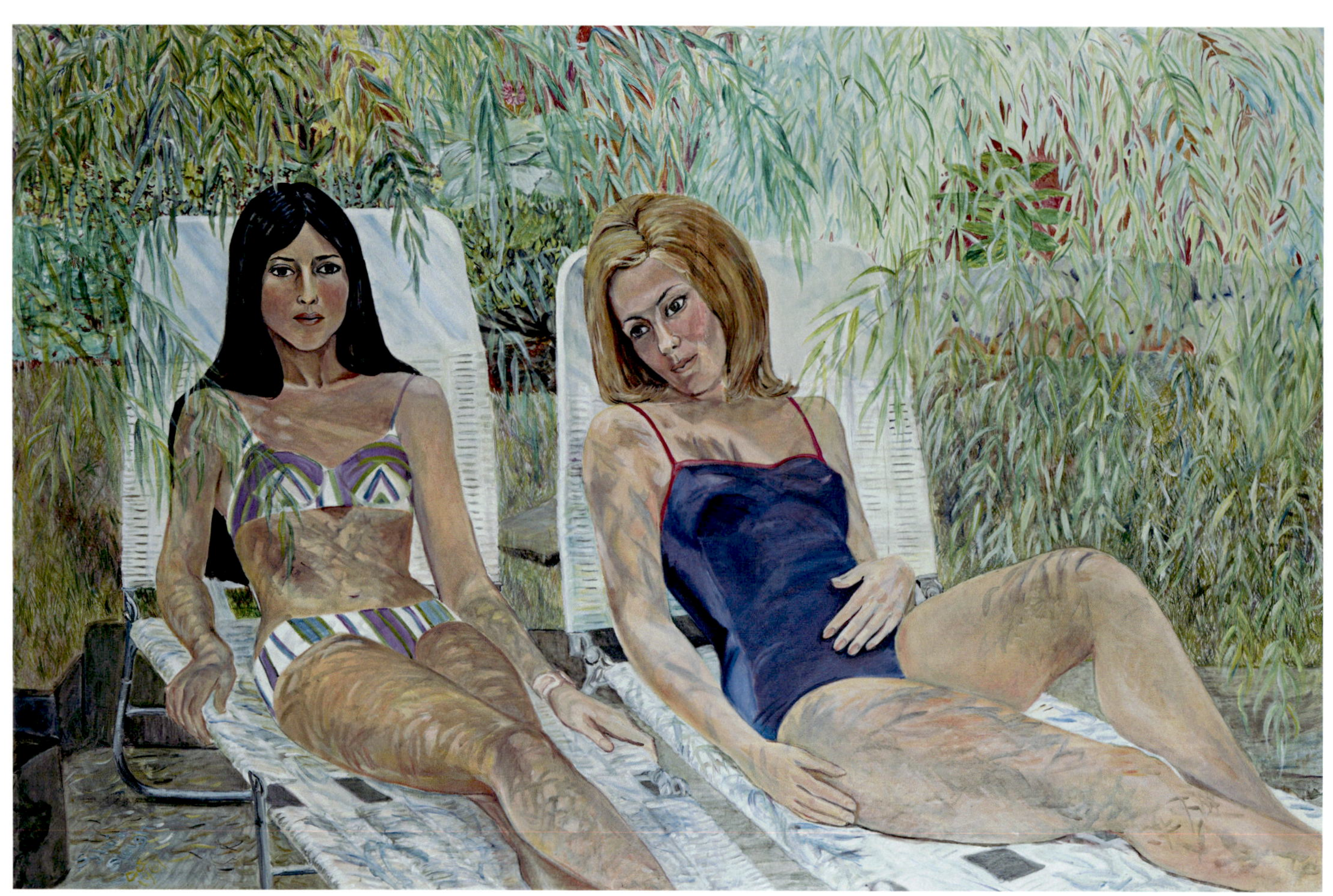

Cat. 11 **Sylvia Sleigh**

The Willows: Sylvia Castro

Oil on canvas, 1967
Gift of the estate of Sylvia Sleigh

SYLVIA SLEIGH

In *The Willows: Sylvia Castro*, a six-foot-wide canvas, the Welsh realist Sylvia Sleigh (1916–2010) painted her friends Sylvia Castro and Marilú Marini sunning themselves on lawn chairs in her backyard (cat. 11). Their tanned skin reflects the lanceolate leaves of the weeping willow, evoking a oneness with nature, and their striking faces are calm. Lounging in a sheltered spot, one is turned toward the other as if in intimate conversation.

Sleigh preferred this casualness and weaving-in-and-out-with-the-setting in her works. Of a similarly themed painting, *Chelsea Garden* (1967), she remarked, "I like my figure subjects to be informal, with precarious compositions, as if the sitters might move or change, but the figures and their environment have to be firmly meshed together." On the sense of privacy that one infers, she confirmed, "The sitters are my friends, because the act of painting someone is very intimate, a personal relationship."[127]

Castro and Marini formed part of the international coterie of artists, dancers, curators, and others who visited Sleigh and her English husband, the influential contemporary art critic, curator, and writer Lawrence Alloway, in their home in Chelsea in New York. Sleigh had arrived in the United States in 1961. She was raised in Hove, Sussex, and trained at the Brighton School of Art from 1934 to 1937, but experienced disappointment when her first husband disapproved of her interest in art.[128]

In about 1967, when this work was painted, Chilean-born Sylvia Castro-Cid (now Sylvia Palacios Whitman), at left, was painting and drawing, and dancing with Trisha Brown in Europe.[129] About the same time, the avant-garde dancer and Argentine-born Marini co-originated *Danse Bouquet* with Ana Kamien in Buenos Aires. The performance was the fruit of their working together in their contemporary dance group, Danza Actual, during the 1960s.[130] Sleigh often made portraits of her friends, and visitors to her home were frequently seen lounging in the garden depicted in her paintings. According to Andrew Hottle, a specialist on Sleigh's work, she exhibited *The Willows: Sylvia Castro* just once, at her solo exhibition at Hemingway Galleries in November 1968.[131]

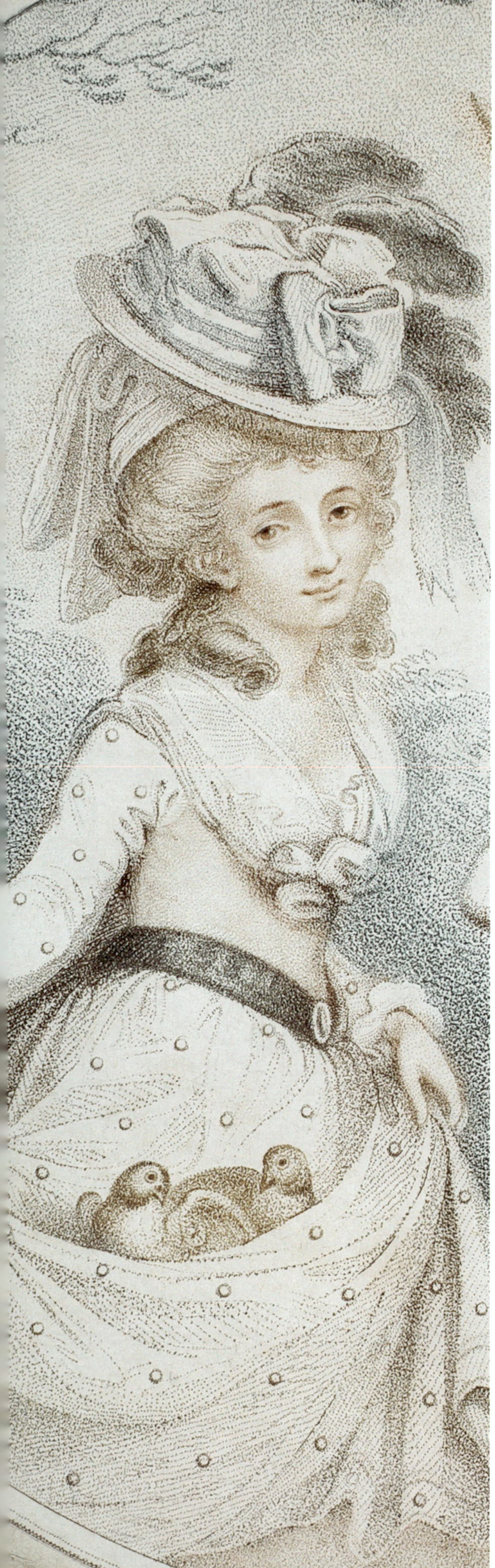

Idyllic Landscapes
Comfort and Security

Florine Stettheimer wrote of her joyfulness in the landscape in this remembrance from her childhood, taken from a longer poem,

In our oleander treed yard on a stage
I sang "Little Maggie May" with bliss.
I dressed up in paper muslin
With fringes and gold stars
In that golden era when to
Adventures there were no bars.[132]

MISS T. BENNETT

Depictions of women mixing with nature and her creatures, such as birds and sheep, were prevalent in English prints of the 1780s, though they were frequently presented in allegorical guises. *Affection and Innocence*, published in March 1785 after a design by Francesco Bartolozzi, features two young women and a cherub in an open landscape. The cherub reaches for a bullfinch held by a string or ribbon (fig. 23). This stipple print, an intaglio technique using small dots to create tonal effects, is one of several that Bartolozzi and his students made after themselves, Élisabeth Louise Vigée Le Brun, Angelica Kauffman, and others portraying women as personifications of rural innocence.

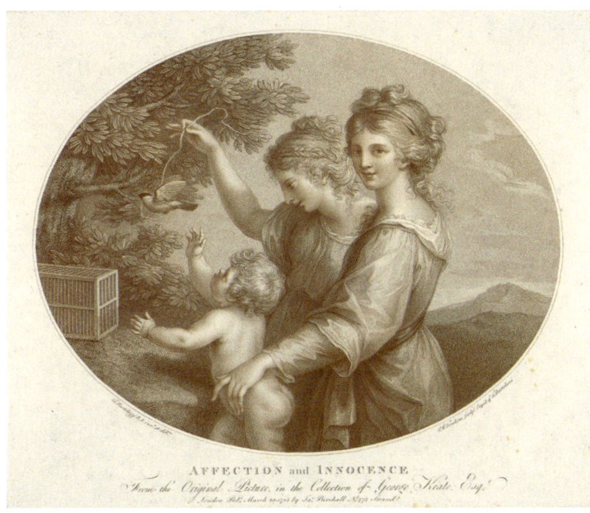

Figure 23. Peltro William Tomkins, after Francesco Bartolozzi, published by James Birchall, *Affection and Innocence*, 1785. Stipple and etching. 12 × 14 in. (30.5 × 35.5 cm). British Museum, Purchased from Louis Bihn 1873, 1873,0809.199

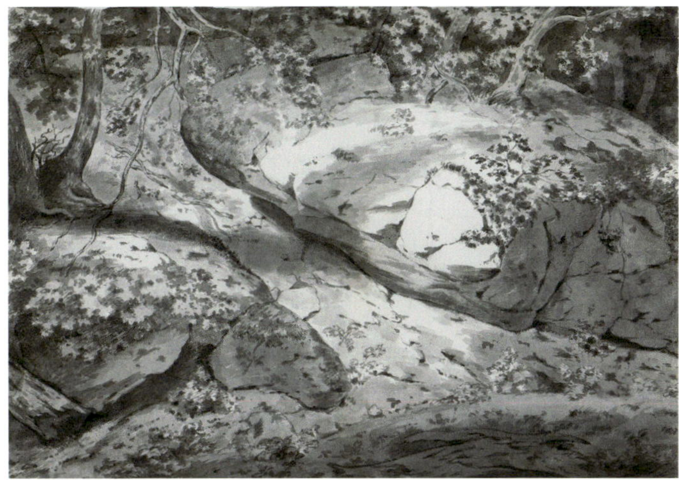

Figure 24. Joseph Wright of Derby, *Study of Rocks and Trees*, 1774 or 1775. Graphite, brush and ink, and wash on cream laid paper. 14¹⁵⁄₁₆ × 21³⁄₈ in. (37.9 × 54.3 cm). Frances Lehman Loeb Art Center, Vassar College, Purchase, Suzette Morton Davidson, class of 1934, Fund, 1966.23.9

In Britain, gentlemen had been drawing for pleasure outdoors since the seventeenth century. Authors of drawing manuals began distinguishing between real and imagined landscapes, and both appear in the eighteenth century.[133] A drawing by Joseph Wright of Derby (fig. 24), for example, describes the features of an actual landscape, while that of Alexander Cozens is imaginary (fig. 25). In the mid-eighteenth century, some women connected to the British royal family sketched landscapes inspired by Cozens.[134]

The connection between the land and women of means took physical and material form, as female land ownership numbered more than ten percent in Georgian Britain.[135] In the eighteenth century, some upper-class women designed their own pleasure gardens and used them as sites of retreat and reflection. The "women-in-nature" theme runs through hundreds of years of art by women, and in the Georgian era—and much later, as well—it is frequently tied to aspects of domestic life.

In about 1785 Miss T. Bennett, a still-unidentified English amateur artist, added an Italianate landscape to the background of a color print. In a scene with a fluted column and slender poplars, two young women play with doves (cat. 12). The figure at left carries the baby birds in a fold of her skirt, while her companion holds a string tied to a flying dove, similar to the print after Bartolozzi. Even the title for the print is uncertain, as variations have appeared in different publications. One, *While, Celia, from the hand . . .*, may reference the characters Celia and her close cousin Rosalind from Shakespeare's comedic play *As You Like It*, while a more descriptive title, *Two Girls with Doves*, has also been published.[136]

Bennett's placement of these two attractive, elite "ladies" showing off their domestic taming skills within a quiet landscape suggests their comfort within the natural world, and perhaps also their taming of nature. Though the scene is idyllic and intimate, its translation into a print implies the upper-class woman who made the design would have participated in the public world of the thriving London print trade.

The printmaker and drawing master Charles White (1751–1785) made this tranquil, round stipple print after Bennett, as the name is engraved in the border. An impression on silk printed from the cut-down plate has survived and isolates the two women above a January 1785 issue date.[137] At the time, White's shop was on Stafford Row, Pimlico, near the Queen's House, a royal residence that attracted the nobility to concerts, balls, and readings.[138]

Fashionable women increasingly purchased prints during these years, especially the decorative stipple prints in gilt frames, and a growing print market developed for feminine themes.[139] In the mid-1770s, stipple prints made after works by the Royal Academician Angelica Kauffman (see cat. 26), who is discussed in more detail below, were popular.[140]

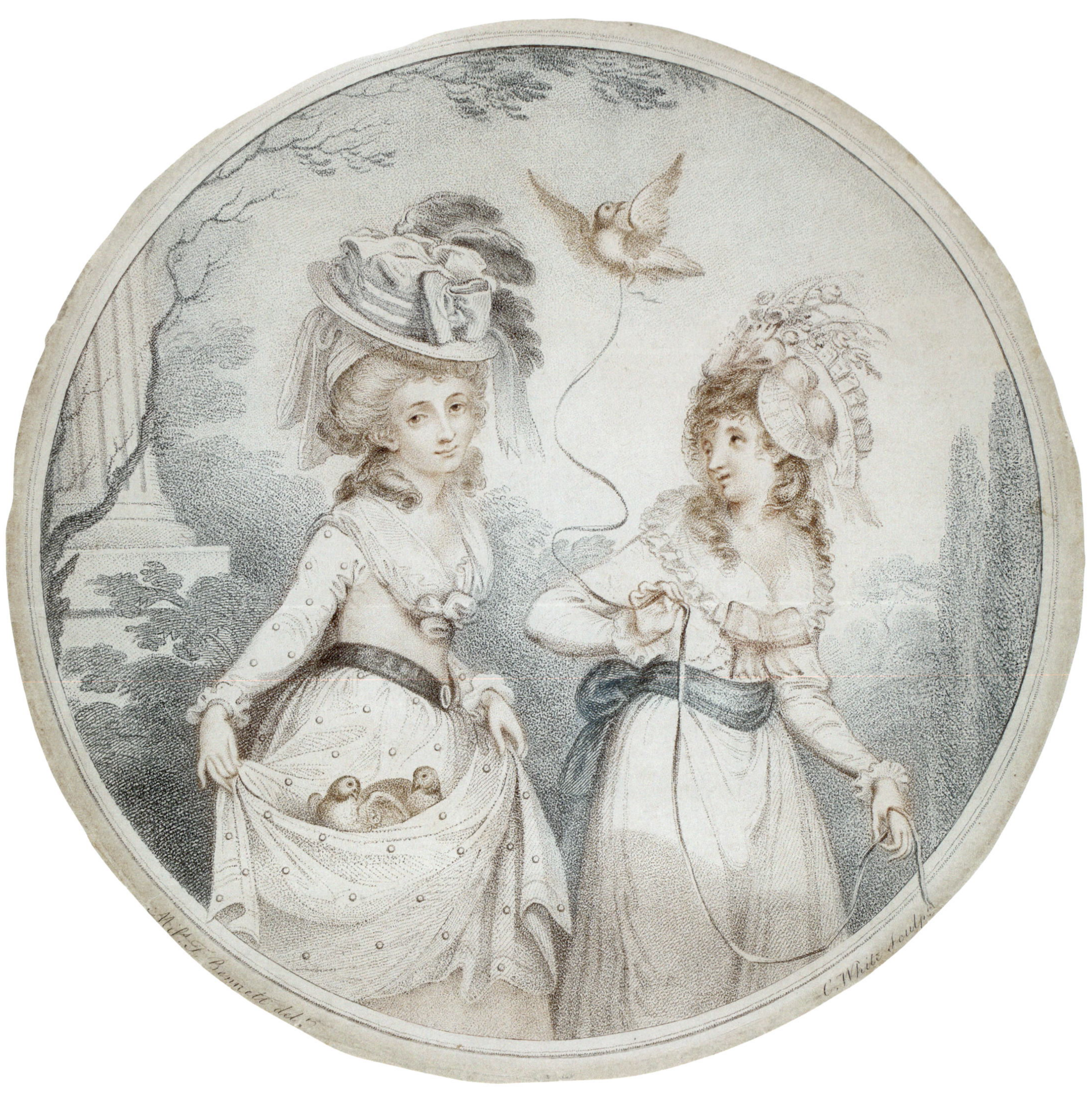

Cat. 12   **Charles White after Miss T. Bennett**

While, Celia, from the hand . . .

Color stipple engraving, 1785

Donor unknown

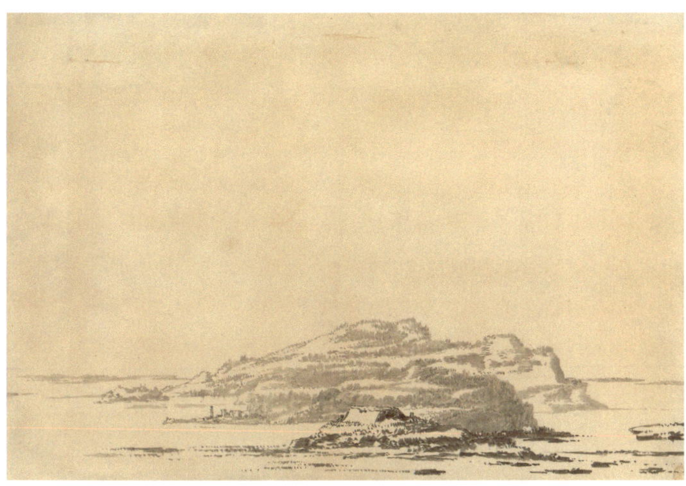

Figure 25. Alexander Cozens, *Fantastic Landscape*, 1780 to 1785. Gray wash, black wash, graphite and buff ground on medium, slightly textured, cream laid paper, mounted on medium, slightly textured, cream laid paper. 12¼ × 17⅜ in. (31.1 × 44.1 cm). Yale Center for British Art, Paul Mellon Collection, B1977.14.139

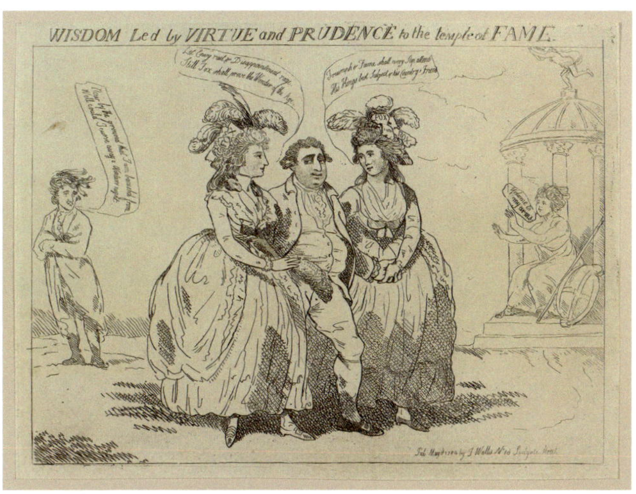

Figure 26. Thomas Rowlandson, published by John Wallis, *Wisdom Led by Virtue and Prudence to the Temple of Fame*, 6 May 1784. Etching. 9¹³⁄₁₆ × 13 in. (24.9 × 33 cm). Royal Collection Trust, RCIN 810081

Amateur women from the nobility, landed gentry, and upper-middle class who pursued drawing as a gentlewomanly pursuit designed many of these decorative prints. These print-makers and print designers emerged from the expanding group of well-to-do young women taking private lessons from drawing masters.[141] Miss Bennett (or Bennet) is one of several mostly amateur women, including Lavinia Bingham, Countess Spencer (1737–1814), the sister-in-law of Georgiana Spencer Cavendish. White translated her designs of "lady imagery" into color stipple prints in the 1780s.[142]

However idyllic the scene in Bennett's design, the depiction may portray contemporary figures, projecting real-life, fashionable personalities, and thus merging imaginative and idyllic landscape with suggestions of portraiture, celebrity, and domestic life. The woman at left, who dons an oversized hat with plumes and ribbons, favors portraits of Georgiana, the Duchess of Devonshire, who was renowned for her ostrich-feather millinery.[143] The duchess and her sister Lady Duncannon, who may be pictured at right, became a familiar pair in watercolors and etchings, especially satirical ones, during the Georgian period.[144] Georgiana endured much scrutiny from the public, graphic satirists, and her mother when she campaigned for votes in the public streets of Covent Garden and surrounding areas. The duchess canvassed for Whig candidate Charles James Fox in the Westminster general election in 1784, and is shown at left in a print with her sister and Fox during polling (fig. 26). This etching is one among many satirical prints that mock Georgiana and her canvassing, and scandalously cast her as a prostitute. Artists placed her in numerous compromising social situations, including hugging butchers and marching with tradesmen for the vote.

ELIZA PHIPPS AND AN UNKNOWN MAKER

Eliza Phipps of the town of Waltham Abbey in County Essex, England, stitched a sampler with a girl playing with a cat in a beautiful garden (cat. 13). She dated the textile March 8, 1828 (or 1818; the year is drawn in very lightly below the vignette). Though little is known about this maker, parish registers include notice of a William Phipps, a tailor on Market Place in Waltham Holy Cross, in 1826.[145]

In Phipps's dreamy landscape, the girl and her pet, along with trees, a fern, flowers, and a peacock, all reside in a pleasant, calm, earth-colored landscape. A lengthy inscription, the maker's name and town, the alphabet, numbers, flowers, arches, and fleurs-de-lis make up the framed remainder. Her age is not given. Above the landscape, Phipps goes beyond the purely visual to express herself. The inscription reveals modesty and aspiration, vulnerability and accommodation, together with ambition:

> *Small is my skill, and tender are my years,*
> *My hopes beat high, but higher beat my fears.*
> *To please, my best endeavours, I have tried,*
> *Happy in such a task to be employed.*
> *Shou'd you dear Parents, but approve my pains,*
> *Great's my reward, and ample are my gains.*

This sampler encapsulated personal hopes and fears, artistic expression, evidence of learning, and sewing skills in preparation for its maker's domestic life in marriage. At the same time, the sampler would become a semipublic visual document and a decorative object meant for display in the home, available for relatives, visitors, and suitors to observe and critique.

In sixteenth-century England, samplers functioned as a dictionary of designs for embroiderers. Pattern books were also published. In the seventeenth century, bands of repeated designs with decorative motifs were included, and samplers were used as teaching exercises for girls. By the mid-eighteenth century, moralizing inscriptions, alphabets, numbers, domestic scenes, and ornamental borders were increasingly added to an oblong to squarish format, and the samplers were hung on the wall in the home or at school. The making of decorative samplers as a kind of domestic diploma for middle- and upper-class teenage girls thrived, mostly under the guidance of female teachers, including those at Quaker and boarding schools.[146] By the nineteenth century, samplers were displaying girls' own compositions and artistic designs. However, in intellectual circles, where the education of girls was debated, some considered samplers outmoded and controversial.[147]

Idyllic landscapes were common subjects in samplers, as were moralizing and religious themes by American girls with a European heritage.[148] Across the Atlantic, an unidentified girl made an unsigned, undated sampler (cat. 14) of a clothed Adam

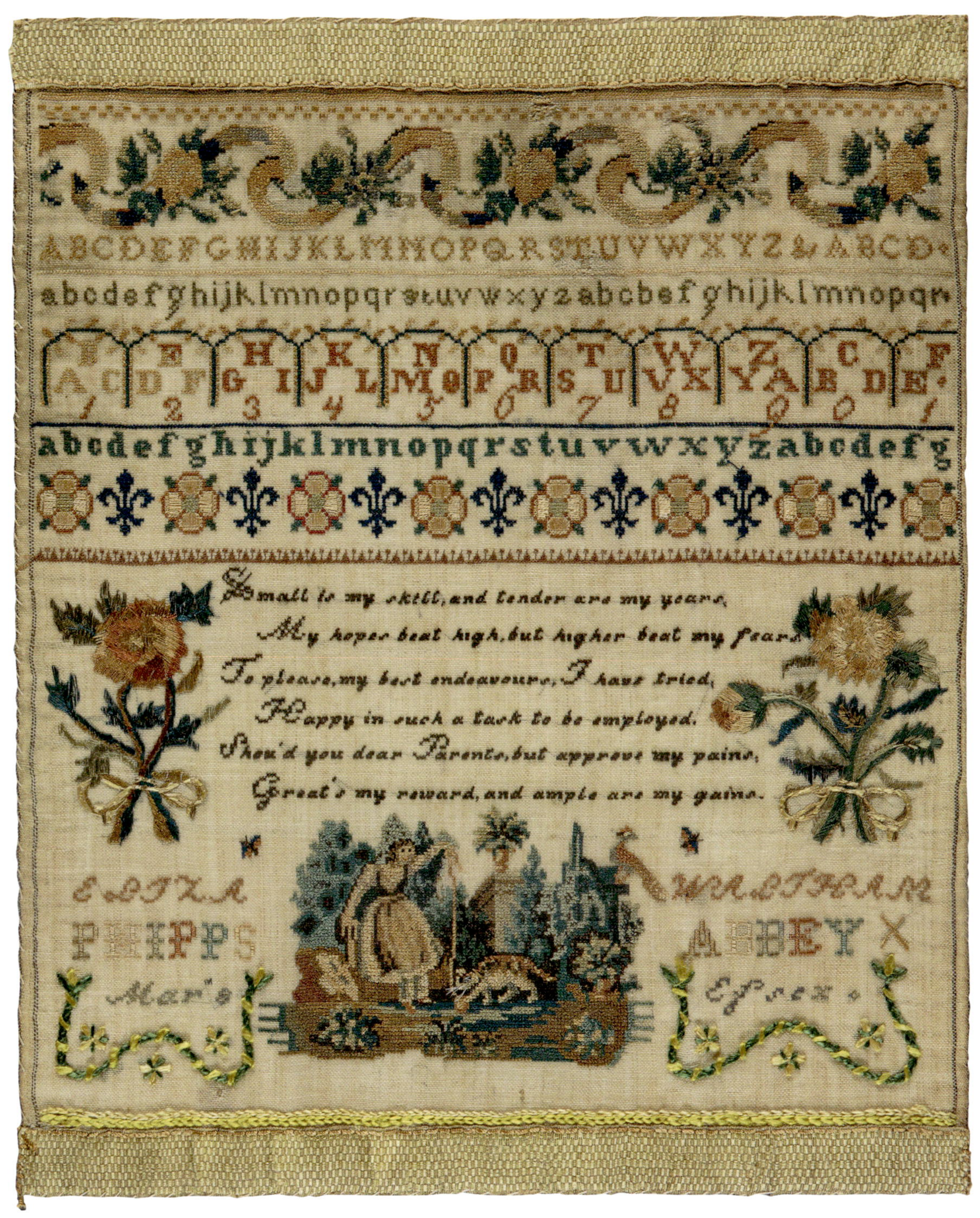

Cat. 13   **Eliza Phipps**

Sampler ("Small is my skill, and tender are my years . . .")

Silk threads, 1828 or 1818

Transfer from Vassar College Libraries, Special Collections, Martha
Clawson Reed Collection

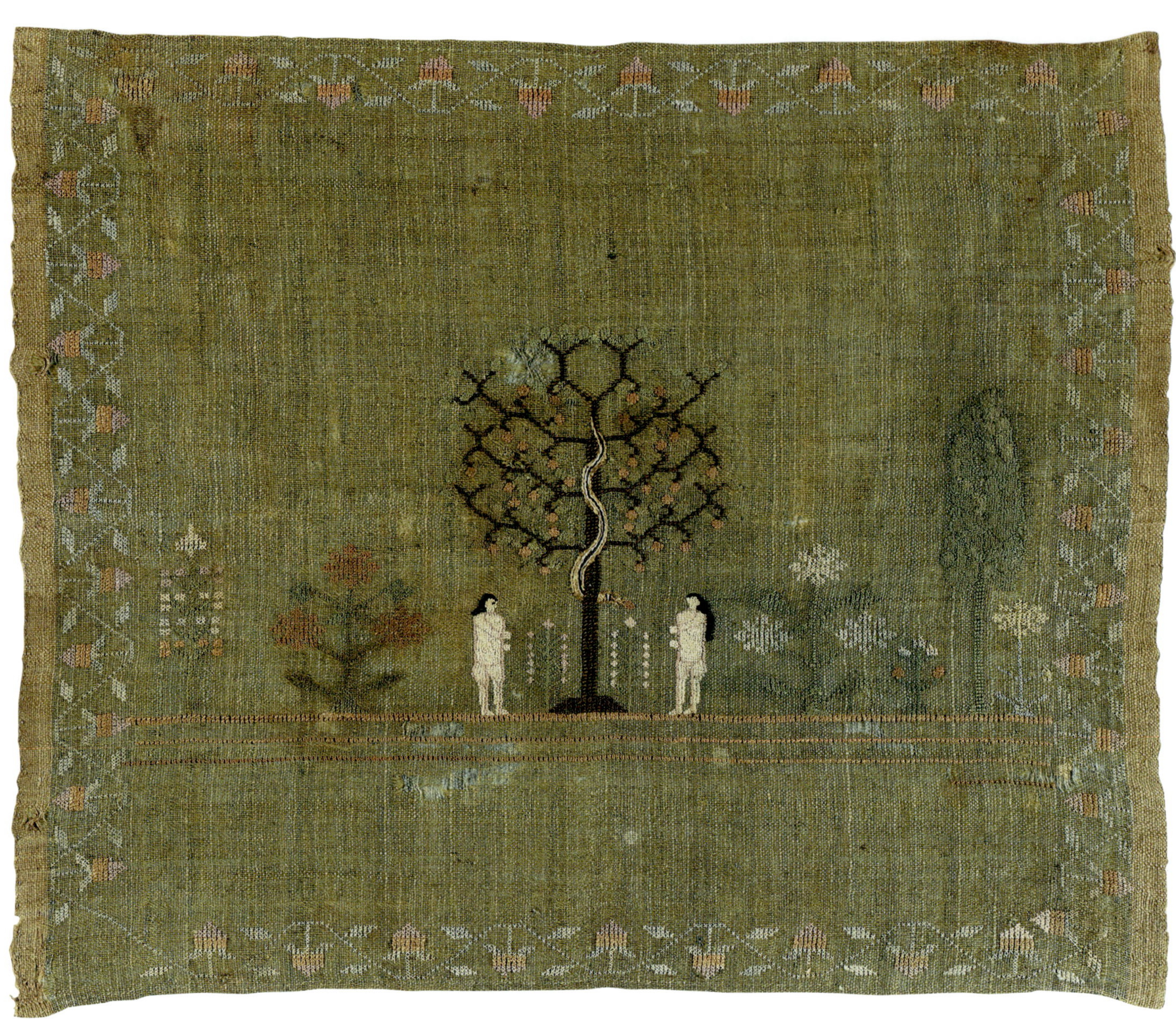

Cat. 14   **Unknown maker**

Sampler (Adam and Eve in the Garden of Eden)

Silk threads, ca. 1808

Gift of Mrs. James W. Packard (Elizabeth Gillmer, class of 1894)

and Eve and an apple tree with its clinging, writhing snake, in this scene from arguably the very first idyllic landscape subject, the Garden of Eden. The work has been catalogued as American and made around 1808.[149] Except for isolated vegetation and the zigzag flower border, the olive green field is reserved mostly for this first couple, with the snake climbing down the Tree of the Knowledge of Good and Evil. The scene shows the moment before Adam and Eve eat the forbidden fruit.

Samplers took hold in seventeenth-century New England, and in the eighteenth century they were being made by young girls as well as older girls in finishing schools. The Adam and Eve with apple-tree motif first appeared in samplers in the Boston area in the middle of the eighteenth century.[150] In this instance, the sampler demonstrates its maker's knowledge of the Bible and expresses her piety.

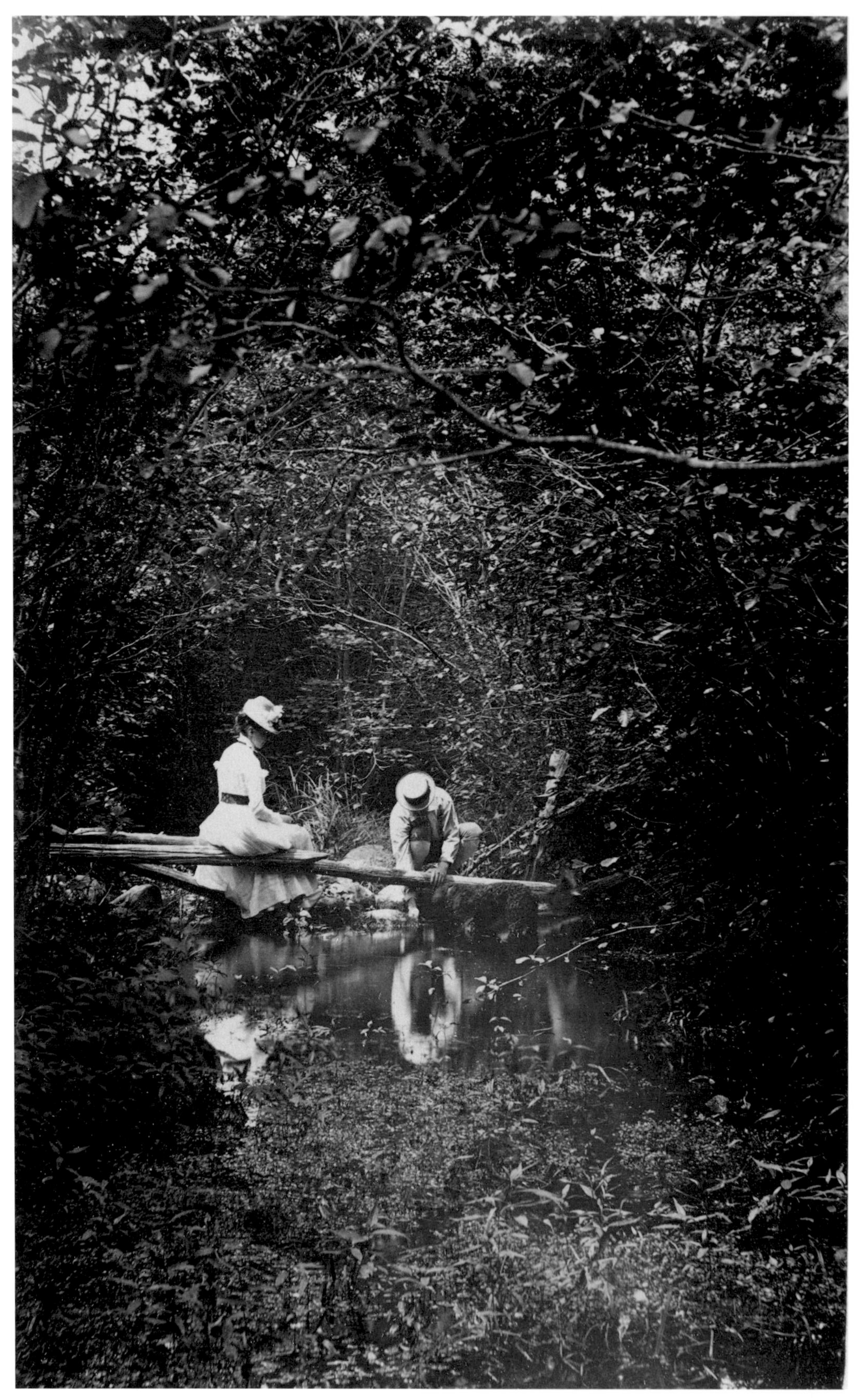

FLORENCE MARIA CUSHING

Through a clearing in the woods, Florence Maria Cushing (1853–1927) photographed a woman, man, and dog by a stream (cat. 15). The woman, in a full skirt, rests on some logs, while the man with his summer boater bends down to the water. The view suggests a couple and their pet enjoying nature on a summer outing. The woman's chignon and her costume's high-neck collar, ruffles, long sleeves, tightened waist, and voluminous skirts reflect fashion of the 1880s.[151]

At first, Cushing seems to have chanced on a private moment. However, this is an albumen photograph, not a Kodak-produced print, and Cushing would have had a glass-plate camera with her, and perhaps a tripod. With the albumen process, for the photograph to be in focus, the figures at the stream would have had to remain still for a few moments, so they very likely cooperated with Cushing in some fashion.[152]

Born outside of Boston, Cushing is a well-known Vassar graduate, class of 1874, who became the first alumna to serve on the Board of Trustees. Cushing House Dormitory is named after her. But she was also a pioneering nature photographer in the 1880s. This landscape follows the Naturalist photography aesthetic, which aimed to capture figures as they naturally appeared in the landscape, with no painted or false backdrops or special costumes, as was then customary. Her brothers-in-law Loring and William Lyman Underwood were early amateur photographers in Massachusetts who subscribed to this approach, and they are said to have been an influence on her.[153]

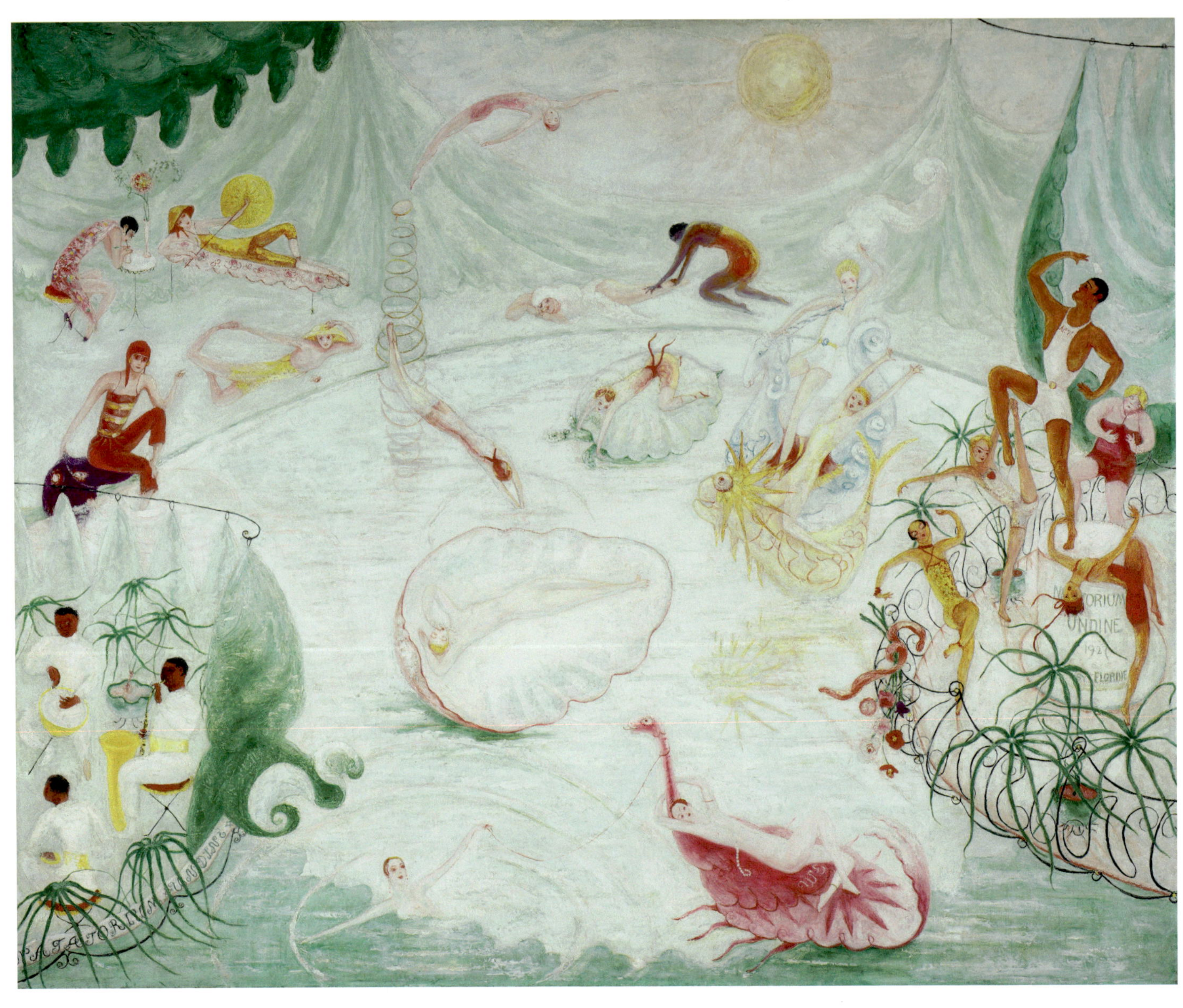

Cat. 16 **Florine Stettheimer**

Natatorium Undine

Oil and encaustic, 1927
Gift of Ettie Stettheimer

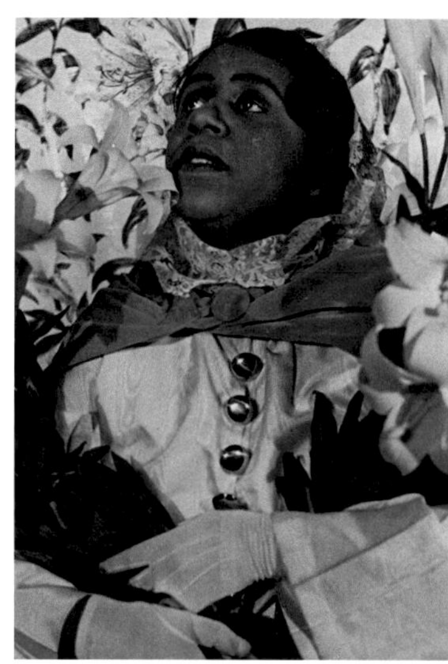

Figure 27. Carl Van Vechten, *St. Theresa*, from *Four Saints in Three Acts*, 1934. Gelatin silver print. 9¾ × 6¾ in. (24.8 × 17.2 cm). Frances Lehman Loeb Art Center, Vassar College, Gift of Pamela Askew, Phoebe DesMarais, and Atwood Allaire, 1996.27.2

FLORINE STETTHEIMER

In *Natatorium Undine*, American artist, poet, and costume designer Florine Stettheimer (1871–1944) presents small-scale portraits of herself, her sister Ettie, and friends in an artificial fantasy landscape (cat. 16). Stettheimer pictures herself with a parasol; Ettie is in a bathing suit at the edge of the pool; and the actress Fania Marinoff, who was married to music critic Carl Van Vechten, is hunched over a table sipping a drink through a straw.[154] The pool contains a Bosch-like mix of water cars—a shell, turtle, dolphins, and a swan-like creature, with passengers—with faux islands on either side decorated with greenery, dancers, and musicians. Here and there, Stettheimer places everyone around or in the pool, and they rest, leap, lounge, and play.

While this painting and much of her art was rather private —the wealthy New Yorker did not need to sell her work for income—Stettheimer was a leading light among the city's avant-garde. She designed the sets and costumes for the 1934 opera *Four Saints in Three Acts* by Gertrude Stein and Virgil Thomson (fig. 27). She co-hosted soirées with her sisters at their family's apartment on West 58th Street and Seventh Avenue, attracting Georgia O'Keeffe, Alfred Stieglitz, Marcel Duchamp, and numer-ous others, and made color-saturated landscapes and interiors that included casual renderings of her close friends and family. In turn, she attended parties hosted by others, including her close

friend Van Vechten, a white champion of jazz and Black culture in Harlem.[155]

Born in Rochester into a Jewish family, Stettheimer did not marry, and she would refine her unusual and original way of painting after years of studying art and immersing herself in the sophisticated material and artistic culture of the city (fig. 28). She lived much of her childhood and teenage years in Germany, study-ing drawing with Sophie von Prieser, director of a boarding school in Stuttgart that advertised itself as having "all the advantages of a comfortable home and superior education."[156] She continued her studies in Berlin and then attended the Art Students League in New York from 1892 to 1895, where she trained in drawing and painting. The artist painted in a studio apartment in Midtown at 80 West 40th Street. She frequently traveled with her mother and sisters to the art capitals of Europe, and painted in Munich.[157]

Though her works are now widely known and celebrated, solo exhibitions of her work were rare until after her death in 1944. She halted a planned show at the Museum of Modern Art in New York in 1916 because she fretted about not having a "painting suitable for the present Museum walls," and she exhibited only in group shows afterward.[158]

Her art was known to her good friends, however, and the intensity of the private vision that her paintings captured matched that of her deep personal vulnerabilities, which persuaded her to

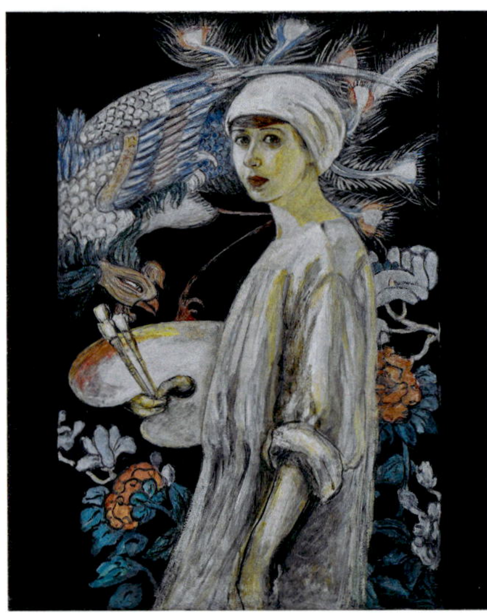

Figure 28. Florine Stettheimer, *Self-Portrait with Paradise Birds*, no date (ca. 1905). Oil on canvas. 39½ × 31¾ in. (100.5 × 80.8 cm). Art Properties, Avery Architectural and Fine Arts Library, Columbia University, Gift of the Estate of Ettie Stettheimer, 1967 (1967.23.13)

mute her real personality for much of the time, as she wrote in this fragment from a poem entitled "To a Gentleman Friend":

When I meet a stranger—
Out of courtesy
I turn on a soft
Pink light
Which is found modest
Even charming
It is a protection
Against wear
And tears
And when
I am rid of
The Always-to-be-Stranger
I turn on my light
And become myself.[159]

In 1948, Kirk Askew at Durlacher Brothers in New York mounted the exhibition *Flowers of Florine Stettheimer*.[160] The following year, her sister Ettie gave *Natatorium Undine* to Vassar College Art Gallery.

ROSELLA HARTMAN

Working in the art colony of Woodstock, New York, after World War I, Rosella Hartman (1894–1993) made drawings, lithographs, and oils of encounters between animals in the countryside, sometimes adding people to her repertoire. In an untitled 1933 drawing, a couple has joined their Siamese cat in front of rushing falls that tumble into a pool edged with rocks (cat. 17). The cat bathes, and the nude couple, one crouching, the other wading, look down at the water, perhaps in contemplation of a swim. Their skin is modeled by crosshatched lines, as in an etching. Makeshift walls of rocks enclose them in a safe shelter. The subject is likely a private, intimate spot in the Woodstock area's woods, an important place for the artist and one she depicted frequently.

Born in Kansas, Hartman trained at the Art Institute of Chicago from 1915 to 1918, and at the Art Students League from 1918 to 1920. She married sculptor Paul Fiene in 1923 after meeting him at the League's summer workshop in Woodstock, where she studied with Andrew Dasburg.[161] Her work received wide attention in the United States during the late 1920s and 1930s, with her first exhibitions in the mid-1920s. She had solo shows at the Whitney Studio Club in 1928, the Daniel Gallery in 1931, and the Rehn Gallery in 1936 and in 1945.[162] Hartman exhibited a drawing entitled *Bathers* at the first Whitney Biennial of Contemporary American Sculpture, Watercolors, and Prints in the winter of 1933–34. She

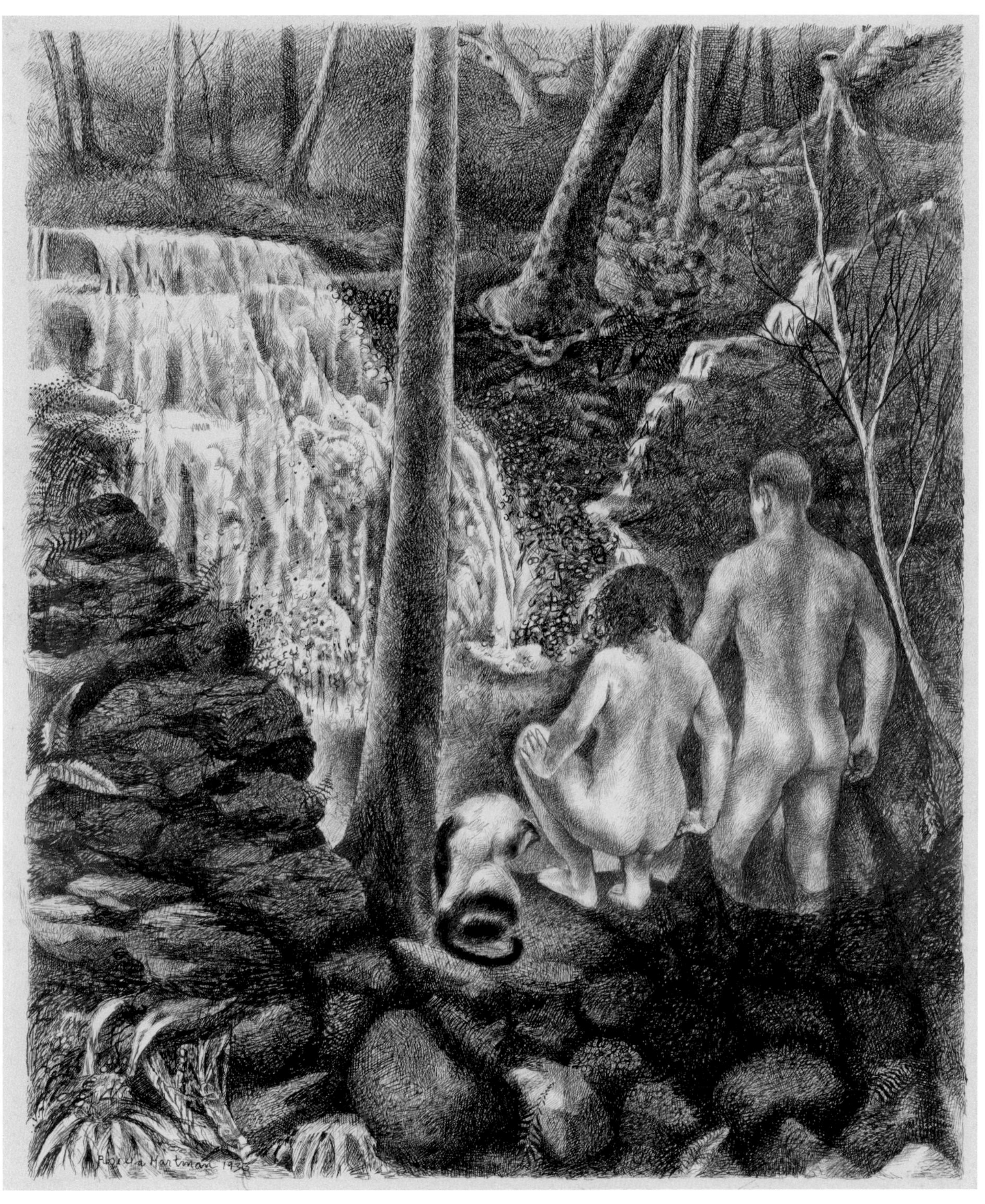

Cat. 17 **Rosella Hartman**

Untitled

Brush and black ink, 1933
Gift of Susan and Steven Hirsch, class of 1971

won two John Simon Guggenheim Memorial Foundation Fellow-ships, one in 1934 to study lithography in Paris and another in 1938. She would make several prints with master lithographer Grant Arnold in Woodstock, a thriving center for printmaking, and with Atelier Desjobert in Paris.[163]

DORIS LEE

The Woodstock art colony appealed to numerous female art-ists, including painter and printmaker Doris Lee (1905–1983) who created a blissful landscape in her *Garden at Night* (cat. 18), painted in about 1950. In the nearly four-foot-high nocturne, flat silhouetted trees, shadows, garden sculptures, and a woman in a long gown float on the canvas in olive green, cloudy sage, and other muted earth tones. Stuart Preston, writing for the *New York Times* in 1949, reviewed Lee's paintings at the Rudolph Gallery in Woodstock, claiming them as "precise fantasies that seem stitched rather than painted."[164] As Lee explained years later, "Many wonderful things happened to me when I started painting. I entered a fascinating new world where my imagina-tion had free reign."[165]

According to a reporter in 1953, Lee relaxed by spending time in the garden and orchard at the Woodstock home she shared with painter Arnold Blanch.[166] Doris Emrick was born into a prosperous and socially prominent family in Illinois and raised in Aledo, close

to the Mississippi River. After graduating from Rockford College in 1927, where she studied painting, she married Russell Lee, the future photographer for the Farm Security Administration, and in 1928 traveled to Europe and trained in art in Paris and Munich. The following year she studied at the Kansas City Art Institute with the painter Ernest Lawson, and followed this with additional training in Europe, including with Cubist painter André Lhote in Paris. After moving to the West Coast, she trained at the California School of Fine Arts in San Francisco with Blanch, who suggested that she use nature or her interests as her main subject. She moved to Woodstock in 1931.[167]

In 1935 she was awarded the Logan Prize for *Thanksgiving*, an American Scene painting, at the Art Institute of Chicago. As a result, Lee's career took off with exhibitions, commissions, reviews, and articles, and she steered her own creative efforts into even more public outlets. Through her association with Associated American Artists, where she made nineteen prints from the 1930s to 1960s, Lee expanded into commercial com-missions, ceramics decoration, book illustrations, greeting cards, and design work for textiles and homewares.[168]

Fantasy landscape remained an interest for Lee throughout these years, as it had with Hartman. Rhapsodic, lyrical mountains and clouds dance across her paintings and prints of farmland and the Catskill Mountains, and they rise over life below (fig. 29). In

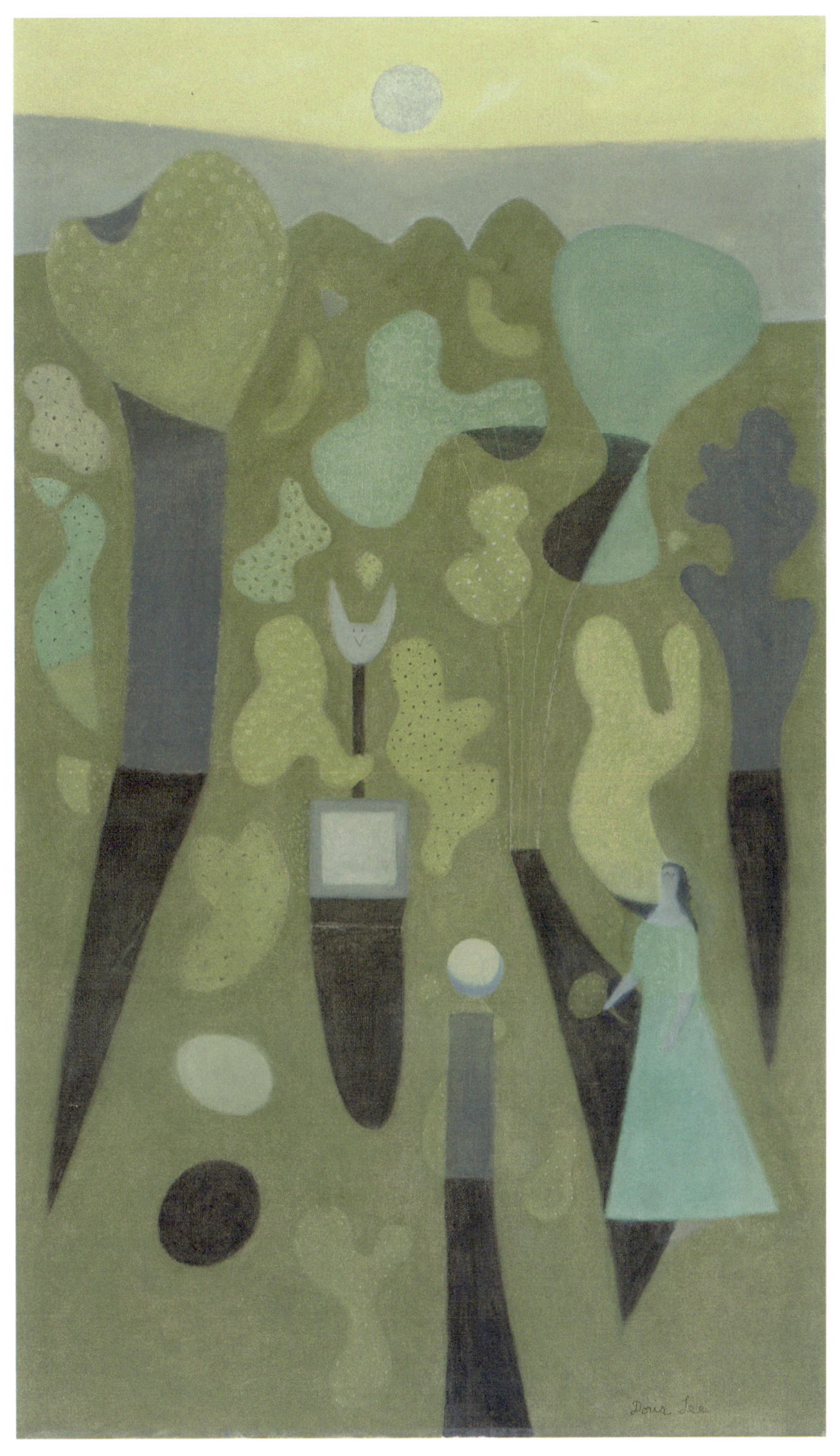

Cat. 18   **Doris Lee**

Garden at Night

Oil on canvas, ca. 1950
Bequest of the artist

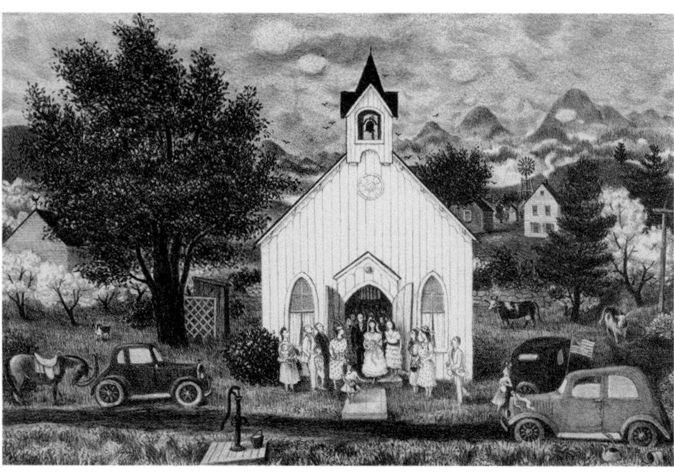

Figure 29. Doris Lee, published by Associated American Artists, *Country Wedding*, 1943. Lithograph. 8 × 11⅞ in. (20.3 × 30.2 cm). Frances Lehman Loeb Art Center, Vassar College, Gift of Mr. and Mrs. Cornelius Osgood, 1959.3.20

the lithograph *Country Wedding*, for instance, the rise and fall of mountain peaks give way to the facade of a picturesque Gothic Revival church festooned with the wedding party and a gaggle of folksy guests. In another lithograph, a helicopter hovers over rows of vegetables. At mid-century, however, the painted and printed forms of her countryside views gradually changed, and she began to dissolve her landscape shapes into flattened silhouettes, though the scenes are still idealized and generally untroubling.

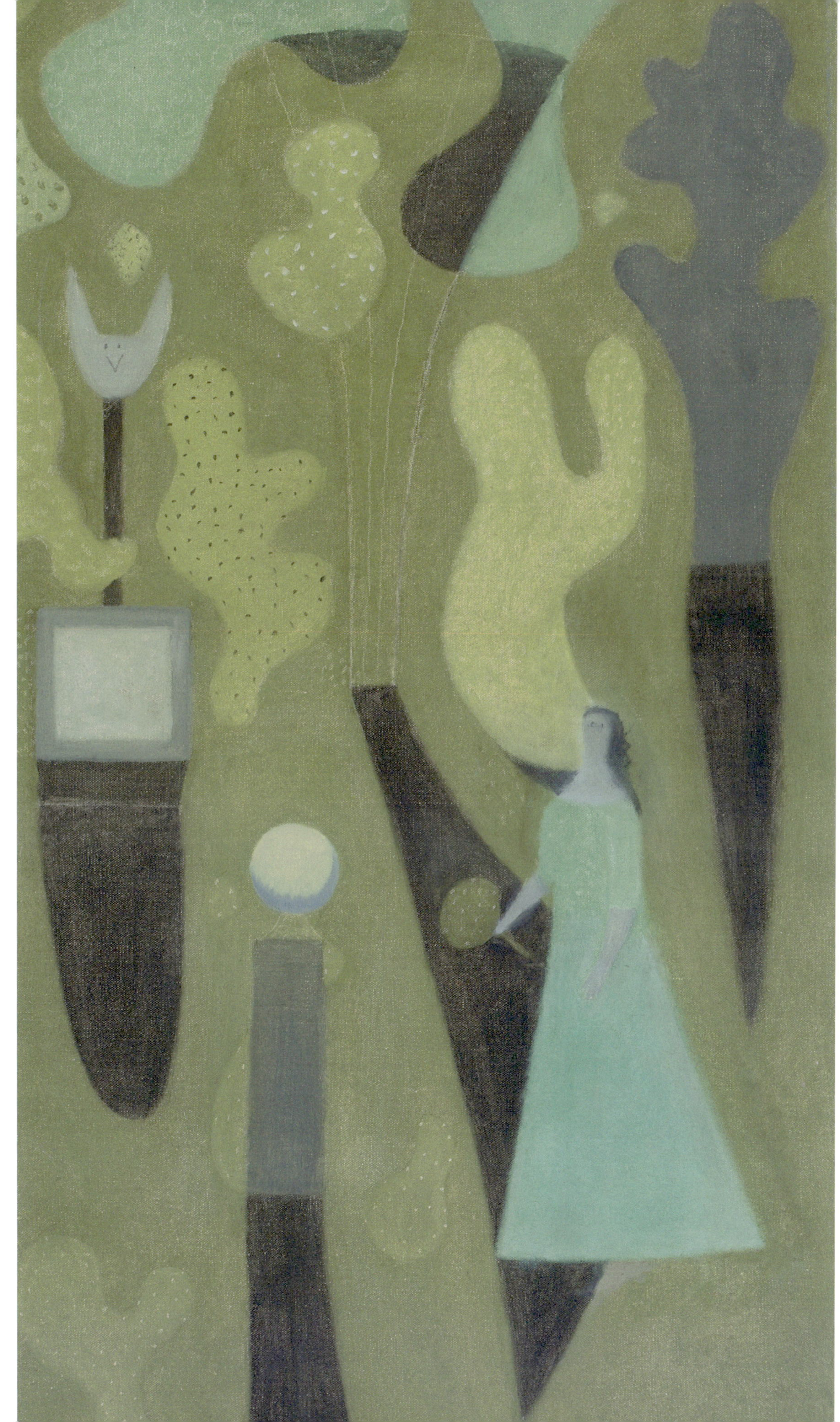

Domestic Scenes
Private and Personal

California artist Joan Brown, who filled her paintings with domestic imagery, noted,

> I feel a deep need to put into visual form all aspects of my own life.

Speaking in 1985, she elaborated,

> When I get too far out with what I'm doing and no longer have any handle, I go back and work from what I can see and what I know, what I am familiar with and it grounds me and roots me.[169]

Miriam Schapiro found her feminist art experiences in the early 1970s to be grounding and profound. Speaking of *Womanhouse*, the first project of the Feminist Art Program at the California Institute of the Arts, she declared in an interview,

> Womanhouse *was conceived of as a house of the dreams and fantasies of women. With no man to censor, what could a woman do in her house? Some artists worked alone, some collaborated with each other. . . . I did a miniature dollhouse.*[170]

MISS CORNWALLIS

An amateur artist, Miss Cornwallis (life dates unknown), depicted the Toke family's private residence, specifically the Great Hall at Godinton Park in Kent, England, that was translated into a highly detailed etching made in the middle of the nineteenth century (cat. 19). The undated print was inscribed as a "Private Plate," that is, the plate and prints produced would have been purchased by the one who commissioned them, and the run may have been small.[171] The manor lies just north of the Great Stour River on the outskirts of Ashford and was built around the older fourteenth-century hall.[172]

The Great Hall was the public face of Godinton Park. Miss Cornwallis may have gone into the Great Hall on more than one occasion and made the original design, facing the ancestral portraits and the room's intricate carvings. The design was subsequently given to John Henry Le Keux (1812–1896), a topographical draftsman and printmaker in London who specialized at mid-century in making reproductive architectural prints. Le Keux played a major role in the formation of Elias Lyman Magoon's art collection—the founding collection at Vassar—acting as Magoon's chief purchasing agent from 1856 to 1860 in London, and buying numerous drawings used in antiquarian publications edited by John Britton.[173]

No concrete information is known about the artist, Miss Cornwallis, or about the transactions involved in making the design into a print. However, not far from Godinton Park lies Linton Place, former home of Lady Julia Mann Cornwallis (1844–1883). Born into an aristocratic family, she inherited a very large Kent estate after the death of her father in 1852. The 15,000–16,000 acres included formal gardens and an eighteenth-century mansion overlooking the River Beult Valley. Her land and residence near Maidstone lie about 20 miles west of Godinton Park.

The idea that this heiress may have made the original design is speculative, but perhaps the idea is not so far-fetched. Drawing would have been one of the pastimes an aristocratic woman such as Julia Mann Cornwallis would have enjoyed as an amateur.[174] In 1862, when she was about eighteen, she married William Archer Amherst, a member of Parliament for West Kent (1859–68), and acquired the title Viscountess Holmesdale.[175] She was also a friend of Lady Mary Filmer (1840–1903) of Kent, an early amateur photographer who made portraits of many of her associates in the 1860s, including several of the Viscountess Holmesdale, and arranged them into albums, sometimes treating them like decorative collage.[176]

This opulent public room at Godinton Park was meant to impress. The enclosed, flamboyantly ornamented space is almost bare of furniture, yet mullioned windows at right wash over a wealth of crowded details, including blazing hearth, paneling, and richly carved mantel and wall screen; portraits of clergy, women,

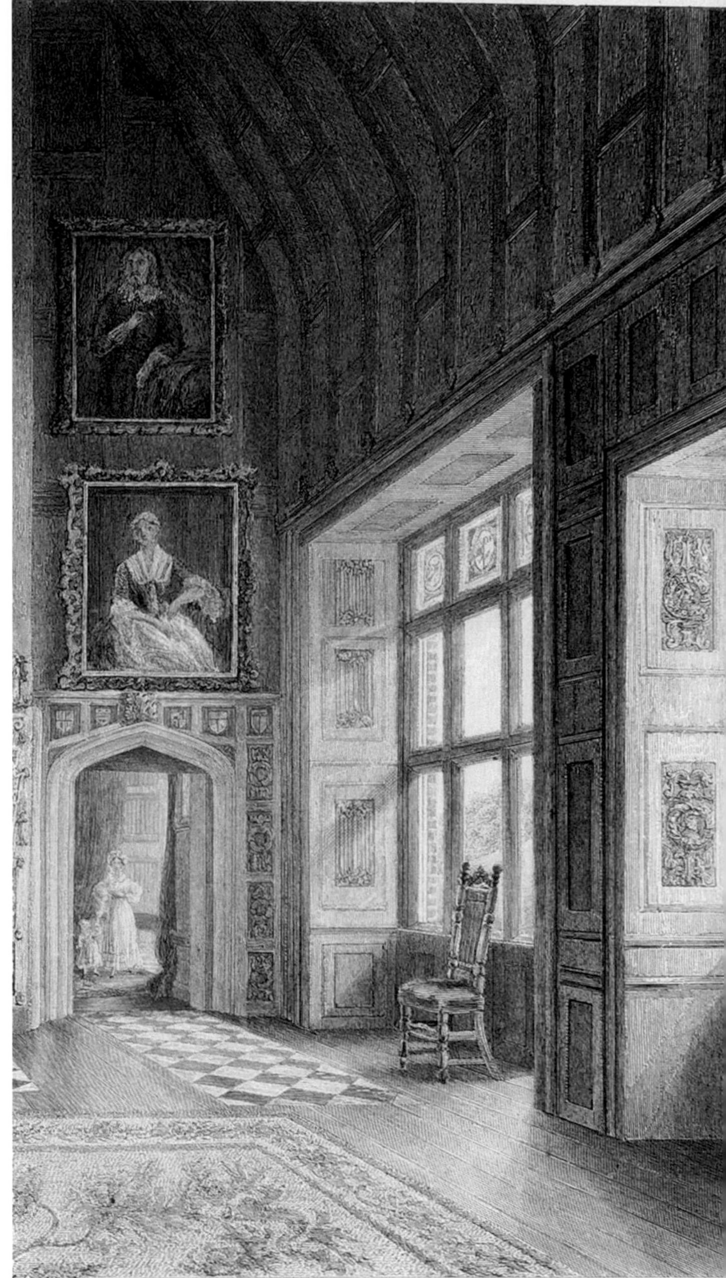

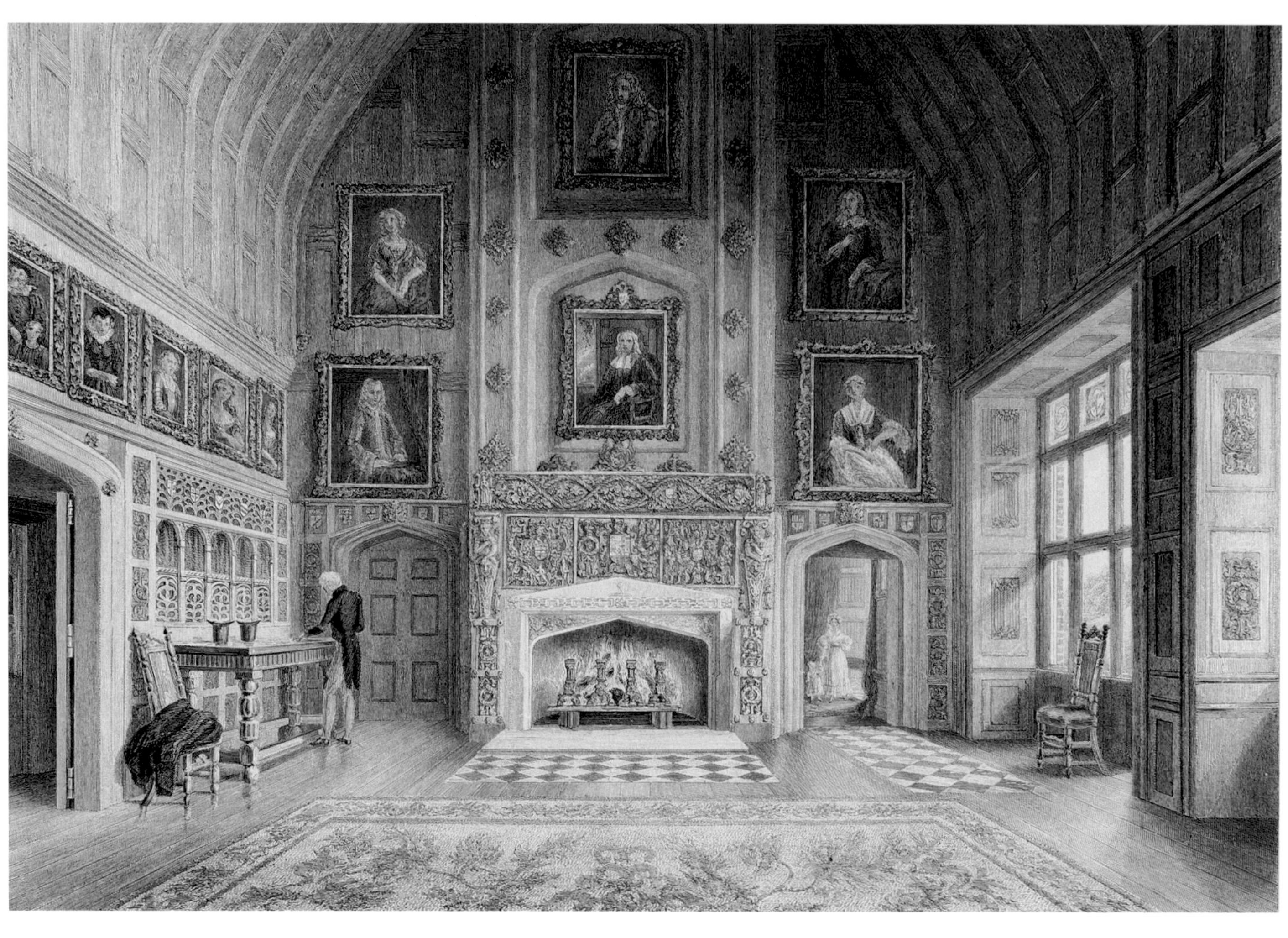

Cat. 19 John Henry Le Keux after Miss Cornwallis, perhaps Lady Julia
Mann Cornwallis, later Viscountess Holmesdale

Godington Hall, Kent (Private Plate)

Etching, probably mid-1850s
Gift of Matthew Vassar

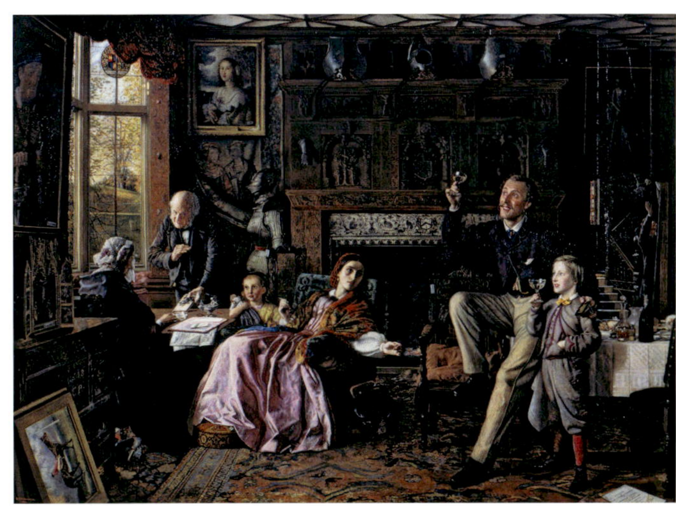

Figure 30. Robert Braithwaite Martineau, *The Last Day in the Old Home*, 1862. Oil on canvas. 42¼ × 57 in. (107.3 × 144.8 cm). Tate Britain, Presented by E. H. Martineau 1896, N01500

and others; a rug; and a gentleman at a carved table perusing a paper or document. This rather public facade projecting history, family, fortune, and lavish taste is pierced, however, by a barely noticeable narrative happening in the arched doorway at right, where a woman holds the hand of a child. Both figures are tiny in comparison to the daunting portraits. The pair suggests a personal life beyond the historical architecture and larger-than-life ambiance of the Great Hall.

Godinton Park, also called Godinton House and Godington Hall, had been the seat of the Toke family since the late fifteenth or early sixteenth century.[177] In the 1620s and 1630s, at about the time that Katherine Manners (cat. 1) and the Duke of Buckingham were renovating the royal palace of New Hall in Essex, the successful sheep- and cattle-farmer Captain Nicholas Toke remodeled Godinton Park. He hired local and Flemish craftsmen to create the decorative paneling, fireplaces, and stairway.[178] Several generations later, in 1855, his descendant, the Rev. William Toke of Godinton, died, and his son, the Rev. Nicholas Toke (1799–1866), inherited the house and land.

By 1855 Nicholas and his Belfast-born wife Emma Leslie had three living children: John Leslie; Nicolas Roundell, born in 1843; and William Arthur, born in 1850, who is perhaps the child represented in the etching. Of note, Emma Leslie Toke, the daughter of the Bishop of Kilmore, penned hymns, and her earliest ones, requested by a friend, were composed in 1851 and published the next year, anonymously, in the hymnal of the Church of England by the Society for Promoting Christian Knowledge.[179]

An early twentieth-century account of the house noted portraits on view at Godinton Park dating to the reign of Henry VIII that were installed in the Great Hall and other parts of the house.[180] The design of the print by Cornwallis seizes on these and on the current installment of family, and other artists took notice, too. The Pre-Raphaelite painter Robert Braithwaite Martineau, a friend of the Toke family, in 1862 completed his painting *The Last Day in the Old Home* (fig. 30), looking to the family and house interior as models for his morality tale of lavish spending and financial woes.[181]

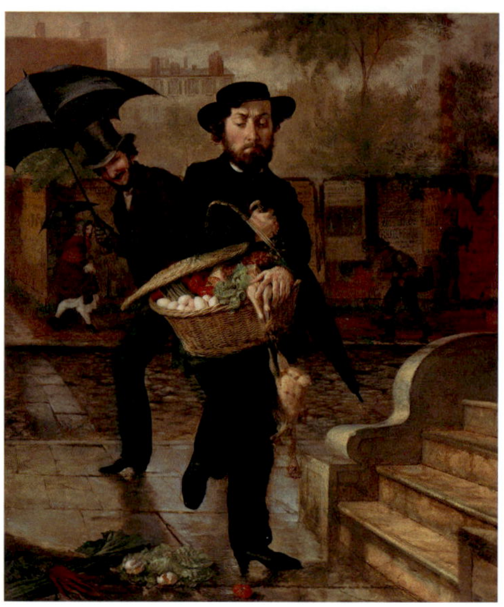

Figure 31. Lilly Martin Spencer, *Young Husband, First Marketing*, 1854. Oil on canvas. 29½ × 24¾ in. (74.9 × 62.9 cm). Metropolitan Museum of Art, Gift of Max N. Berry, 2015, 2015.401

LILLY MARTIN SPENCER

The leading mid-nineteenth-century American genre painter Lilly Martin Spencer (1822–1902) constructed a scene of a woman inside an open doorway, working with a spinning wheel and enjoying the view outside (cat. 20). Caught in a personal moment, and alone except for two playful kittens, Spencer's frontier woman spins as she looks out on greenery and flowers, the pink blossoms having landed on the floor and on her bonnet. In April 1894, when she signed this work, the artist was living almost unknown in Poughkeepsie and painting for a living at age seventy-two.

The canvas matches the description found in a letter Spencer wrote that mentions a painting with "a country lass of about the same [colonial] period, singing to the hum of her spinning wheel, that she has drawn to the log cabin door, to enjoy, in her gaiety of heart, the bright sunshine and fresh rose-scented breeze of a summer of long ago!" Though Spencer seems to have entered it into competition at the National Academy of Design in about 1897, it was apparently rejected, and she emphasized in a submission letter how long it had been since she had exhibited.[182]

Becoming well known at mid-century, Spencer pursued mostly portraits and domestic-subject paintings and prints attractive to American middle-class audiences rising in prosperity and education.[183] Distinct from most male genre painters of the time, she pursued women and their chores and children as major themes, staging intimate moments in the kitchen or with a baby in a bedroom. Some paintings also featured men, such as *Young Husband, First Marketing*, of 1854 (fig. 31).

Born in Exeter in the southwest of England to French parents with socially progressive views, she moved with them to the United States in 1830, and to a farmhouse near Marietta, Ohio, three years later. Her parents followed the principles of French utopian socialist Charles Fourier (1772–1837), and they co-founded in 1845 the Trumbull Phalanx utopian community in Braceville, Ohio. Showing much artistic promise in Marietta and with her parents' encouragement, the teenager moved in 1841 to the regional art center of Cincinnati, where she exhibited and studied painting with James H. Beard, a sought-after portrait painter.[184]

Spencer began painting domestic themes for a popular audience when she married in Cincinnati in the 1840s and had children, eventually bearing thirteen, seven of whom reached adulthood. From an unconventional upbringing, she provided for the family financially, and her husband, the tailor-trained Benjamin Rush Spencer, assisted her with domestic affairs and her art, handling the business side.[185] By mid-century, when they lived in New York and then New Jersey, she had become known and respected by the public for her genre paintings, but snubbed by those in more serious art circles for her sometimes unrefined drawing and comical, teasing humor, which underplayed the conventional

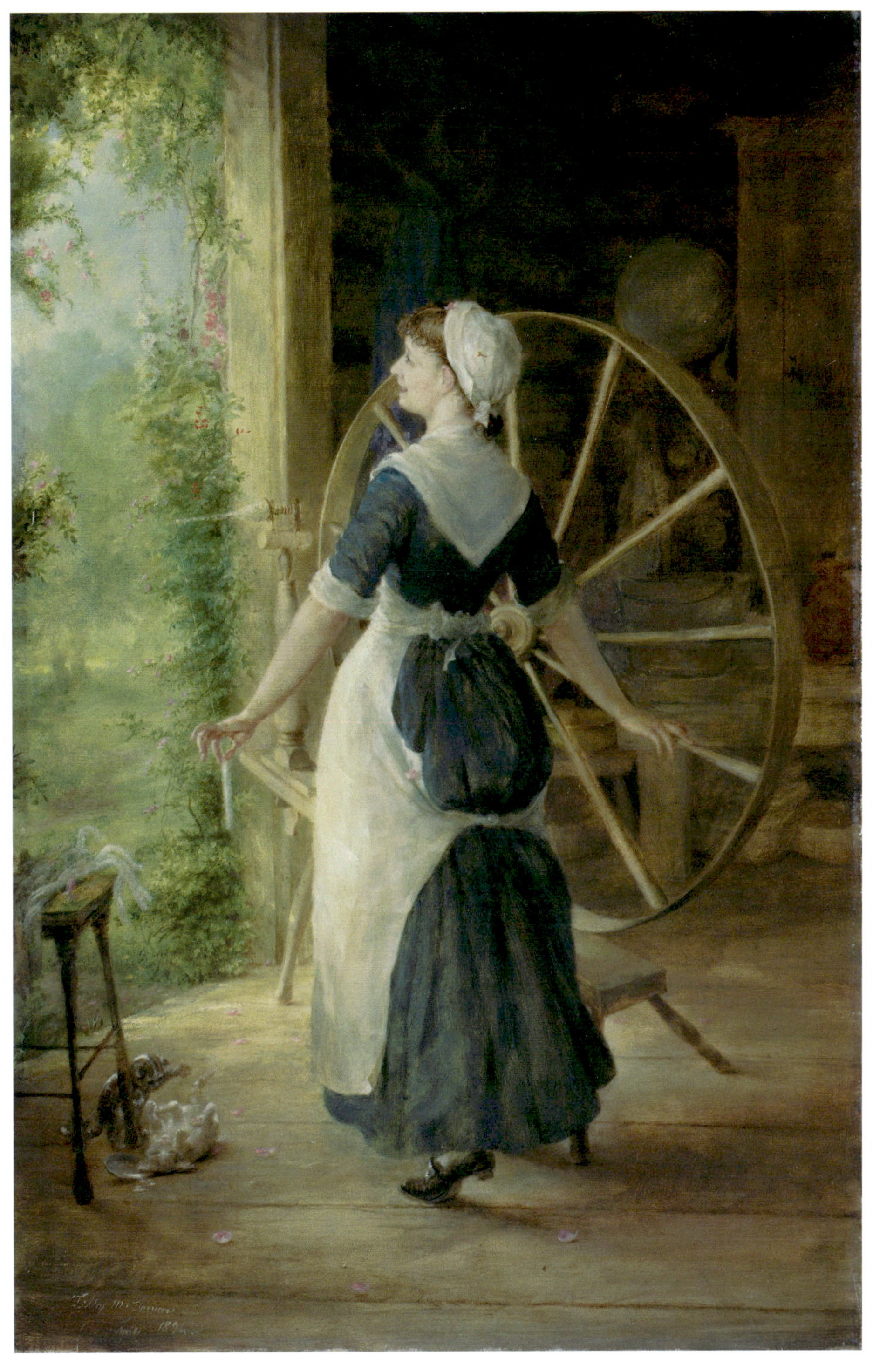

Cat. 20   Lilly Martin Spencer

The Spinner

Oil on canvas, 1894

Gift of Mr. and Mrs. Herbert L. Shultz (Barbara H. Rodie, class of 1942)

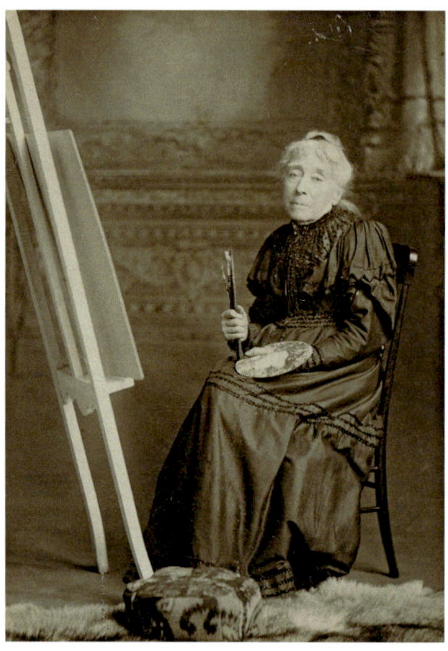

Figure 32. Herve Homer, photographer, *Lilly Martin Spencer*, ca. 1900. Photograph. 6¹¹⁄₁₆ × 4⁵⁄₁₆ in. (17 × 11 cm). Lilly Martin Spencer papers, 1828–1966, Archives of American Art, Smithsonian Institution (DSI-AAA)6342

womanly virtues of modesty, truth, and self-sacrifice.[186] Writing to her mother of a critical review in the *New York Tribune*, she comforted her,

> *. . . don't mind it dearest Mother. I don't, it is not the only foolish attack I have got in the papers. . . . I depend entirely on my own truthful and persevering efforts to improve, and my own natural powers whatever they may be—on this raft of quiet and comfortable self resilience, I float completely amidst all these vain attempts from jealous shafts, to keep me down.[187]*

However, her work appealed to the masses, and she engaged lithographic firms to translate her genre canvases into prints. Art unions also reproduced her paintings through prints, and prints after her designs were advertised in art magazines and circulated widely.[188]

The vogue for genre painting collapsed after the Civil War, but Spencer persisted in the Vassar painting with an ideal colonial subject, though she abandoned the close brushstrokes, intricately patterned fabrics, and chiaroscuro of her earlier works. She replaced them with a more current European, cosmopolitan emphasis on light, air, and invigorating park-like greenery. As for the painter's central focus in this work, spinning for the most part had migrated from the home to new factories by the 1830s

in New England.[189] It was still practiced in the country home in Ohio, however, as witnessed by British observer Frances Trollope (1779–1863), whose *Domestic Manners of the Americans*, published in 1832, may have been a source of imagery for some of Spencer's paintings. Trollope's description of an isolated log cabin with the self-sufficient wife and another woman busily spinning may have also been helpful here.[190]

Spencer completed the oil in 1894, late in her career, when she was apparently living in Poughkeepsie, decades after she had made a name for herself (fig. 32). According to the author of a December 1898 newspaper article, few townspeople knew she was living in the city and painting there. The writer noted, "About fifteen years ago she moved with her family to the farms on the other side of the river [Highland], and for the past five years has been a resident of this city, living in a modest way, with her son Charles, and daughter, Lillie, at No. 97 Cherry Street. . . . Mrs. Spencer's studio, at her home, has in it a number of beautiful specimens of her skillful touch." By 1898, the artist was reportedly in ill health, and the writer indicated that Spencer was suffering from malaria but still painting portraits.[191] There is no hint of illness in the Vassar painting, but rather a hopeful gaze by the spinner into an idyllic world of fresh air and warm-weather flora.[192]

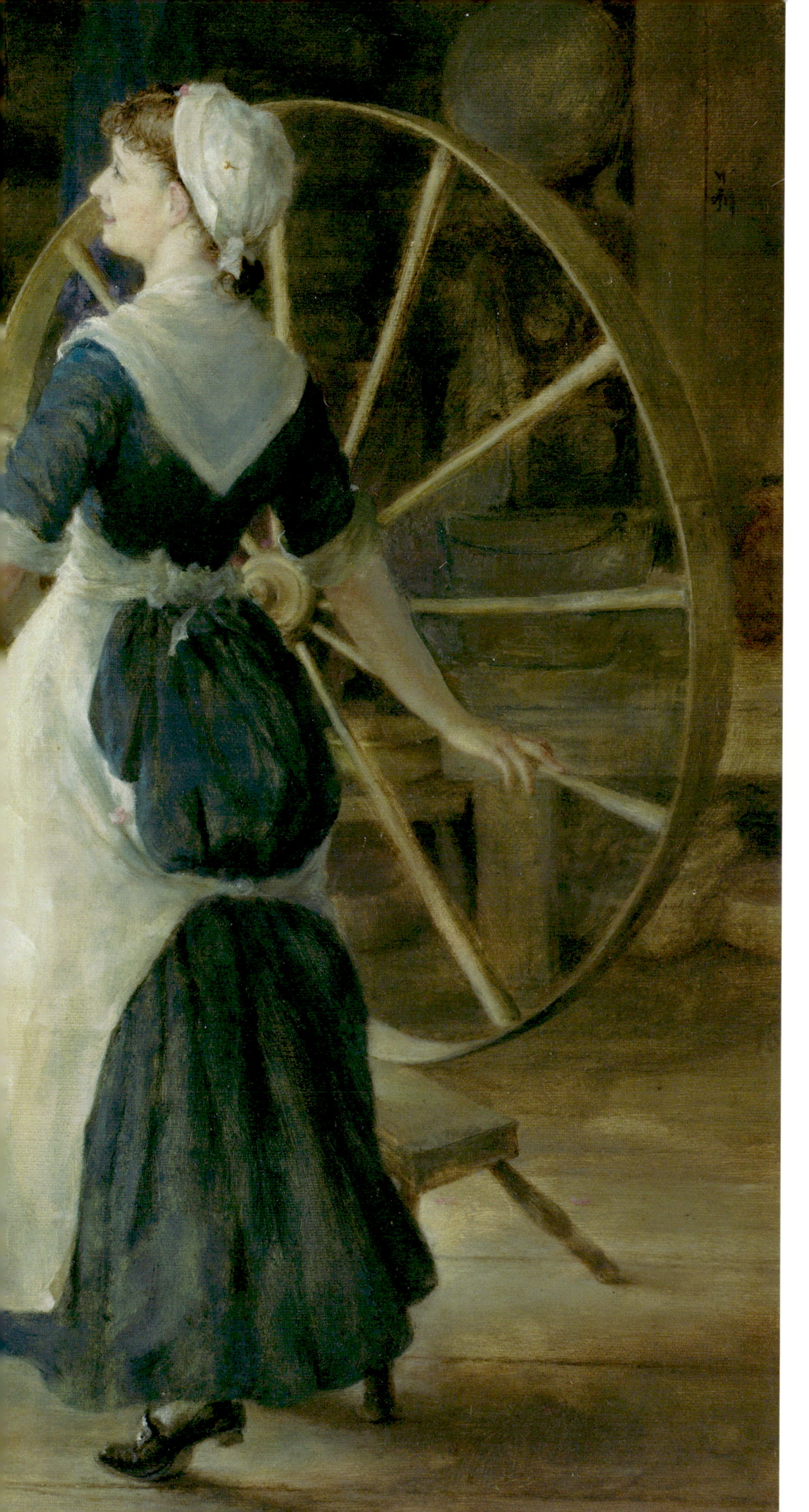

MARY CASSATT

For *Denise Holding Her Child* (cat. 21), Mary Cassatt (1844–1926) scratched her drypoint needle into a bed of resistant copper, attempting to fix in the plate a pleasant, private glimpse of a well-behaved child clinging to her mother. In its apprehensive, grasping embrace, the child lays claim to its mother as they both look to our right at some unknown person or scene. Cassatt seems to have captured the core of their features and hair at the same time, as those areas are similarly defined. Printing transformed those inked furrows into a delicate image of a child seeking maternal security, while printmaking, a medium for multiples, allowed that glimpse of Cassatt's child and model to circulate among the public.[193]

Cassatt valued printmaking for its unforgiving way of teaching drawing, telling her first biographer, when standing in front of her etching and aquatint *Under the Lamp* (see fig. 17), "Voilà qui vous apprend à dessiner!" (That is what teaches you to draw!).[194] From the late 1880s, as she exhibited with the new Société des Peintres-Graveurs, she specialized in this modern Madonna theme in her prints, paintings, and pastels, propelled in part by a ready audience built by her dealer Paul Durand-Ruel.[195] For Cassatt, as she wrote him in 1903, the drypoints she was making were "Less difficult to place."[196]

Reared in Allegheny City (near Pittsburgh), Philadelphia, and Europe, Cassatt came from a wealthy and worldly family. Her father was head of an investment company that specialized in cotton.[197] While Matthew Vassar was developing and opening Vassar College, Cassatt was training at the Pennsylvania Academy of the Fine Arts from 1860 to 1865. Unable to apply to the École des Beaux-Arts in Paris because of her gender, she continued her studies privately with several painters in Paris and Rome. In the 1870s she undertook commissions for making copies of paintings, like many American female painters at the time, and exhibited at Salons in Paris and shows in the United States. She first exhibited at the Salon in 1868 as an art student. By the mid-1870s Cassatt was living in a Paris studio by herself and inviting Americans there for making their portraits.[198] After the conservative juries of the Salons of 1875 and 1877 rejected her works, she accepted the invitation from Edgar Degas to join the Impressionists, with whom she first exhibited in 1879. Her work received much press notice, and she began to learn printmaking. She entered into professional associations with print dealer Samuel Avery in the United States and Durand-Ruel in Paris.[199]

In time she would move from romantic painted subjects into glimpses of upper-class women's leisurely moments as represented by posed models, sometimes family. By 1900 Cassatt had become the most celebrated of contemporary American women artists with her mother-and-child imagery.[200]

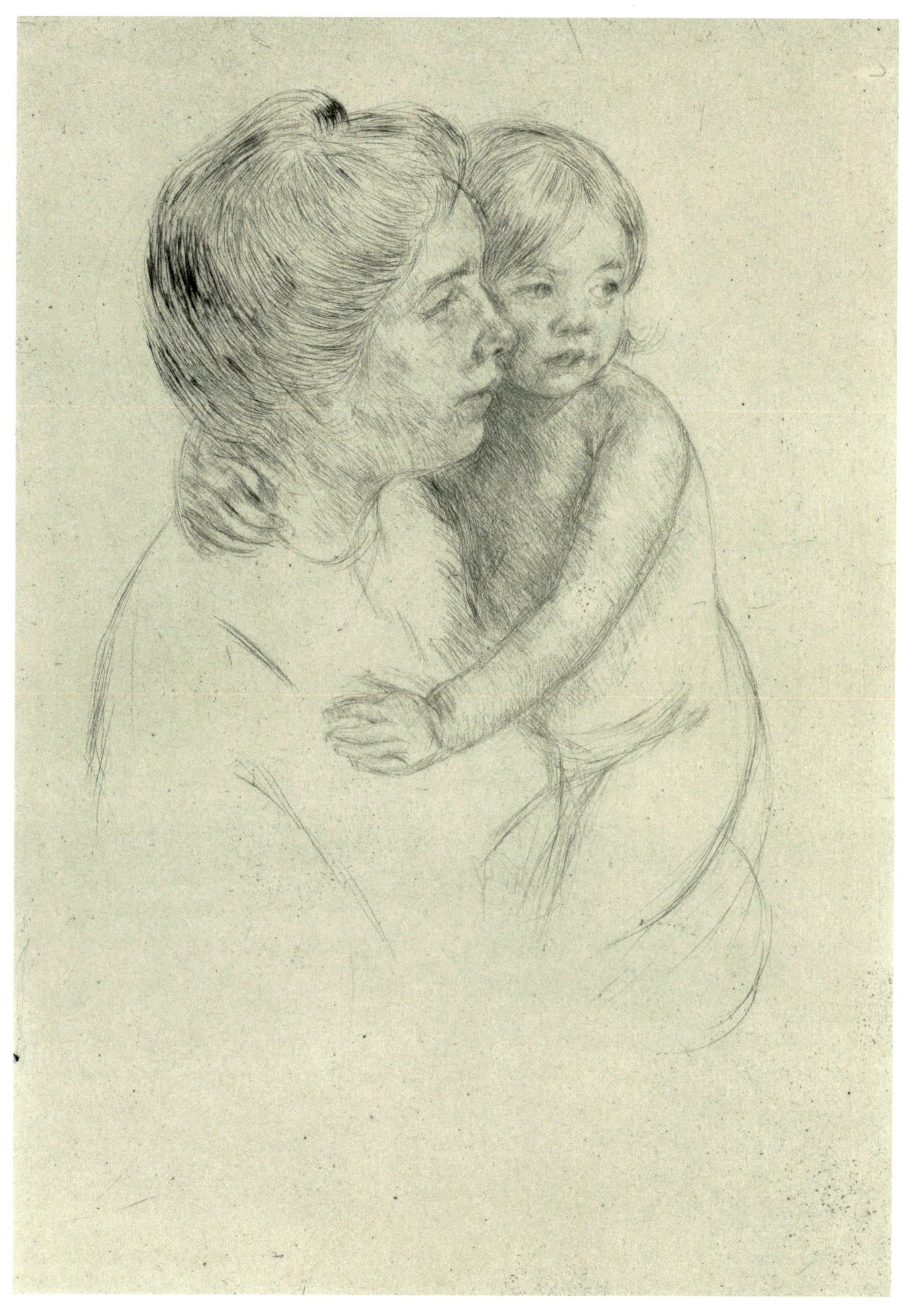

Cat. 21 **Mary Cassatt**

Denise Holding Her Child

Drypoint, ca. 1905
Gift of Alicia Craig Faxon, class of 1952

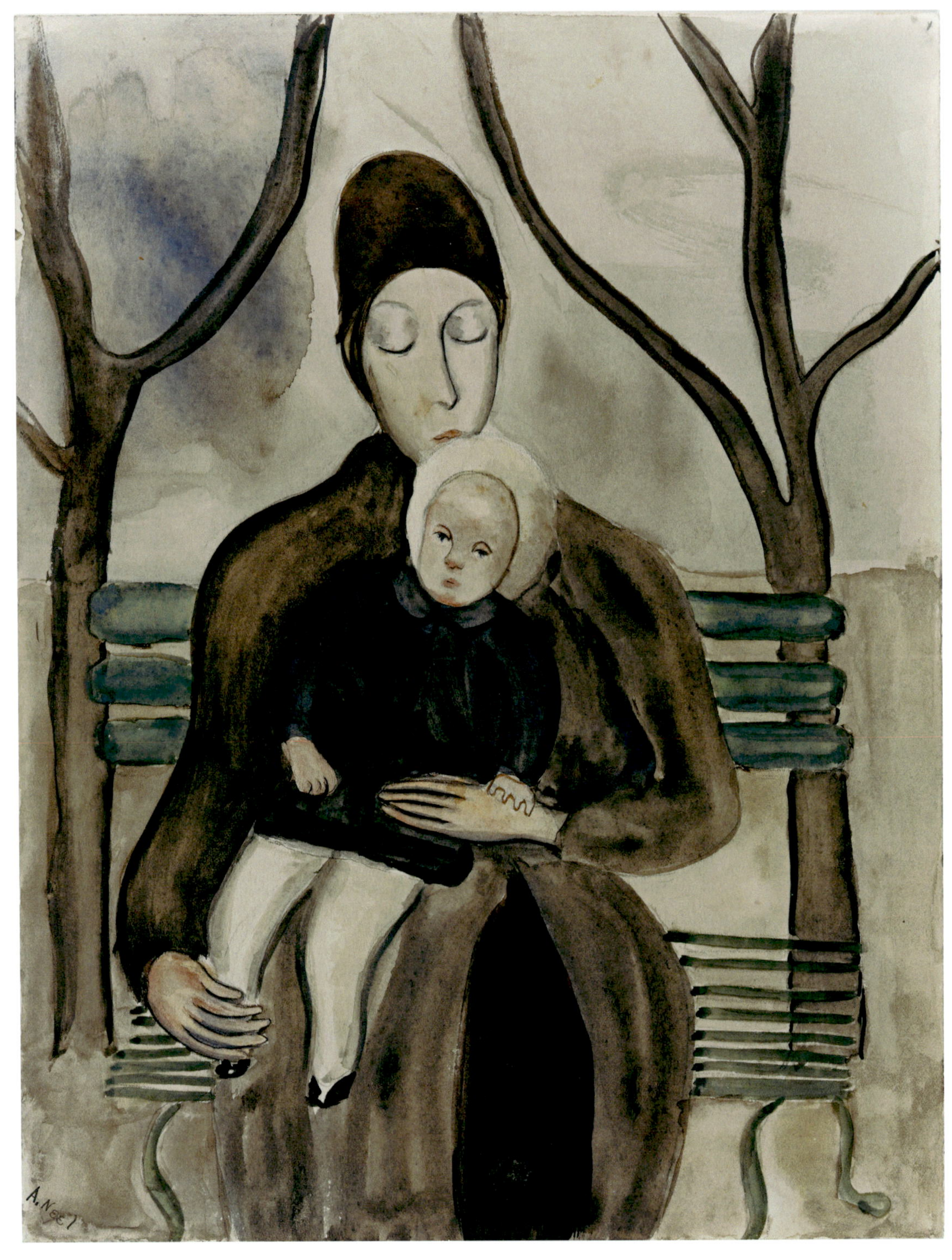

Cat. 22 **Alice Neel**

Mother and Child

Brush and watercolor over graphite, 1927

Gift of Mrs. John Benson Brooks (Frances K. B. Jones, class of 1940)

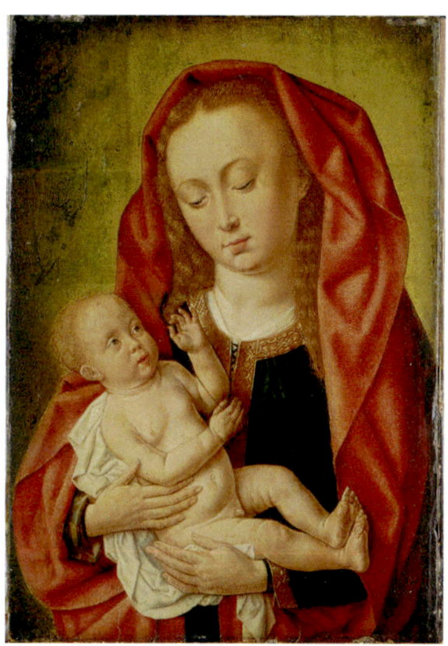

Figure 33. Master of Saint Giles, *Virgin and Child with a Dragonfly*, ca. 1500. Oil and tempera (?) on paper laid down on oak panel. 10½ × 7⅛ in. (26.6 × 18.2 cm). Metropolitan Museum of Art, New York, Robert Lehman Collection, 1975, 1975.1.131

ALICE NEEL

Alice Neel (1900–1984) painted a personal moment between herself and her baby daughter Santillana in *Mother and Child*, a watercolor from 1927 (cat. 22). The infant was born in Havana in late December of 1926 and died in New York almost one year later. With eyes cast downward, a serene Neel holds an impassive Santillana looking out at us, while they sit on a park bench. The dark, watery brown indicates cold weather, and the scene is relieved somewhat by the rising trees stretching to the sky, providing a protective niche. The baby looks unwell, and Neel embraces her like a sixteenth-century Madonna (fig. 33). Neel, in a sense, brings her baby's illness to the public eye by painting her in her lethargic, almost lifeless state out in the open for an audience to witness. Flattened and sinuous, the modern composition amplifies the moods of both of them and reflects the Art Deco designs of the period with their smooth, swelling curves in fashion, sculpture, furniture, and architecture. Beginning in the last months of 1927, Neel worked at an Art Deco shop on Madison Avenue.[201]

Only two and a half years out of art school when she made the watercolor, Neel had done well in portrait painting, winning awards.[202] She is most well known for her portraits, in which her penetrating, disarming approach creates an "incisive or critical realism," as Linda Nochlin put it. But as others have pointed out, portraits of mothers with children thrive within her oeuvre.[203]

Raised in small-town Colwyn, Pennsylvania, in a constraining, proper family, the sensitive Neel attended the School of Industrial Art in Philadelphia at night while working part time. Beginning in 1921 she studied at the Philadelphia School of Design for Women, graduating with a fine arts degree in 1925. She kept her painting interests private, away from her family, saying, "I had my own secret life at art school."[204] She especially admired the school's collection of plaster casts of ancient sculpture, and the drawing classes were foundational for her, especially the life classes with male and female nude models.

While at the women's school, she was strongly influenced by *The Art Spirit*, written by Robert Henri, who taught there in the 1890s. In his book, Henri, leader of the Ashcan School of artists, called for realism and the portrayal of everyday life. During these years Neel also took classes at the Graphic Sketch Club, where ordinary people were used as models, and she went out into the streets of Philadelphia to sketch, following Henri's teachings. During a summer course in open-air painting in 1924 in Chester Springs, an outpost of the Pennsylvania Academy of the Fine Arts, she met Cuban artist Carlos Enríquez, whom she would marry in 1925.

As Neel made clear, she was pulled between concentrating on her painting and focusing on a husband and a family. She told Patricia Hills much later, "I always had this awful dichotomy.

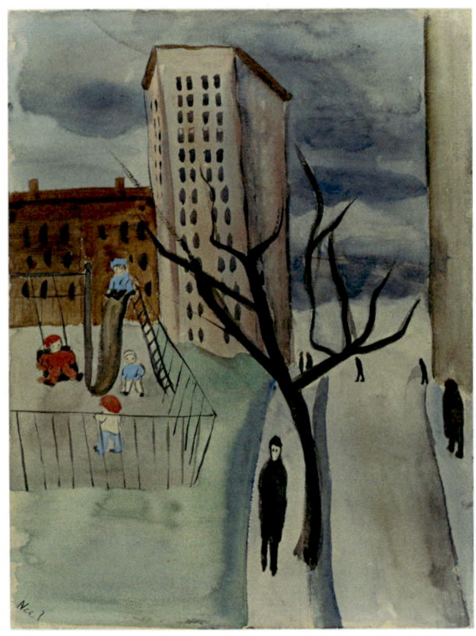

Figure 34. Alice Neel, *After Death of the Child*, 1927. Watercolor, gouache, and graphite on paper. 11¾ × 8¾ in. (29.9 × 22.2 cm). Frances Lehman Loeb Art Center, Vassar College, Gift of Mrs. John Benson Brooks (Frances K. B. Jones, class of 1940), 1990.19.6

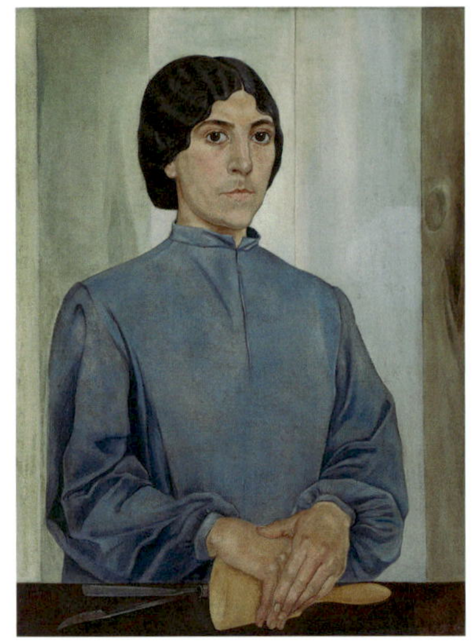

Figure 35. Stefan Hirsch, *Portrait of Concetta Scaravaglione*, 1927. Oil on canvas. 29¾ × 21¼ in. (75.6 × 54 cm). Frances Lehman Loeb Art Center, Vassar College, Gift of Dr. Edward Scarvalone, 1976.82

I loved Isabetta [her second daughter], of course I did. But I wanted to paint."[205] In 1926 she joined her husband in Havana. Her introduction to Cuba included her engagement with Vanguardia, a movement of artists using modernist styles with Cuban subject matter. She exhibited with the group, but returned to Colwyn alone with Santillana in spring 1927. In the fall she moved with her husband to West 81st Street in New York, where she would paint watercolors during a period of dire poverty. Finally, with the baby deathly ill, she returned to Colwyn.[206]

In *After Death of the Child* of the same year (fig. 34), Neel depicted a pedestrian with a skull face, a haunting—and taunting—specter, standing near children in a playground. A deathlike figure on a public sidewalk is imaginative, but the watercolor, with its bleak mood and contemporary setting, presages the social-realist work with which Neel would become engaged in the next decade in Depression-era New York.[207]

CONCETTA SCARAVAGLIONE

In *Girl with Cocks*, Concetta Scaravaglione (1900–1975) carved the figure of a girl petting a chicken, with another at her feet (cat. 23). She created the sculpture during her Rome Prize Fellowship residency at the American Academy in 1947–50.[208] The warm color, vital spirit, and rural subject evoke southern Italy, the homeland of her parents.

Born in New York in 1900, Scaravaglione (fig. 35) studied at the National Academy of Design, the Educational Alliance Art School, and the Art Students League. To pay her fees at the League, she worked in perfume and lampshade factories.[209] When she left for Maine in the summer of 1925 to study with sculptor Robert Laurent (fig. 36), her mother cautioned her to "see that you are always with a lady companion."[210]

Scaravaglione did not marry. She lived in New York and exhibited at the Salons of America, the Jewish Art Center, Whitney Studio Club, Museum of Modern Art, the Brooklyn Museum, the Metropolitan Museum of Art, the Whitney Museum of American Art, and numerous other museums. She also participated in government art programs, making several bas-reliefs and sculptures for the Works Progress Administration's Federal Art Project, the Section of Fine Arts, and the New York World's Fair. Locations for her New Deal–era commissions include the U.S. Post Office Department (now the Clinton Federal Building) and Federal Trade Commission in Washington, D.C.; the Federal Building at the New

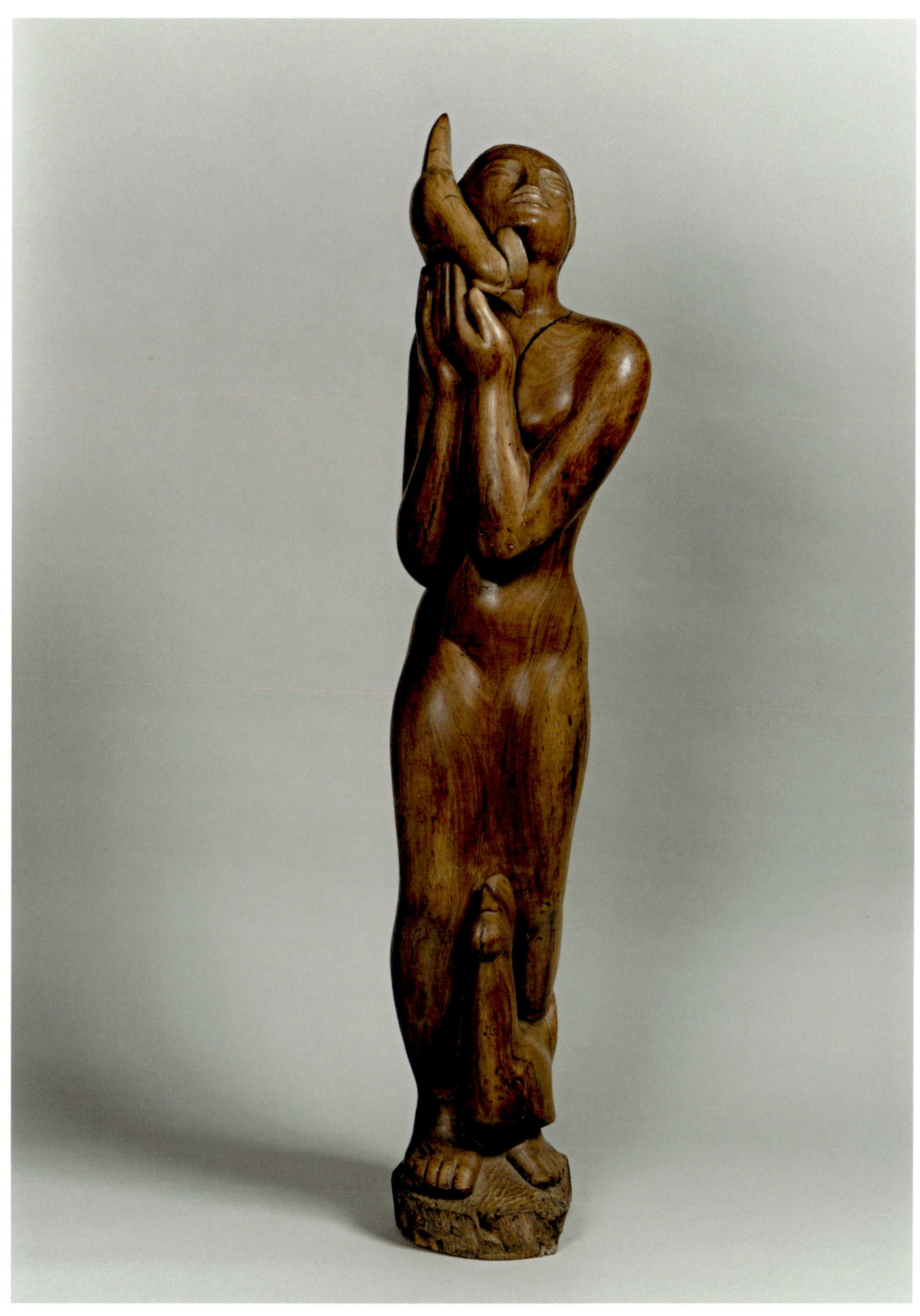

Cat. 23 **Concetta Scaravaglione**
Girl with Cocks

Italian walnut, 1947–48
Gift of Mr. John M. Stratton, in honor of his daughter Mrs. Tuxton B.
Pratt, Jr. (Elizabeth Stratton, class of 1950)

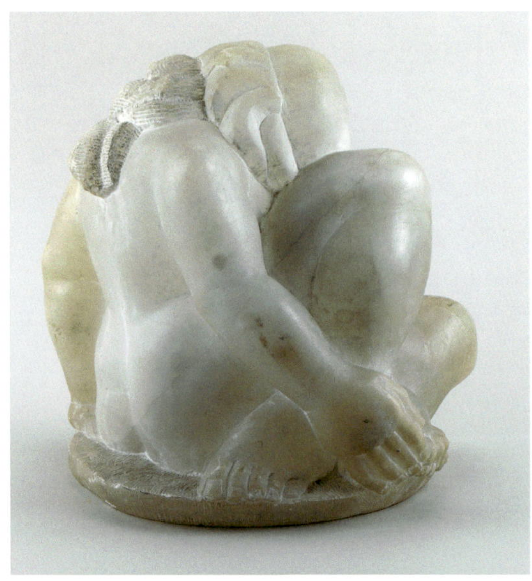

Figure 36. Robert Laurent, *Sleep*, 1938. Alabaster. 14⁹⁄₁₆ × 12½ × 11 in.
(37 × 31.8 × 27.9 cm). Frances Lehman Loeb Art Center, Vassar College,
Museum purchase, 1941.5

York World's Fair; and the Drexel Hill, Pennsylvania, post office. Throughout her life she also reached out to younger generations and joined the faculty at several institutions, including the Educational Alliance, New York University, Sarah Lawrence College, Black Mountain College, and Vassar College, retiring from the last named in 1967.[211] The artist favored solid, rounded, nude sculptures of women and children, their stoicism reminiscent of Archaic Greek kouroi. *Girl with Cocks* exudes a more energetic, contemporary domestic subject.

JOAN BROWN

Joan Brown (1938–1990) pictured a semi-clad woman in a private space in *Getting Ready for the Bath* (cat. 24; not illustrated), a large painting from 1961.* Wearing only a striped top, she balances her weight against a standing tub, with a green bra, printed red clothing, and a pair of red shoes resting nearby. The painting is more than five feet high and wide, and public viewers—strangers—confront this almost nude, frank body and orderly and brilliantly colored bathroom head-on.

Domestic subjects and habitats are key to Brown's art, which is largely autobiographical. "I feel most of my work, if not all of it, is like keeping a diary," she noted.[212] The bathroom, studio,

* Cat. 24 is not illustrated per the Estate of Joan Brown

kitchen, living room, tables, interiors with portraits, self-portraits, couples, cats, dogs, and children appear frequently. The early 1960s were a turning point for her as she emerged from abstraction back to figuration. Her portrayals of a comfortable home life are rendered in thickly applied paint, especially reds and yellows. Her instructor at the California School of Fine Arts, Elmer Bischoff, had urged her to study and paint the everyday things around her.[213]

During these years, 1960–62, the San Francisco painter lived with artist Manuel Neri, her husband, and they shared a studio for much of this time. She earned her M.F.A. from the California School of Fine Arts and joined the faculty there, and exhibited locally and nationally. During this time she also traveled in Europe for three months, visiting Italy, Spain, France, and England, and had a child.[214] Most of her paintings of these years were large, their size and brilliant colors making a public statement. She liked working on these big canvases because, as she later stated, "I found out it was very personal because I feel on a large scale that I'm a participant. I can step into the paintings that are my size or larger; I can really walk in there."[215]

Getting Ready for the Bath brings to mind another painting by Brown, *Aida at the Bath* (Hirshhorn Museum and Sculpture Garden, Washington, D.C.), also of 1961. That work was prompted by memories of the opera she had seen in Rome, where the lead character

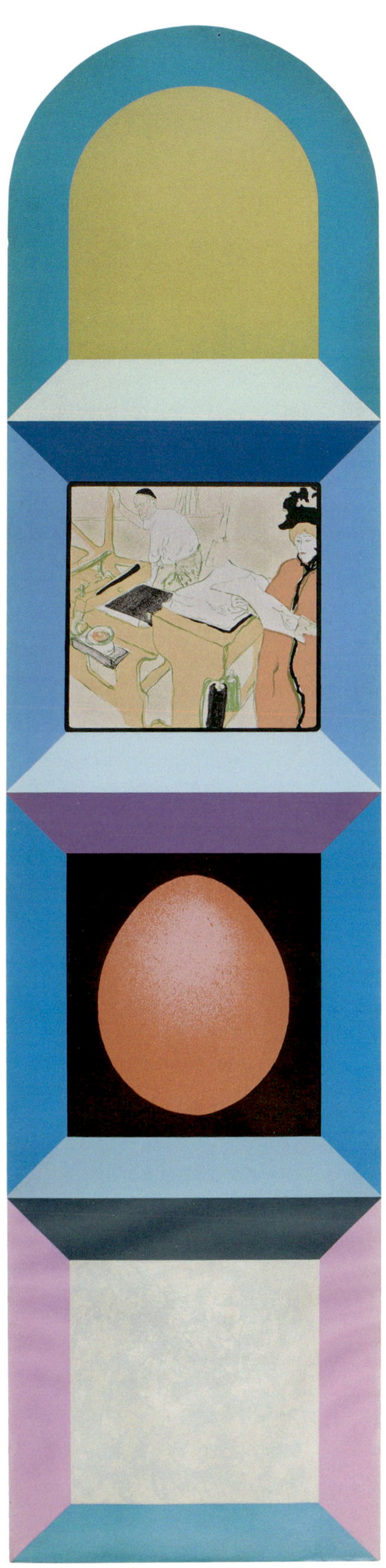

Cat. 25 **Miriam Schapiro**

Shrine

Four-part color lithograph, 1964
Gift of Dorothy Seiberling Steinberg, class of 1943, and Leo Steinberg

bathes in a checkerboard-like setting of rectangular pools and large square tiles. In *Getting Ready for the Bath*, Brown posed the model in an ordinary setting but retained the checkerboard flooring, which has been explained as an expression of her admiration for the sixteenth-century Italian painter Tintoretto and a desire for order. These two paintings presage her series of paintings on the female nude the following year.[216]

MIRIAM SCHAPIRO

Shrine (cat. 25), by American feminist artist Miriam Schapiro (1923–2015), embodies symbols of her life as a woman, mother, and printmaker. At the same time, her reference to the portfolio *L'Estampe originale*—the high point of collaborative printmaking in Paris in the 1890s, especially for color lithography—placed her aspirations on a very high level. Schapiro made this print in 1964 at Tamarind Lithography Workshop in Los Angeles during its early days of introducing lithography to American artists, sponsored with funds from the Ford Foundation.[217] For her print, Schapiro drew upon her earlier Shrine paintings, which were "shrines to painting—to the ways and whys of painting," explained Paul Brach, the artist's husband, in 1962.[218]

By 1973 Schapiro spoke of the female-charged nature of the Shrine paintings as "Layers and layers of provocative association and connotation—much of it female-engendered. By that I mean

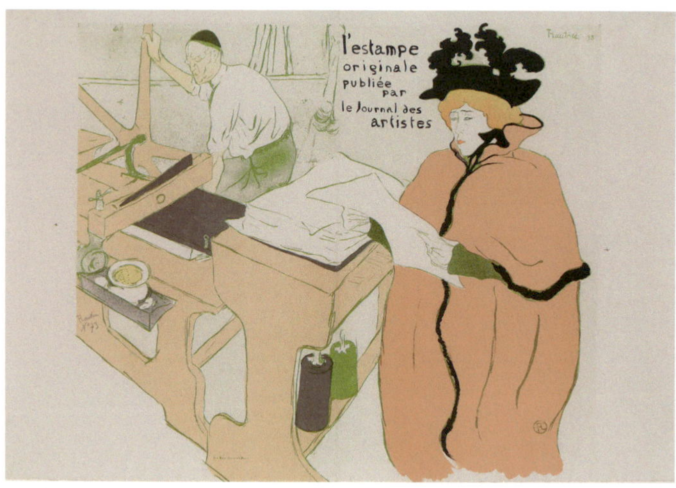

Figure 37. Henri de Toulouse-Lautrec, cover for *L'Estampe originale*, Album 1, published by le Journal des Artistes, 1893. Lithograph printed in six colors on folded wove paper; only state. 23 × 32⅝ in. (58.4 × 82.8 cm). Metropolitan Museum of Art, Rogers Fund, 1922, 22.82.1-1

that I made a real attempt to have the egg symbol be a metaphor for me as a woman and as a creative woman at that."[219] The egg shape can be seen as an emblem of fertility and motherhood in both the Shrine paintings and the lithograph. By the time the print was made, the couple's son, Peter Adam Brach, was about nine.[220] And, yet, with its various windows, *Shrine* may be seen as an expression of Schapiro's attempt to compartmentalize her art life and her domestic life, due to a personal crisis in about 1959 when she felt the need to move her studio out of the house and into a neutral space that was hers alone.[221]

Schapiro loaded her autobiographical content in the *Shrine* lithograph with an iconic image of the 1890s that would have spoken to her close collaborations with fine art printers. Raised in a Russian Jewish family in the Flatbush area of Brooklyn, Schapiro was trained in art initially by her father, and later studied drawing at the Museum of Modern Art and in classes sponsored by the Works Progress Administration.[222] She then went to Hunter College and transferred to the State University of Iowa in Iowa City, where she studied with Argentine-born Mauricio Lasansky. A Jewish printmaker who specialized in intaglio techniques such as engraving and soft-ground etching, he had refined his printmaking studies with Stanley William Hayter at Atelier 17 in New York. Schapiro became Lasansky's first assistant. She received her B.A. and M.A., and finally her M.F.A. in painting in 1949.[223]

At Tamarind, Schapiro would have worked with fine art printers and possibly trainees on developing the four separate prints that make up *Shrine*, checking each impression after it was pulled from the press. Such is the case, too, with the scene in the color lithograph from *L'Estampe originale* of dancer Jane Avril, a star of the Moulin Rouge cabaret in Paris, inspecting an impression while the Jewish printer Père Cotelle is in the midst of printing yet another one on the lithographic press (fig. 37).[224] Made by Avril's friend Henri de Toulouse-Lautrec for the cover of the inaugural album of prints, this earlier color lithograph unites a printmaking expert with a highly creative woman, and Schapiro's adoption of it seems to signal an equivalent situation with her print project at Tamarind.

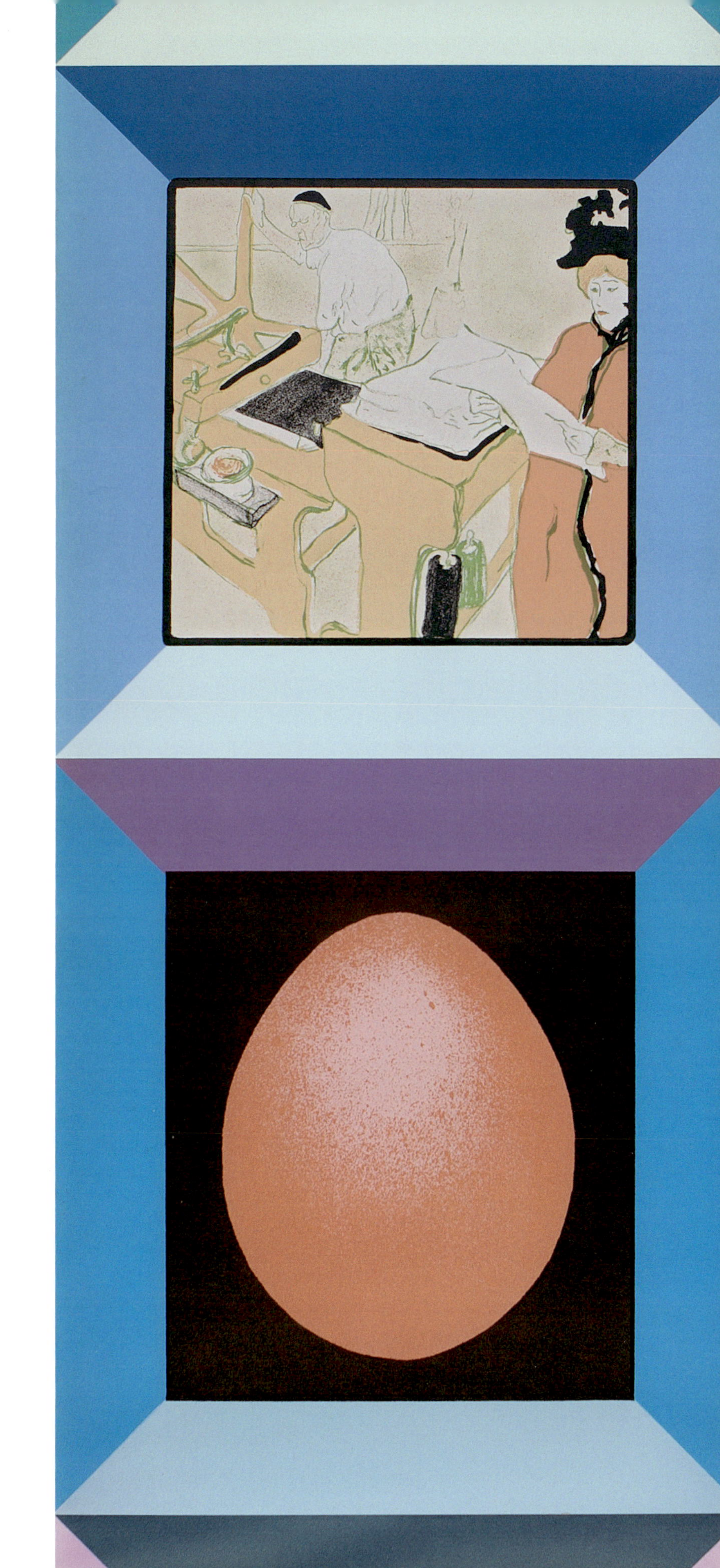

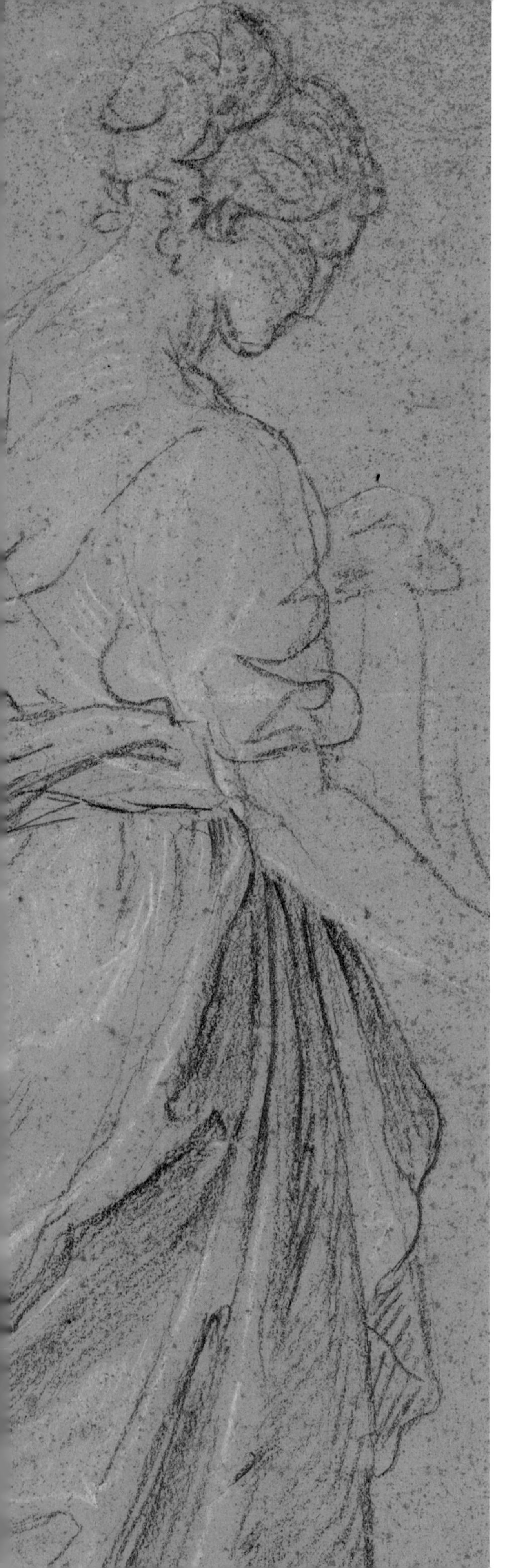

Narratives
The Stimulus of Ideas

In a letter from 1805, the London printmaker Caroline Watson confided,

> *I have always led a reclusive life, studiously attentive to my profession. I sought for no pleasure but what reading presented me with, & in that I always felt delight. I was intirely [sic] persuaded that in conversing with the ideas of great men, in contemplating the intellectual world, & searching for the riches contained there, the mind attains its truest happiness.*[225]

Elba Huffman (later Bouslog), a Vassar student from Indiana, wrote her mother in 1869,

> *These colleges poke fun at Vassar because she wants to make this institution stand for as much for women as Yale and Harvard do for men. The same text books are used, but our sex and youth as a college are against us.*[226]

And after being at Vassar for a few months, Huffman declared to her mother,

> *To an eager ambitious girl, set for a year in an environ- ment so foreign to the quiet life of her little home town, it is certainly an inspiration to come in close friendly*

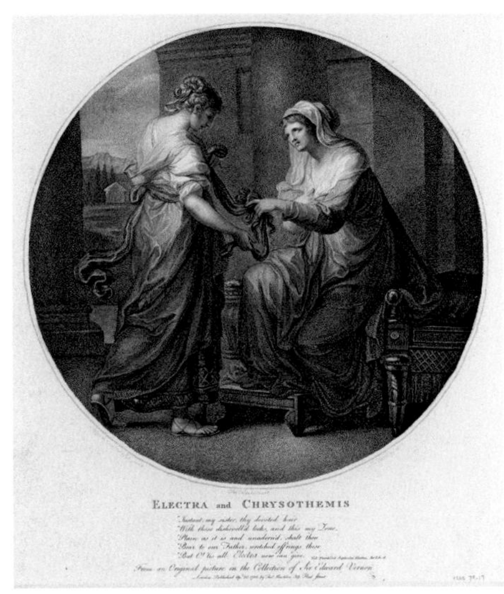

Figure 38. Sylvester Harding, after Angelica Kauffman, published by Thomas Macklin, *Electra and Chrysothemis*, 1786. Stipple engraving. 15¹³⁄₁₆ × 13¹¹⁄₁₆ in. (40.2 × 34.8 cm). Frances Lehman Loeb Art Center, Vassar College, Purchase, Suzette Morton Davidson, class of 1934, Fund, 1979.17

contact with such teachers as these two men—Van Ingen and Backus—whose names so often appear in my letters. In the world of Art and Endeavor which they represent and we are studying about, it is always what man has done or can do that interests and invites. . . . the future is calling to me and lies upon my soul.[227]

ANGELICA KAUFFMAN

Swiss neoclassical painter and etcher Angelica Kauffman (1741–1807) drew the profile of a woman, her hair in a chignon, in long flowing skirts and a sash (cat. 26). Drawn when Kauffman was living in London, the sheet suggests an intense interest in drapery studies materialized in chalk on paper with loops, tussles, and slashes of grainy black and white. The drawing takes up almost the entire sheet.

The work is a preparatory study for the painting *Electra Giving Her Sister Chrysothemis Her Girdle and a Lock of Hair from Orestes for the Grave of Agamemnon* (private collection), of about 1778.[228] The elegantly drawn drapery reflects Kauffman's interest in the antique, and it is a trademark characteristic of her paintings and prints and the more than three hundred mostly English, single-issue engravings made after her work.[229] In 1786, Thomas Macklin published *Electra and Chrysothemis* (fig. 38), a stipple engraving by

Sylvester Harding after the painting, which was then in the private collection of Sir Edward Vernon.[230] The subject is taken from Act 1, Scene 4, of Sophocles's *Electra*, translated by University of Cambridge professor Thomas Franklin, whose volumes on the ancient Greek dramatist were published in 1759. Intent on pinning down the pose and classicizing clothes in her drawing, Kauffman excluded an identifiable background, which was standard practice in preparatory drawings of the single figure, but most likely she drew the model in her studio at her home along the Golden Square in Soho.[231] By this time she had become extraordinarily well known and revered in London, though exhibition critics gave mixed reviews of her history paintings, judging variably her contrast of delicate and brilliant tones and her drawing ability and interpretations.[232] Twelve years earlier she had been on the Continent, where she had gained a following and a flourishing clientele among those on the Grand Tour, painting their portraits and winning membership into the prestigious Accademia di San Luca.

In London she continued her highly public career, painting local and international patrons from royalty, the aristocracy, and others who were socially well connected. Her neoclassical history paintings (fig. 39) were an unusual intellectual enterprise for a female artist, as women were not permitted to draw male nudes at the academies and art schools, which were foundational to history painting.[233]

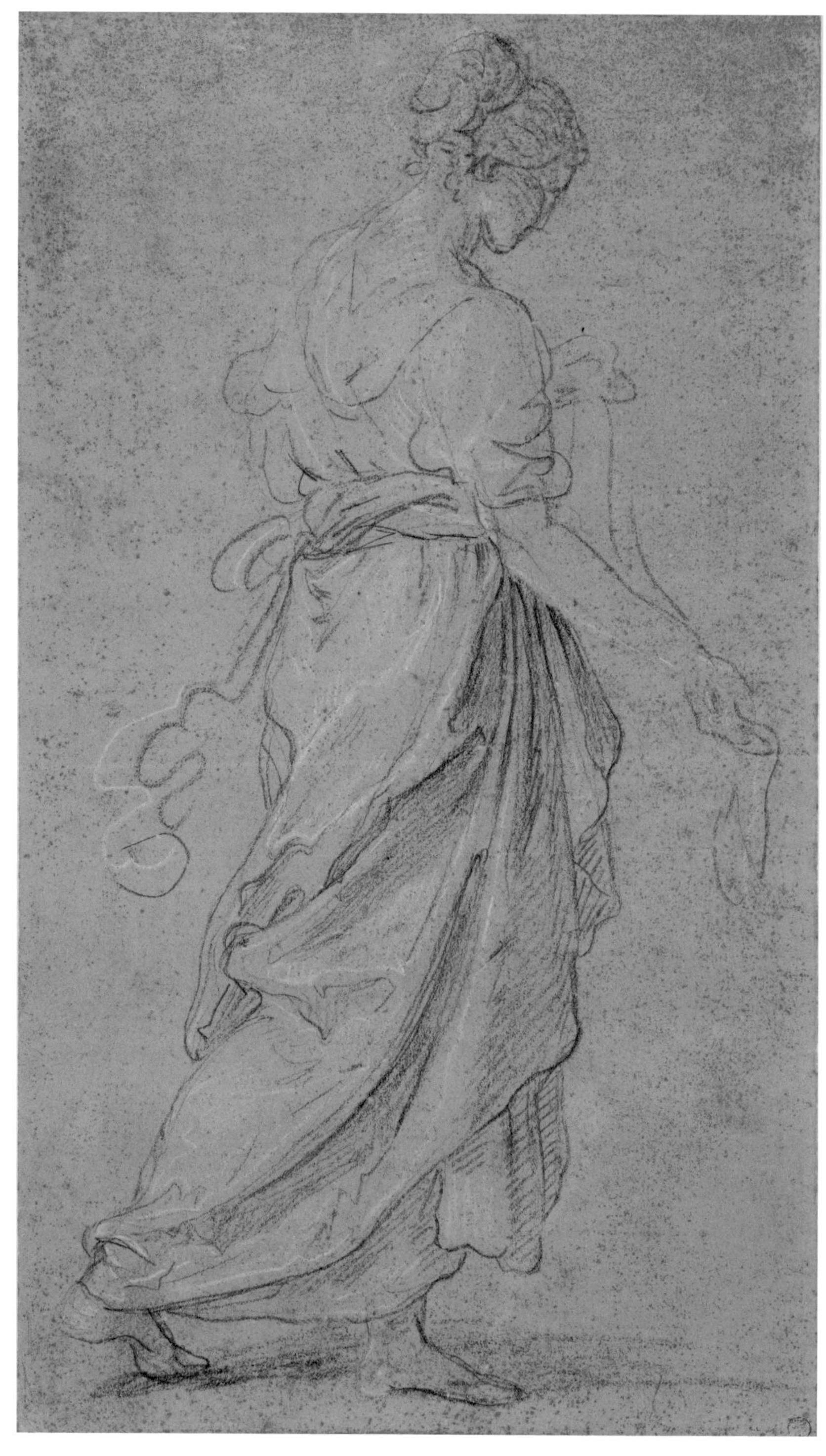

Cat. 26 **Angelica Kauffman**

Chrysothemis

Black chalk, heightened with white chalk, ca. 1778
Purchase, Suzette Morton Davidson, class of 1934, Fund

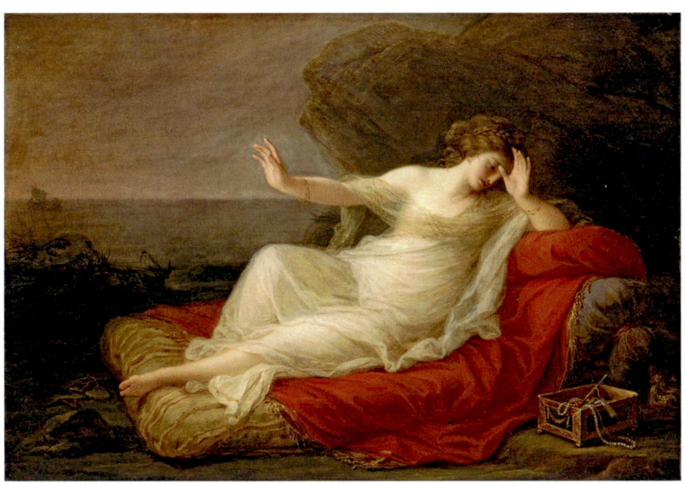

Figure 39. Angelica Kauffman, *Ariadne Abandoned by Theseus*, 1774. Oil on canvas. 25⅛ × 35¹³⁄₁₆ in. (63.8 × 90.9 cm). Museum of Fine Arts, Houston, Gift of Mr. and Mrs. Harris Masterson III in memory of Neill Turner Masterson, Jr., 69.23

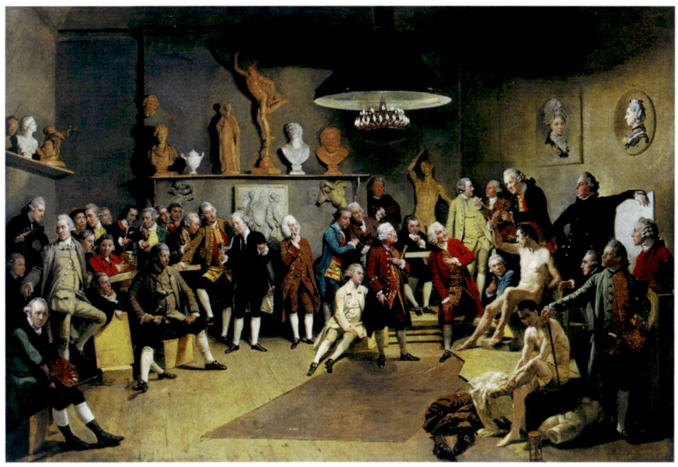

Figure 40. Johan Joseph Zoffany, *The Academicians of the Royal Academy*, 1771–72. Oil on canvas. 39¾ × 58¹⁄₁₆ in. (101.1 × 147.5 cm). Royal Collection Trust, RCIN 400747

Kauffman traveled in prominent artistic circles in London, and in 1768 she co-founded the Royal Academy of Arts. Johan Joseph Zoffany painted the members of the Royal Academy in 1771–72 in the life-drawing room when the Academy was housed at Old Somerset House (fig. 40). He placed her portrait high on the wall behind the nude male model and across from shelves of plaster casts, facing a portrait to the right of the only other female member at the time, Mary Moser. The members below turn to the model and each other in a vivid display of conversation and male fashion. An artist whose knowledge and application of classical history was associated more with male than female artists, Kauffman could not attend the drawing classes but could show works of art at the Academy's annual exhibitions.[234] Kauffman exhibited there into the late 1790s when she was again in Rome, and like modern-day architects and painters, she also worked with associates and manufacturers to incorporate her designs into furniture, teapots, porcelains, and other domestic objects, like Doris Lee would do in New York in the mid-twentieth century.

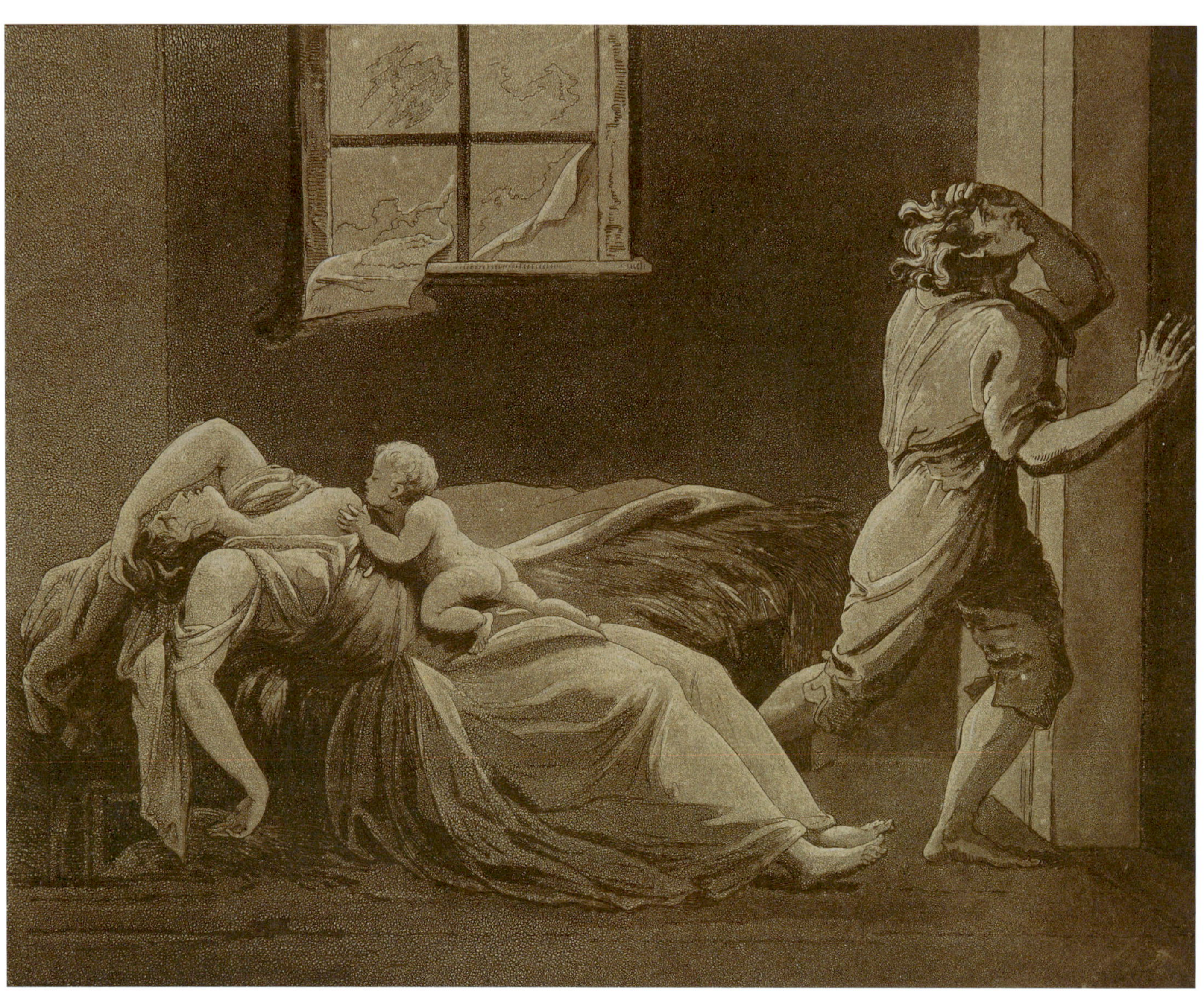

Cat. 27   **Caroline Watson after Maria Cosway**

Mis'ry's Victims

Etching and aquatint, 1803, from the folio *The Winter Day*, 1804

Purchase, Suzette Morton Davidson, class of 1934, Fund

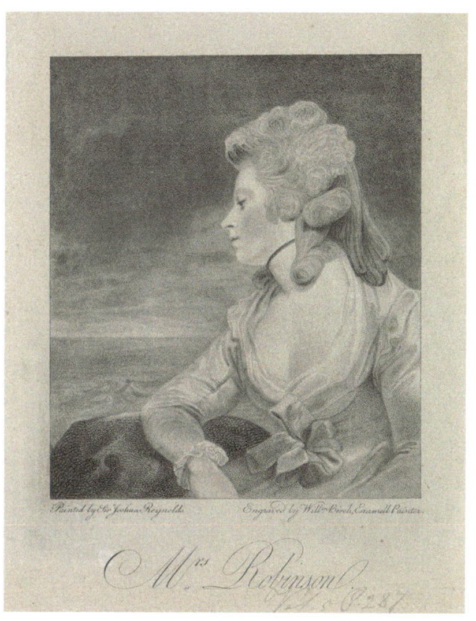

Figure 41. William Birch after Sir Joshua Reynolds, *Mrs. Robinson*, 1792. Stipple engraving and aquatint on medium, slightly textured, beige laid paper. 7 × 5⁷⁄₁₆ in. (17.7 × 13.8 cm). Yale Center for British Art, Paul Mellon Collection, B1977.14.10201

CAROLINE WATSON AND MARIA HADFIELD COSWAY

In the early 1800s, London printmaker Caroline Watson (1760/61–1814) pictured a family in a small, dilapidated room of their home, with what appear to be oiled-paper windowpanes (cat. 27). The bed, at the time the most important piece of furniture, is in the center, its mattress shedding straw. Since about 1720–30, owners of new buildings in Europe had begun to use glass glazing, so the paper windowpanes, the disrepair, and the drama of a desperate woman dying with a baby at her breast illustrate the growing, appallingly poor population in London at the turn of the century.[235] The aquatint shows sensitivity to critical health and social conditions for women and families in England.

Though Watson made the print, it belongs to a publication project called *The Winter Day*, which she created with painter Maria Cosway (1759–1838), who designed the original illustrations; Mary Darby Robinson (1757–1800) (fig. 41), the prominent writer, intellectual, proto-feminist, and actress, wrote the poem that inspired the set of twelve sepia prints with verse.[236] The poem contrasted the beau monde, or fashionable society, and their lavish surroundings with the hopeless circumstances of the poor, and was a call for upper-class women to open their eyes to the wider world, sentiments also voiced by Robinson in her anonymously published *A Letter to the Women of England, on the Injustice of Mental Subordination* in 1799. In *Mis'ry's Victims,*

Robinson's verse appears below the image and compares "*Fashion's* idle votaries" in the preceding plate with a "cheerless naked room, / Where mis'ry's victims wait their doom," as pictured in the print.[237]

Rudolph Ackermann's Repository of Arts published the edition in London in 1804, though the prints carry the year 1803. A writer for the *Literary Magazine* in 1804 lauded the genius of these three women in this "very curious work" and opined that English "women have assumed, in some degree, the equality with men," an intense issue in the writings of Robinson and others.[238]

Watson, encouraged by her mezzotint-engraver father, made 118 prints and is considered the first woman in Great Britain to be a prominent and independent professional printmaker. She specialized in stipple prints after historical scenes and portraits by George Romney, Joshua Reynolds, and others, and gained much renown for her work, with Queen Charlotte giving her the title "Engraver to the Queen" in 1785.[239]

As a child prodigy in art and music, the Florence-born and well-educated Maria Louisa Catherine Cecilia Hadfield visited galleries and studied with eminent artists, encouraged by her English father, who was an owner of Florentine inns frequented by visitors on the Grand Tour. Upon returning from her own visit to Rome, she was elected to the Accademia delle Arti del Disegno in Florence, but after her father died she moved with her family

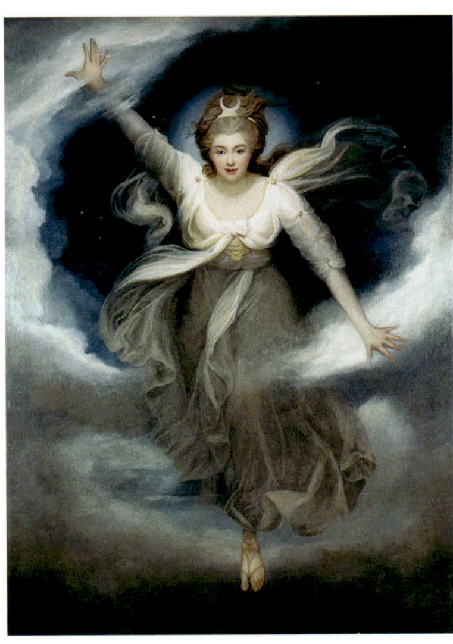

Figure 42. Maria Hadfield Cosway, *Georgiana as Cynthia from Spenser's "The Faerie Queene,"* 1781–82. Oil on canvas. 86½ × 63 in. (219.7 × 160 cm). © The Devonshire Collections, Chatsworth

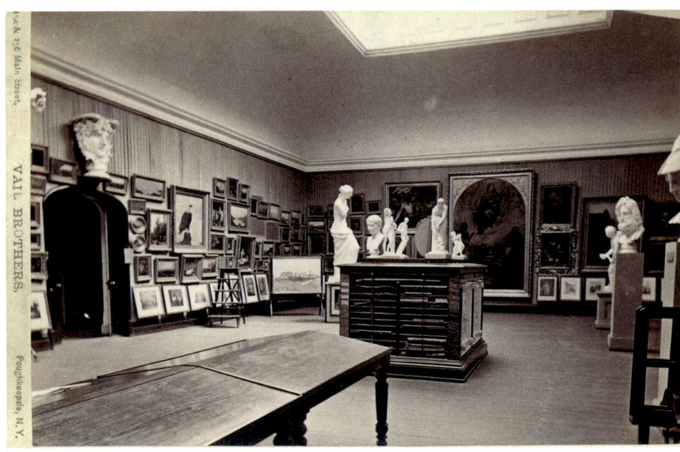

Figure 43. Vail Brothers Photography Studio, Poughkeepsie, NY, *Avery Hall Art Gallery, Vassar College*, between 1875–1914. Photograph. Vassar College Archives and Special Collections Library, Main Library

to London in 1779. There Angelica Kauffman became her mentor, and the younger artist began exhibiting at the Royal Academy and embarking on portrait commissions, including an allegorical portrait of Georgiana, the Duchess of Devonshire (fig. 42).

In financial distress, she married in 1781 the well-to-do miniature-portrait painter and art dealer Richard Cosway (1742–1821), who at first discouraged her from pursuing a professional art career, urging her instead to host her own high-society soirées.[240] Maria Cosway's designs of entertained and entertaining women of the upper class find resonance in a pair of her moralizing books with prints made after her drawings, *The Progress of Female Dissipation* and *The Progress of Female Virtue*, both of 1800. Their themes center on frivolous women and their trifling activities versus virtuous women focused on domestic life and home duties, as championed in conduct books of the era.[241]

EMMA CONANT CHURCH

In 1862 American artist Emma Conant Church (1831–1893) copied Baroque painter Carlo Dolci's *Madonna and Child* (cat. 28) in the Palazzo Corsini in Rome, carefully gauging the weight of her brushstrokes and the mixing of her colors. She would sell her copy, done on commission for Vassar College, and another reproductive painting to the school for its future art collection, while college founder Matthew Vassar would purchase a third

copy—a large painting after Raphael—for the college.[242] This copy of Dolci's Madonna adoring the baby Jesus would have served as an apt model of behavior for the students. It was exhibited along with Church's two other reproductive paintings and plaster casts of ancient and Italian Renaissance sculptures, first in Main Building, and then starting in 1875 in Avery Hall, the second location of the art gallery at the college (fig. 43).

Church was the daughter of a Baptist minister, the Rev. Dr. Pharcellus Church, who published sermons and religious books, and was editor of the *New York Chronicle* from 1855 to 1865.[243] His daughter engaged with the art world of her time and would have been vulnerable to criticism from newspaper reviewers or patrons and those who belittled women emerging into the public sphere. It is still not known where Church received her art training, but by 1860 she was busy—one reporter wrote, she "finds as much work to do as she has time to work in"—with studio space in the Dodworth Buildings in Brooklyn, and active as an exhibitor, with six paintings shown at the National Academy of Design exhibition in 1861, when she was thirty.[244] She was among numerous women artists in the New York area who specialized in portraiture, landscape, or genre who exhibited at the Academy. A writer in the *Springfield Weekly Republican* noticed this emergence of female artists, writing, "There are a good many women among the rising artists of New York and Brooklyn, including Miss Emma

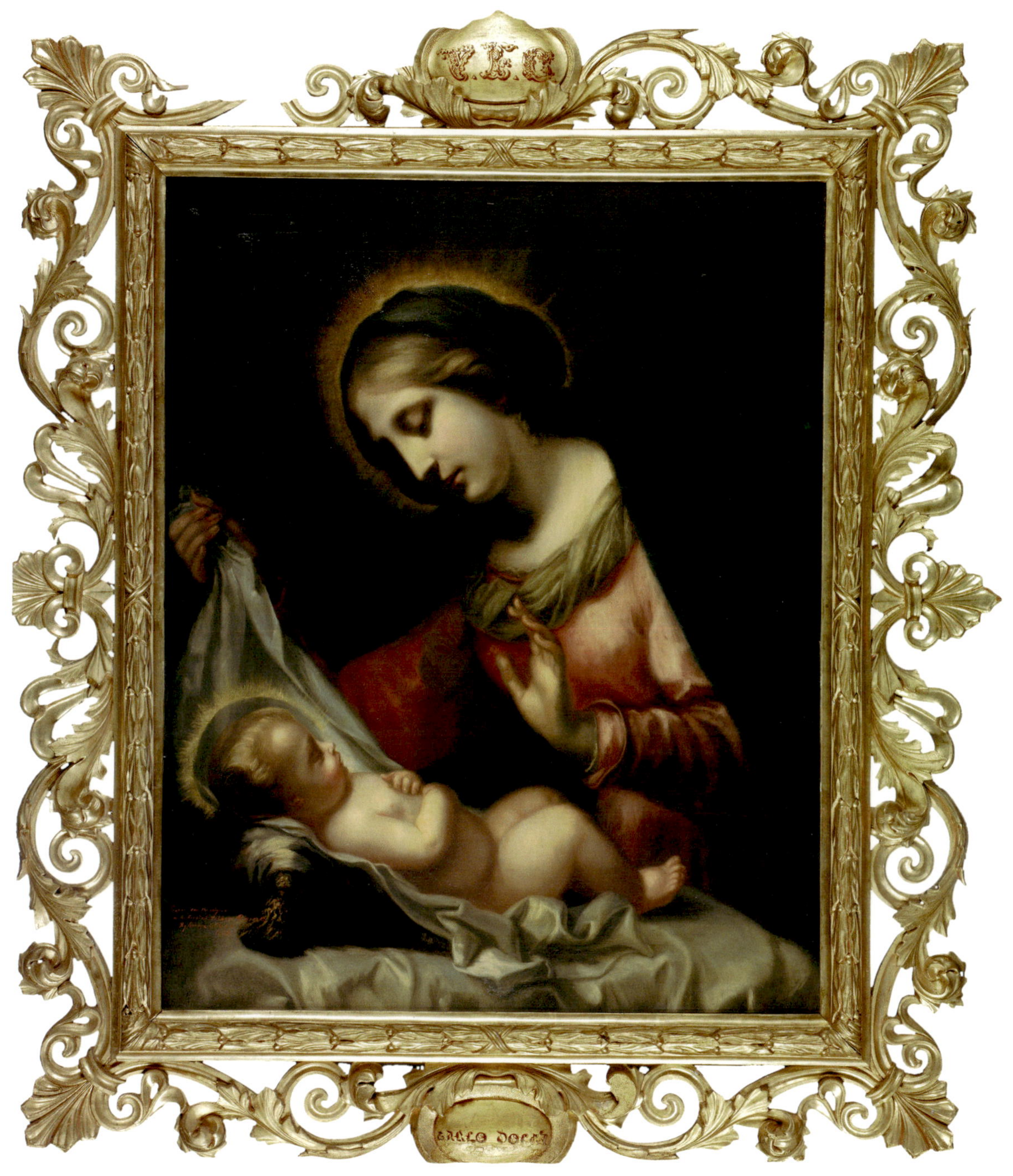

Cat. 28   **Emma Conant Church after Carlo Dolci**

Madonna and Child

Oil on canvas, 1862

Gift of Matthew Vassar

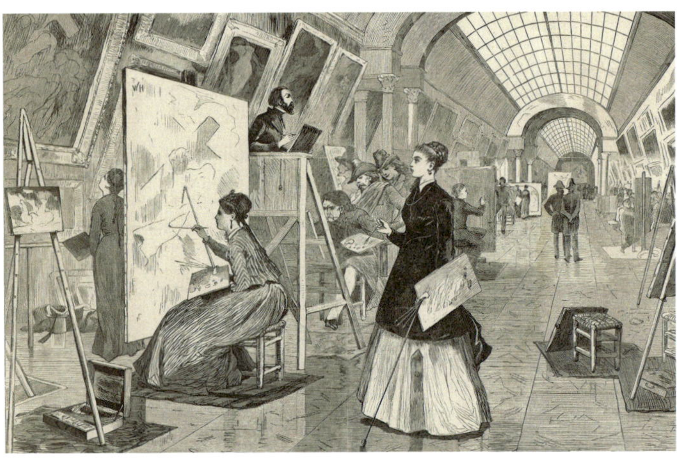

Figure 44. Winslow Homer, *Art-Students and Copyists in the Louvre Gallery, Paris*, published in *Harper's Weekly* (11 January 1868). Wood engraving on newsprint. 11¼ × 16⅜ in. (28.6 × 41.6 cm). Frances Lehman Loeb Art Center, Vassar College, Purchase, Louise Woodruff Johnston, class of 1922, Fund, 1974.22.1

Church."[245] In late 1860, Church went abroad and became a copyist, like Mary Cassatt, duplicating Old Master paintings at the Louvre in Paris or museums and collections in Rome, where there were networks of American women painters and sculptors. Of the thirty-eight copyists listed in Bonfigli's *Guide to the Studios in Rome* for 1860, only five were women.[246] Winslow Homer illustrated the crowded copyist situation in his wood engraving for *Harper's Weekly* early in 1868 (fig. 44), emphasizing the small group of upstart women interrupting what had generally been a male activity. As Jacqueline Marie Musacchio demonstrates, ample literature encouraged women to travel in Europe, though they were advised to exercise caution.[247]

Church took commissions to earn her living, and in 1862, when the new Vassar College president, the Rev. Milo P. Jewett, visited her in Rome, she agreed to deliver painted copies of four eminent Old Master paintings to the college as part of a new art collection. Early in 1863 Church wrote to Matthew Vassar that she would gather advice on which paintings to copy from adviser-friends in Rome, namely, Charlotte Cushman, Harriet Hosmer, and Emma Stebbins.[248] However, the copy after Dolci, dated 1862, was probably already finished by this time.[249] Alas, Church did not make a fourth copy. Vassar himself paid for the third copy, the large painting after Raphael, partly to assuage the head of the Committee on Fine Arts, the Rev. E. L. Magoon, who

had not been consulted on the commission of the reproductive paintings and adamantly opposed the purchase of copies rather than originals.[250]

Returning to New York, Church exhibited at the Brooklyn Art Association and National Academy of Design, and received critical praise. She soon returned to Europe, however, to revisit European capitals, including Rome, Paris, and London. In 1874 she married a businessman, James Long, who died in 1876 in Paris. Church died in 1893 in Port Chester, New York.[251]

ELBA HUFFMAN BOUSLOG

As a young Vassar student, Elba Huffman (1850–1933), from Peru, Indiana, wrote a series of letters home to her mother in 1869–70 that give a vivid, personal account of life and academics for an aspiring upper-middle-class young woman. For ten months, she penned these letters that show her sparkling wit, interactions with others, and thoughts on society's expectations for women. In 1915 Vassar would publish them under the title *Letters from Old-Time Vassar*, with the author given as anonymous.

Like dozens of advanced young women at the school who wanted to supplement their studies, Huffman was pursuing special courses beyond the regular preparatory classes that Elizabeth Coffin (see cat. 3) and others were taking. Offered a scholarship by principal Hannah Lyman (fig. 45) for the following year, Huffman

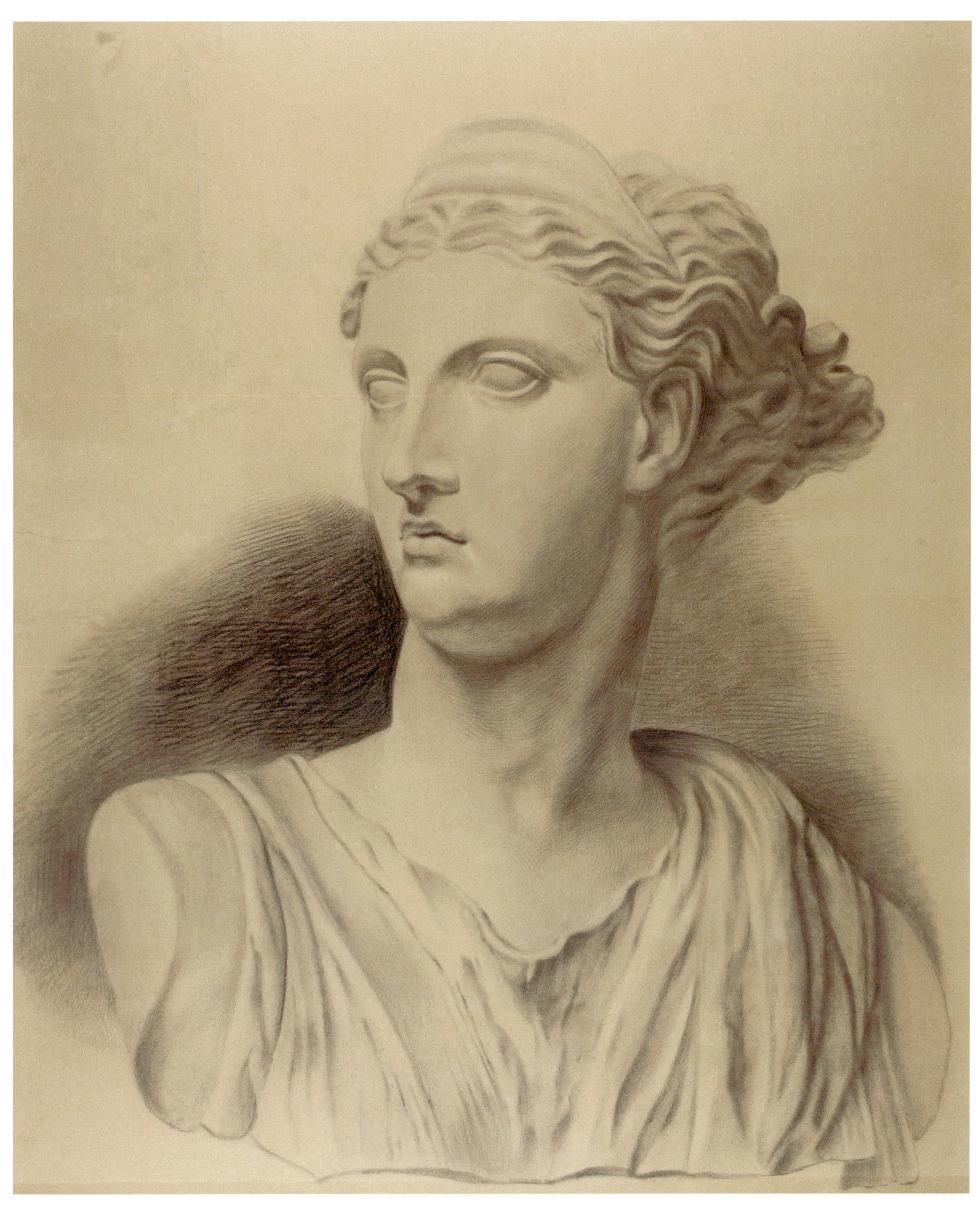

Cat. 29   **Elba Huffman Bouslog**

Diana

Charcoal, ca. 1869–70
Gift in memory of the artist Elba Huffman Bouslog, by
Patsy Denton Corbett, granddaughter of the artist

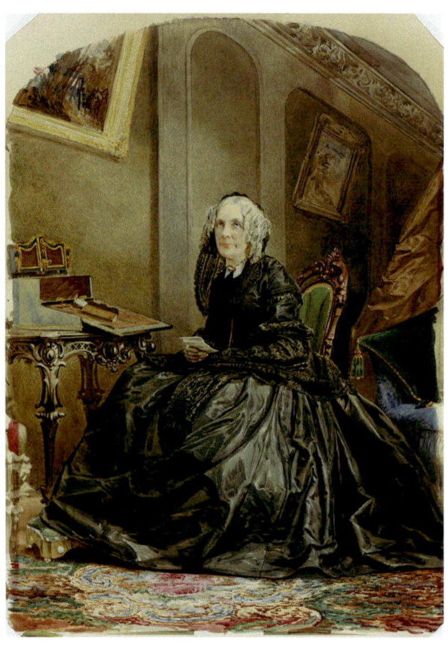

Figure 45. American, 19th century, *Hannah W. Lyman*. Watercolor. 19 × 27½ in. (48.3 × 69.9 cm). Frances Lehman Loeb Art Center, Vassar College, X.168

was elated, though she seems to have changed her plans about returning and was advised by Miss Lyman instead on "a life-course for me built along lines she had traveled."[252] Miss Lyman, born in Northampton, Massachusetts, had taught at Gorham Academy in Maine and Mrs. Gray's Seminary for Ladies in Petersburg, Virginia, before forming her own seminary for young ladies in Montreal that was modeled on high religious principles.[253]

Huffman's letters relayed her experiences and her excitement at the prospect of attending Vassar: "I feel so excited, so emancipated," she wrote in the first letter before she had arrived. She would go on to take several classes that fall, including on the Bible, elocution, Latin, chemistry, mineralogy, and drawing, as well as gym. She took drawing again in the spring, taught by the Dutch painter Henry Van Ingen, head of the art department.[254]

One of the "Art girls," as she described herself, she wrote frequently about her instructor.[255] In the fall semester Huffman took a drawing class with Van Ingen in the art studio on the fifth floor of Main Building. Van Ingen recognized Huffman's talent, and praised her "good eye for proportion, light and shade."[256] In the spring semester she described being "promoted" to the Art Gallery, where she set up an easel one day and was busy "putting on crayon with one hand while stumping with the other." She would also go with the sketching class twice to the Highlands

Mountains with Van Ingen, and another time "over fences, thro' creeks and plowed field."[257]

In one letter, Huffman discusses making two charcoal drawings from a plaster cast of the Venus de Milo, which was on display in the Art Gallery and later in Avery Hall when the art gallery moved in 1875 (fig. 43).[258] Another drawing, believed to be from her school days at Vassar, pictures what appears to be a cast of the goddess Diana (cat. 29). The drawing shows that the young student drew carefully with soft charcoal, almost filling the page, and creating sculptural effects with feathery crosshatches, light outlines, and shadowy smudges of charcoal.

An admirer of women's rights leaders Elizabeth Cady Stanton and Susan B. Anthony, Huffman became involved in progressive reforms around children's education and well-being. She did not become an artist. The daughter of a Methodist minister, she was educated by a private tutor in her early years. She attended public school when they were established. At sixteen she completed high school and then taught there for two years, then passed examinations that placed her in the junior class at Vassar, though she enrolled in senior subjects as well. In 1874 she married John Howell Bouslog, and in 1880 they had a son who died not long afterwards. After their first daughter was born, the family moved to Springfield, Missouri, in about 1882. Subsequently, she became immersed in rallying for children's issues, speaking and lobbying for state bills on child labor and compulsory education. Out of necessity, she established a school, Bouslog Academy, at her home due to the financial hit the family took with the Panic of 1893 and because of the illness of her husband, a victim of typhoid fever. In about 1898 the family moved to Bay St. Louis, Mississippi, residing in a French Colonial house called "Elmwood." With her husband's death in 1912, she would live with a daughter and her family in Bay St. Louis until her own death in 1933.[259]

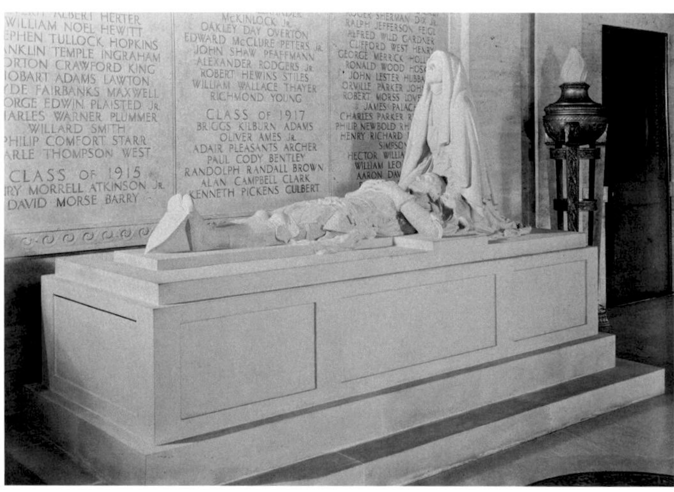

Figure 46. Malvina Cornell Hoffman, *The Sacrifice*, 1922. Caen marble. 84 × 148½ × 70½ in. (213.4 × 377.2 × 179.1 cm). Harvard University Portrait Collection, Gift of Mrs. Robert Bacon to the University, 1922, S93

Figure 47. Anna Coleman Ladd, *Women's Overseas Service League*, 1921. Cast bronze plaque. Diam.: 5⅝ in. (14.4 cm). American Numismatic Society, New York, 0000.999.40668 obverse

MALVINA CORNELL HOFFMAN

Malvina Hoffman (1885–1966) made a small bust in 1923 of an allegorical character, Pax, or Peace, that was cast at Roman Bronze Works in Brooklyn the following year (cat. 30).[260] The petite bronze head depicts an attractive, solemn woman in a winged headband and scarf looking downward, as if surveying a scene below. She seems lost in reverie.

The subject, connected to the Great War, was not new for Hoffman. Before World War I, Adolph Ochs of the *New York Times* had proposed that she create a peace monument, and Hoffman made designs and models for her "Modern Acropolis," but the war ended those plans. Instead, she worked for the Red Cross in New York, including fundraising for artists in Paris through the Appui aux Artistes (Aid to Artists) and coordinating letter writing to families in Europe. She did, however, produce some war-related sculptures, including a marble commission called *The Sacrifice* in 1922 (fig. 46). Originally titled *La Douleur est la Mère de la Beauté (Sorrow is the Mother of Beauty)*, the memorial depicts a woman in long draperies kneeling before a prostrate crusader.[261] Civic-minded, Hoffman traveled to Yugoslavia in 1919 as secretary of the American Yugo-Slav Relief Society to assess the needs of the children and report back to U.S. government officials and the American Red Cross in Paris. Her return to Paris shocked her:

I felt years older—the life of Paris appeared artificial and I found it painful to answer the many questions that every one asked. They all seemed to be so far removed from this recent world of smoking lava and victims of the bloody volcano of war, pestilence, famine, death—the Four Horsemen of the Apocalypse in ghastly reality, still ravaging the face of the earth.[262]

Artists commemorated peace through a wide number of different mediums. Boston sculptor Anna Coleman Ladd, for instance, made a bronze plaque for the Women's Overseas Service League, an aid society for women who had served in the war, which featured the head of a young woman wearing a winged hairband between a submarine and battleship (fig. 47).[263]

Hoffman was a major sculptor of the early and mid-twentieth century who used a flexible approach to her portrait busts, figurative works, and memorial commissions that was based in precedents as varied as classical, Renaissance, neoclassical, and naturalistic styles.[264] Women were frequent subjects for her, especially the Russian prima ballerina Anna Pavlova, with whom she had a long friendship. As an art student in Paris, Hoffman first saw Pavlova in summer 1910 while on holiday in London.

Born into a prominent musical and social family, Hoffman received early training at the Art Students League, drawing nude

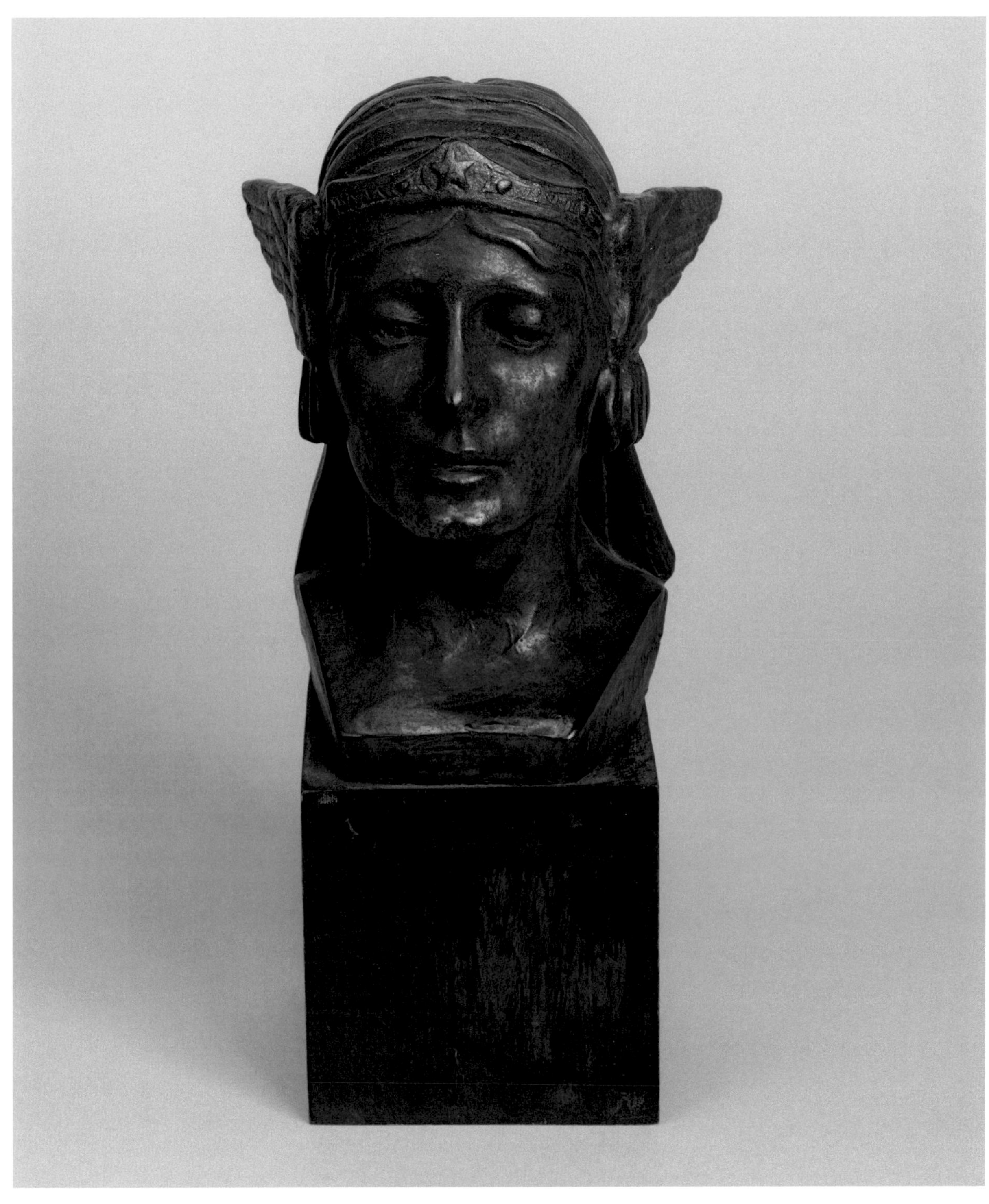

Cat. 30 **Malvina Cornell Hoffman**
Pax

Bronze, 1923, cast in 1924
Gift of Mrs. Hobart Cale (Marion L. Davis, class of 1929)

models in a life class, and at the Women's School of Applied Design in New York. She learned about sculpting and modeling from George Grey Barnard and Herbert Adams, and painting with John White Alexander at the private Veltin School for Girls in New York. She also studied with sculptors Gutzon Borglum and Ivan Meštrović, and in Paris with Auguste Rodin and in classes at the Académie Colarossi.[265] To better understand the human form, she studied anatomy in New York at the Cornell College of Physicians and Surgeons.[266]

After her father's death in 1909, Hoffman took over financial responsibilities for herself and her mother and, with funds from a bequest from her godmother, they traveled to Europe, where they lived for an extended period. Back in New York she settled into studio life, attracted a lively social set, and supported herself with sculpture commissions. Later, in 1924, she would marry British violinist Samuel B. Grimson, with whom she had had a long relationship. Beyond her popular works on Anna Pavlova, Hoffman is also well known for *Races of Mankind*, her series of anthropological sculptures for the Hall of Man at the Field Museum of Natural History in Chicago, produced in the late 1920s and early 1930s. Though critics considered them race-based and problematic, more recent audiences have appreciated the artist's sensitivity toward her subjects.[267]

MARION GREENWOOD

During the Great Depression, American artist Marion Greenwood (1909–1970) drew a socially conscious study in thick, black sweeps of the conté crayon (cat. 31) for a mural at a new market in Mexico City. The everyday kraft paper she used bears desperate images: gaunt women standing, sitting, and waiting in front of skyscrapers and smokestacks; a phalanx of men trudging among workers crushed in collapsed mines; and a worker turning gears in support of industry and U.S. dollars. Up above, the fat hands of a capitalist grasp a strip of ticker tape bearing dollar signs instead of stock prices. With its polemical imagery, this early drawing belongs to the era of anti-capitalist, left-wing proletarian art in the early 1930s. The style was perhaps most familiar in the United States through paintings, murals, prints, and political cartoons by artists active in the John Reed Clubs, where worker exploitation was a key theme and newspaper and magazine cartoons were the chief weapons.[268]

With a great sense of adventure, Greenwood went to Mexico, where she found uncensored artistic freedom with this and earlier mural projects. The country, with its mural and printmaking programs and more tolerant attitudes, attracted numerous American artists, including Elizabeth Catlett (cat. 9) and Margaret Burroughs (cat. 32). Greenwood's travels sparked an archive of imagery from villages, towns, and the countryside, including casual, intimate sketches of Indians and other people and scenes along the way.

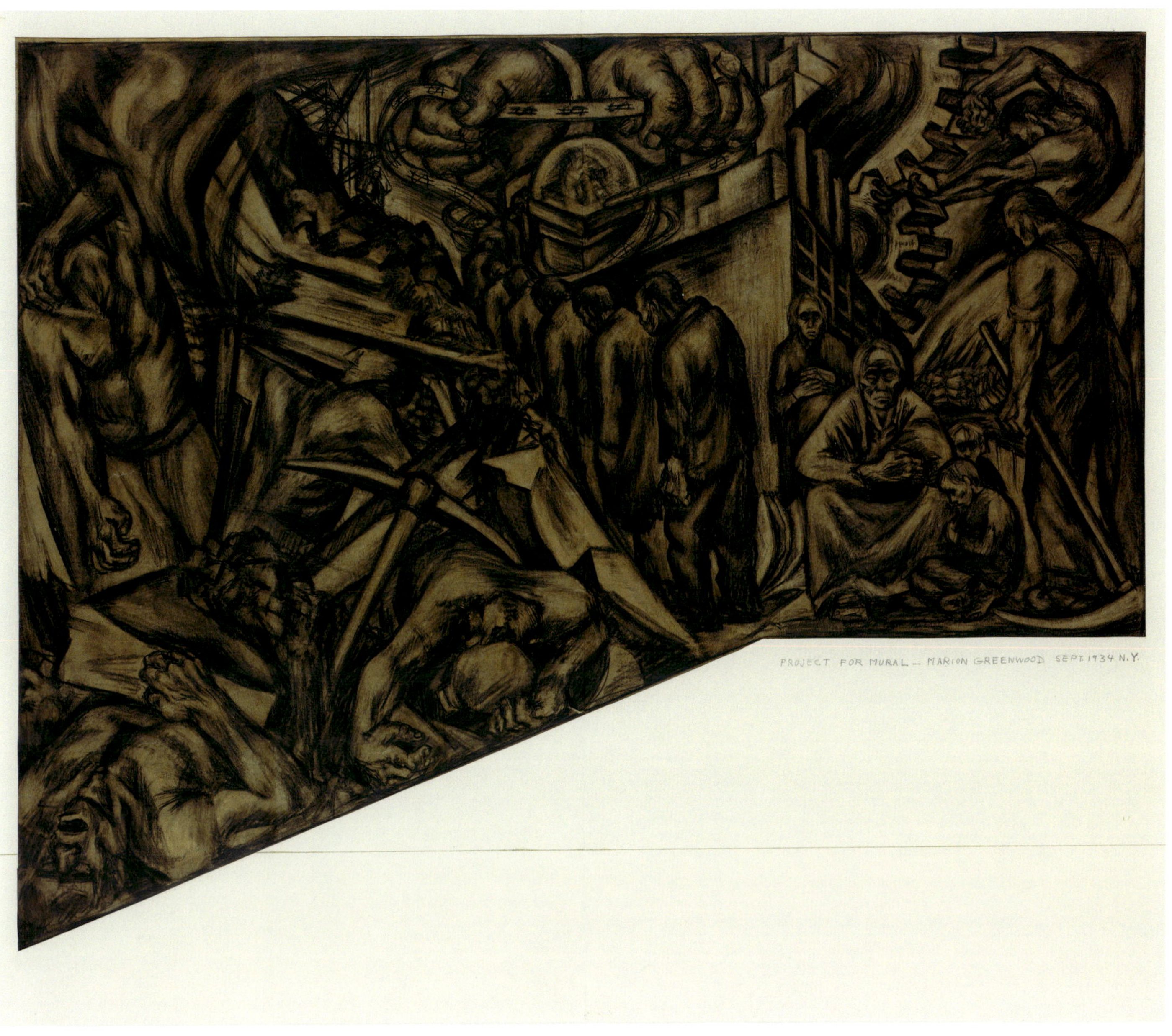

PROJECT FOR MURAL — MARION GREENWOOD   SEPT. 1934 N.Y.

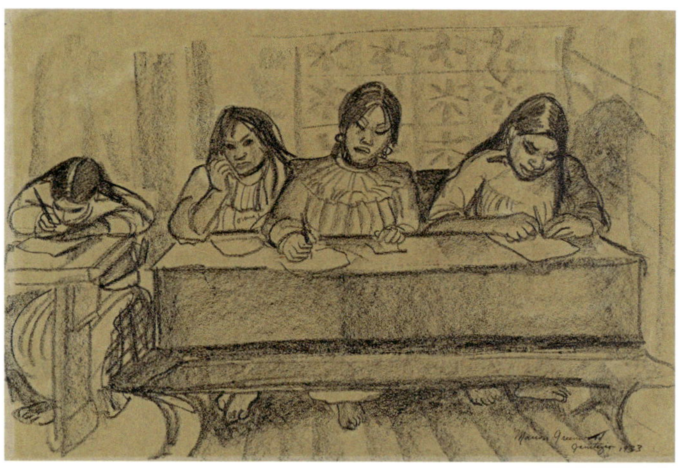

Figure 48. Marion Greenwood, *Four Mexican Schoolgirls*, 1933. Crayon on beige wove paper. 13⅛ × 19 in. (33.3 × 48.3 cm). Frances Lehman Loeb Art Center, Vassar College, Gift of Mrs. Al Paul Lefton, 1974.25.5

These include *Four Mexican Schoolgirls* (fig. 48), drawn in 1933 in Janitzio, an island in Lake Pátzcuaro, west of Morelia. There she completed a mural on Tarascan Indian life at the University of San Nicolás of Hidalgo. However, she endured personal restrictions, saying,

> *The only lack of freedom was of course privately. I had to stay in my hotel room like a prisoner at night because it was Latin America, and I had to be very much aware of what they were thinking of me in the whole little town, or rather it's a small city. There was a lot of unhappiness connected with it, and I did receive letters and phone calls to leave the place anonymously. I had a lot of hostility to overcome, and the students didn't want me to paint because . . . they had some idea that I wasn't for the kind of political regime that they wanted. I don't know where they got that idea.*[269]

Invited to contribute to the mural project for the market in Mexico City, she completed her preliminary drawing for the Mercado Abelardo L. Rodríguez Civic Center in September 1934 while she was still in New York. The previous June, American artist and fellow muralist Pablo O'Higgins, a Mexican citizen and the artists' supervisor, had urged Greenwood and her sister Grace to concentrate on the here and now for their murals, to

> *Emphasize local conditions, actual struggle, and present-day reality of exploitation, misery, and social retrogression, . . . and the necessity for struggle and means of struggle against these conditions, that will touch the everyday problems of the people.*[270]

In his letter, he told the sisters about unrest by miners and petroleum workers in Tampico. American and British companies had made deep inroads into Mexico, and Greenwood would have found much relevant material when researching her subject. By 1932, Standard Oil Company of New Jersey controlled the Huasteca refining company, and by 1919 Royal Dutch Shell had a controlling interest in the El Águila company.[271] Both of these Mexican firms were major employers in the Tampico area, an important port on the Gulf of Mexico for oil and ores, and in January 1934 they balked at paying minimum wages to workers, as required by a new law.[272] Earlier, in 1932, unemployed men and women from Tampico described as "hungry and jobless" led a march of thousands bound for Mexico City to ask for relief.[273]

When Greenwood returned to Mexico and engaged with the project firsthand, she studied Renaissance mural painting, joined in long intellectual discussions with other artists, and ultimately revised the design, focusing on agricultural farming and production instead, and strategically painting symbols of mining and

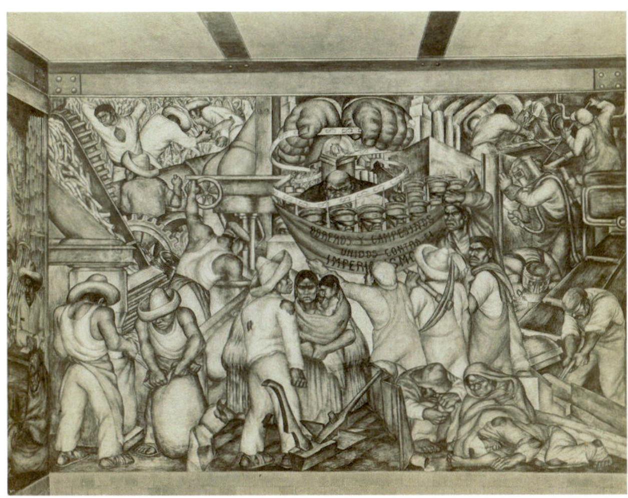

Figure 49. Lola Alvarez Bravo, Section of Marion Greenwood's fresco *The Industrialization of the Countryside*, in Mercado Abelardo L. Rodríguez Civic Center, Mexico City. Gelatin silver print. 19 × 23½ in. (48.3 × 59.7 cm). Frances Lehman Loeb Art Center, Vassar College, Gift of Mrs. Patricia Ashley, 1976.44.24

steel production near her sister's mining fresco. Inspired by Diego Rivera's *Mexico Today and Tomorrow* at the Palacio Nacional in Mexico City, Greenwood executed her fresco, *The Industrialization of the Countryside*, on site, borrowing several elements from him (fig. 49). Rivera, a technical adviser for the market murals, mentored Greenwood, her sister Grace, and the other artists on the project, and approved their drawings. She worked on her two walls for a year and a half.[274]

In the United States, Greenwood painted several murals with social themes for the federal government from the early 1930s to 1940. Born in Brooklyn, she studied at the Art Students League with John Sloan and George Bridgman, and formed important friendships at the Yaddo artist retreat in Saratoga Springs, New York. Other instruction included training at the Académie Colarossi, which Malvina Hoffman (cat. 30) also attended, an alternative art school formed in the late nineteenth century in Paris, where women artists could attend and draw the male nude.[275]

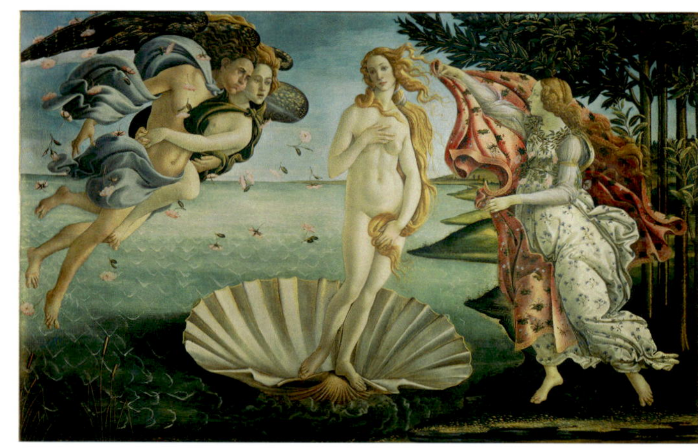

Figure 50. Sandro Botticelli, *Birth of Venus*, 1486. Tempera on canvas. 67¹⁵⁄₁₆ × 109⅝ in. (172.5 × 278.5 cm). The Uffizi, Florence, Inv.1890 no. 878

MARGARET TAYLOR GOSS BURROUGHS

Artist, writer, teacher, and community leader Margaret Taylor Goss Burroughs (1917–2010) made an allegorical linoleum cut in 1957 entitled *Black Venus* (cat. 32), her personal take on Sandro Botticelli's *Birth of Venus* (fig. 50). Burroughs displaced the white Tuscan beauty with an exalted Black woman taking the reins and symbolizing a rebirth. The artist's parody had deep emotional roots. Burroughs knew from experience as an African American student in Chicago public schools that the history of Black people, especially Black women, was ignored, and she hungered to learn as much as she could about them.[276] With her further studies in art education and her championing of Black art and culture, the artist created this new icon, adapted in part from the Old Masters.

Burroughs dedicated herself to advancing awareness of African American art and culture. She became a public figure in Chicago, co-founding in 1940 the Southside Community Art Center and in 1961 the pioneering Ebony Museum of Negro History and Art, which later became the DuSable Museum of African American History. In 1937 she earned a teaching certificate from Chicago Teachers Normal College (Chicago State University), and later received B.A. and M.A. degrees in art education from the School of the Art Institute of Chicago.[277] She began a career teaching art in public schools in Chicago—grade school, high school, and then junior college—from the 1940s to the 1970s.[278]

Burroughs was born into a working-class family in St. Rose, Louisiana, on the outskirts of New Orleans, in the segregated South. Her mother, a domestic worker, taught Black children in the back of the Baptist church, and her mother's mother told stories about their ancestors as slaves.[279] In 1922, the young girl and her family relocated to Chicago, with its fractious racial conditions, prompted by the killing of a relative by the Ku Klux Klan. The Taylors formed part of the mass migration of African Americans from the South to other regions of the country. They lived on the South Side of Chicago in the Bronzeville area, a section densely populated with Black families, and growing up there her mother and a white art teacher encouraged her to draw.[280]

In Bronzeville, during the Great Depression and into the fifties, generations of Black artists actively voiced their concerns about social justice and inclusion. This Chicago Renaissance fused art with left-wing politics and drove an awakening and advocacy of Black art, writing, and culture that included Burroughs, her friend Elizabeth Catlett (cat. 9) and her husband Charles White, Archibald Motley, and many other artists.[281] Burroughs was intimately involved in the Renaissance, and early on looked to others as role models for the politically engaged artist. At the age of seventeen she began a lifelong friendship with singer and activist Paul Robeson, who inspired her political activism.[282]

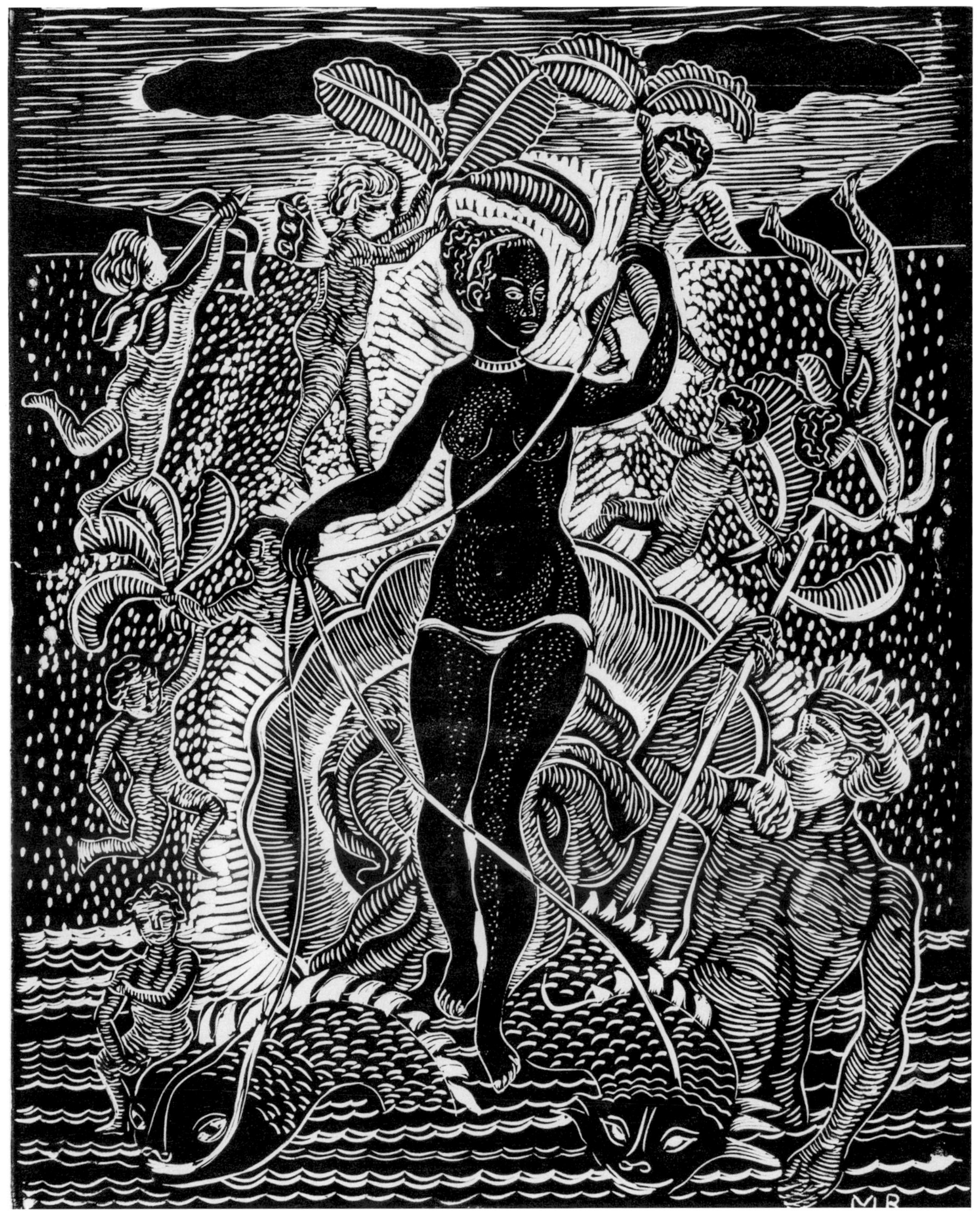

Cat. 32   **Margaret Taylor Goss Burroughs**

Black Venus

Linoleum cut, 1957
Purchase, Betsy Mudge Wilson, class of 1956, Memorial Fund

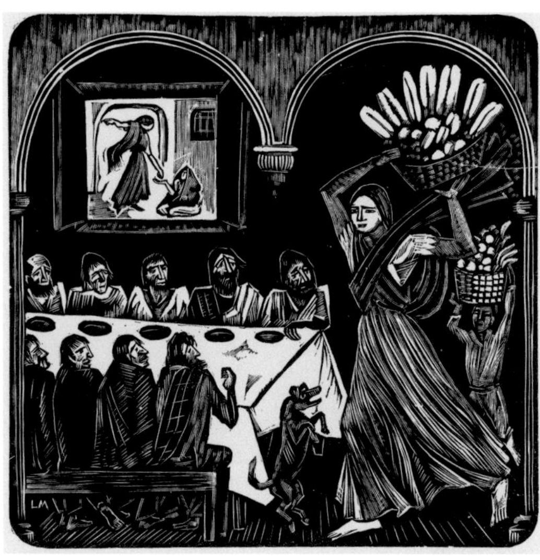

Figure 51. Leopoldo Méndez, *The Banquet*, 1932. Woodcut. 4⅞ × 4⅞ in.
(12.4 × 12.4 cm). Frances Lehman Loeb Art Center, Vassar College, Gift of
Professor and Mrs. Laurence Schmeckebier (Alexandra Kluge, class of 1930),
1976.52.4

In the 1930s Burroughs attended protest rallies in Bronzeville against lynching and in support of the Scottsboro Boys, a group of young Black men accused of raping two white women in Alabama and a major leftist cause in the early thirties.[283] From art classes at the South Side Settlement House, she and other students formed the Art Crafts Guild. They were instrumental in fundraising for a building to house the South Side Community Art Center, which was sponsored by the Works Projects Administration.[284] Burroughs was a driving force, organizing the Art Center and its programs with an eye to promoting Black culture and art with a broad social message. This corresponded to the Popular Front campaign, an international effort to galvanize a wide coalition of cultural groups and individuals to oppose war and fascism.[285] Writing an anti-war article in the *Chicago Defender*, she called African Americans to action to create a new world for themselves:

If all of the black men and women would mass themselves in a solid flank, to abolish the poll tax in the south; to end lynching and peonage; to do away with jimcrowism and segregation; to enforce the Constitution as it is written —if all black men and women would mass themselves in solid opposition to war we would see America really being America to BLACK AMERICANS. . . . Fighting for this ideal black women would be laying a firm foundation for the future of this country lifting ourselves up and off the lowest rung of the economic ladder and insuring that one-third of the nation which is ill-housed, ill-clothed and ill-fed [gets] a new birth.[286]

In the arch political and social conservatism of America in the 1950s, Burroughs was attacked for her progressive attitudes. In a partial response, she sought to recuperate from the toxic climate of suspicion at the school where she was teaching, as she explained, "there was an awful lot of pressure put on anybody who was the least bit militant. They'd claim that you were a Communist and would try to take your job away from you. So I asked for this sabbatical and got it for 1952."[287]

During her year's sabbatical in Mexico City, Burroughs, like Catlett, learned how to make linoleum cuts while studying at the Taller de Gráfica Popular, the workshop making prints steeped in the language of social concern. Leopoldo Méndez (fig. 51) was among its founders. Burroughs had learned the more traditional printmaking processes at the Art Institute and took the opportunity to make her own inexpensive social art.[288] She had not used linoleum before to make prints, but explained, "You take a piece of linoleum, battleship linoleum, just like we have on the floor, and you have these sharp tools, and you make your drawing on linoleum."[289] On her first trip to Mexico the year before,

Burroughs had found the country refreshingly liberating, she recalled, with none of the prejudices experienced by Blacks north of the border, that "being Negroes, we rather melted right in with the rest of the population. No one stared at us when we went to eat at the fancier places. We received the best and cordial service."[290] For Burroughs, the personal freedom she found there was transformative.

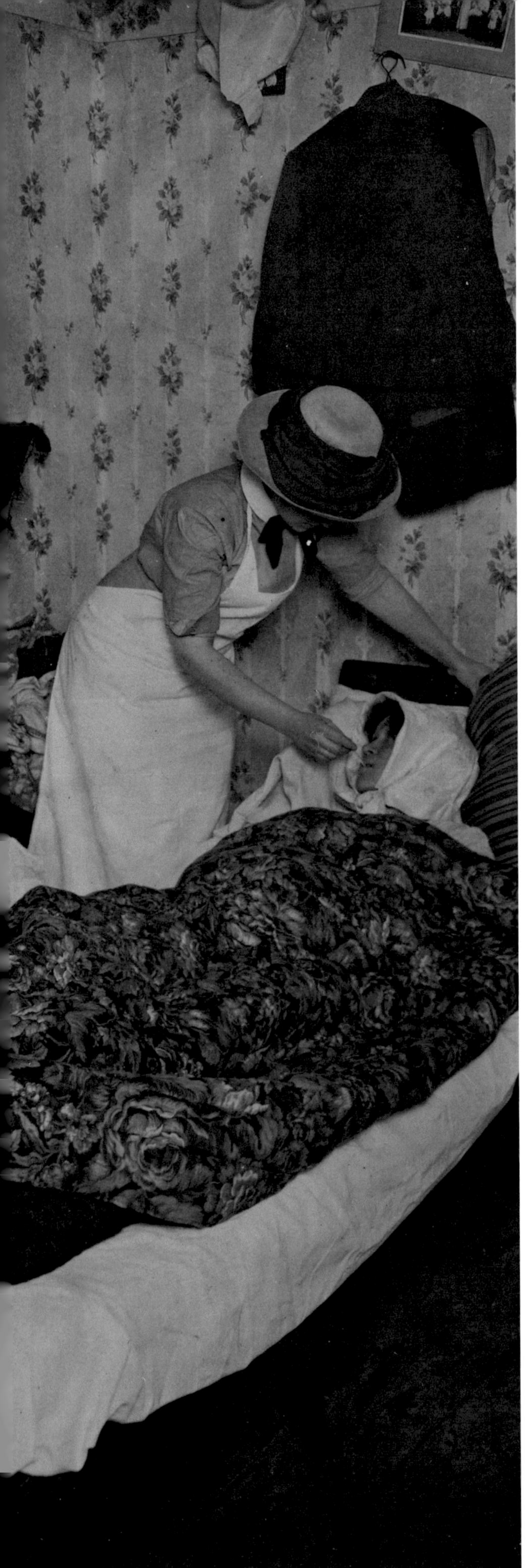

Documentary Photographs
Into the Streets

News photographer Jessie Tarbox Beals circulated at the 1904 St. Louis World's Fair, writing,

> *Many a mile have I walked in a day taking sixteen to thirty photos of every description. Those who have grown weary tramping around the Fair carrying a little 4 × 5 camera will understand the difference of doing the same thing with a heavy 8 × 10 camera and a tripod to match, the 12 holders with glass plates alone weighing about 30 lbs. Palace to the Pike, Stadium to the States Terrace, with intramural skirting around the edge of things, taking an hour to go nowhere was an experience calculated to wear out the strongest, but full of interest and the joy of success.*[291]

Margaret Bourke-White explained a headiness she felt starting out in Cleveland:

> *No one gave me any direction. I was free to use my own imagination, develop my own style. During this formative period when I had so much to learn about photography, I was free to make my own experiments and my own mistakes.*[292]

JESSIE TARBOX BEALS

In the tenement bedroom of an immigrant, a woman in a head covering lies in bed (cat. 33). According to the two calendars that are visible, the photograph was probably taken in January 1914. The room, decorated with family pictures, keepsakes, a feather fan, an advertisement, dishes and cups, a pitcher, and a goblet, also includes a crust of bread on the chair. At the moment, neighbors or relatives spy on her through the door, a nurse takes her temperature and adjusts her pillow, and the professional photographer Jesse Tarbox Beals (1871–1942) is inside this private space, too, taking the picture.

Born in Ontario, Canada, to a well-to-do family of Huguenot heritage that met financial ruin, Beals turned to teaching as a young woman in Williamsburg, Massachusetts. For diversion, she sought her first camera by convincing a neighbor to subscribe to a magazine, *Youth's Companion*, so that she could get the prize object. In time she began purchasing her own cameras, first a Kodak, then a 4×5 view camera with which she started selling her photographs in 1889, when she was eighteen. After moving to teach at a larger school in Greenfield, she would meet and marry photographer and amateur botanist Alfred Tennyson Beals and get her first newspaper assignment as a photographer. Together the two left for Vermont and the life of itinerant photography, with her husband as a strategic partner processing and printing the photographs. Beals had several prints published in newspapers with her byline and persisted in carrying heavy camera equipment around with her, all the while wearing full, ankle-length skirts.[293]

After settling in Buffalo, New York, Beals was hired as staff photographer for two local daily newspapers, using an 8×10 view camera to shoot courtroom scenes, fires, and less dramatic events. She became the first female news photographer on staff in the nation. In 1904 the couple left Buffalo for St. Louis, where for six months she photographed the St. Louis World's Fair and attracted national newspaper clients, especially in New York, where the couple established a studio the following year. In the city, Beals reflected on the attitude needed for her to compete: "Mere feminine, delicate, Dresden China type of women, get nowhere in business or professional life. They marry millionaires, if they are lucky. But if a woman is to make headway with men she must be truly masculine."[294] Her work would expand to mainstream magazines.

She also kept a diary and, like Florine Stettheimer (cat. 16), wrote poetry and associated with other artists in Greenwich Village.[295] These artists, writers, and poets, such as Edna St. Vincent Millay (fig. 52), gave her more license to rely on her own thoughts and tentative ideas in her professional life, and she confided later,

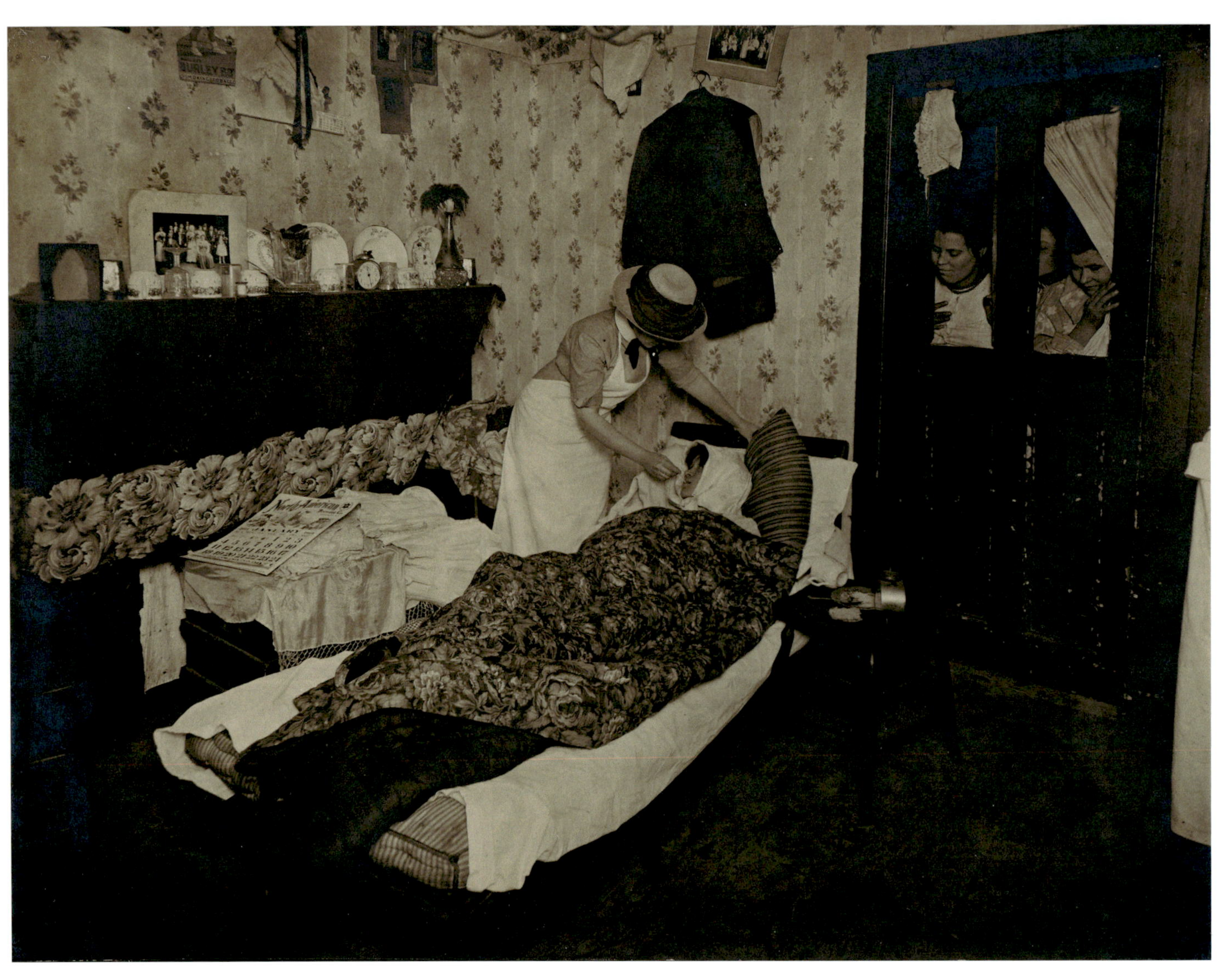

Cat. 33   **Jessie Tarbox Beals**

Nurse Attending to Ill Women at Home

Gelatin silver print, ca. 1914
Gift from the Michael and Joyce Axelrod collection (Joyce Jacobson,
class of 1961)

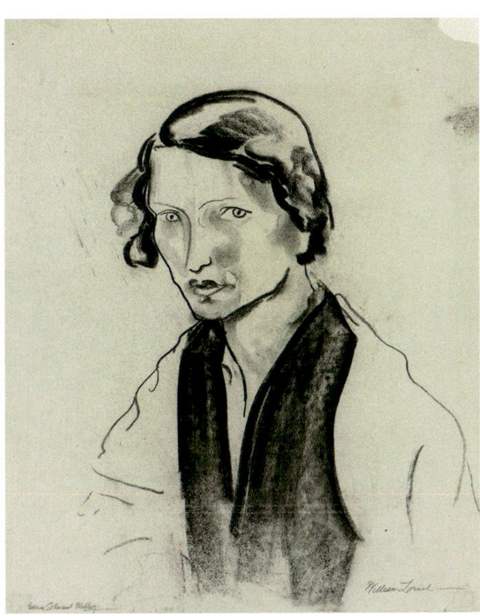

Figure 52. William Zorach, *Portrait of Edna St. Vincent Millay*, ca. 1918. Charcoal on paper. 21 × 15⅜ in. (53.3 × 39.1 cm). Frances Lehman Loeb Art Center, Vassar College, Gift of Tessim Zorach, 1971.11

just to be among them and talk with them inspired me to strike out and do the kind of work I had been yearning to do. I had never known intimately artistic folk before. They gave me confidence in myself and a wonderful optimism which no disappointment since has been able to rob me of.[296]

In the early 1910s, when she bore a daughter, Beals began photographing children in "tenement house conditions for the purpose of reform."[297] She was part of a group of photographers, including Jacob Riis and Lewis Hine, who documented social conditions for the New York Association for Improving the Condition of the Poor and for the Charity Organization Society. *Nurse Attending to Ill Women at Home* fits within these parameters and provides an intimate introduction to an immigrant's life in the city in about 1914.[298]

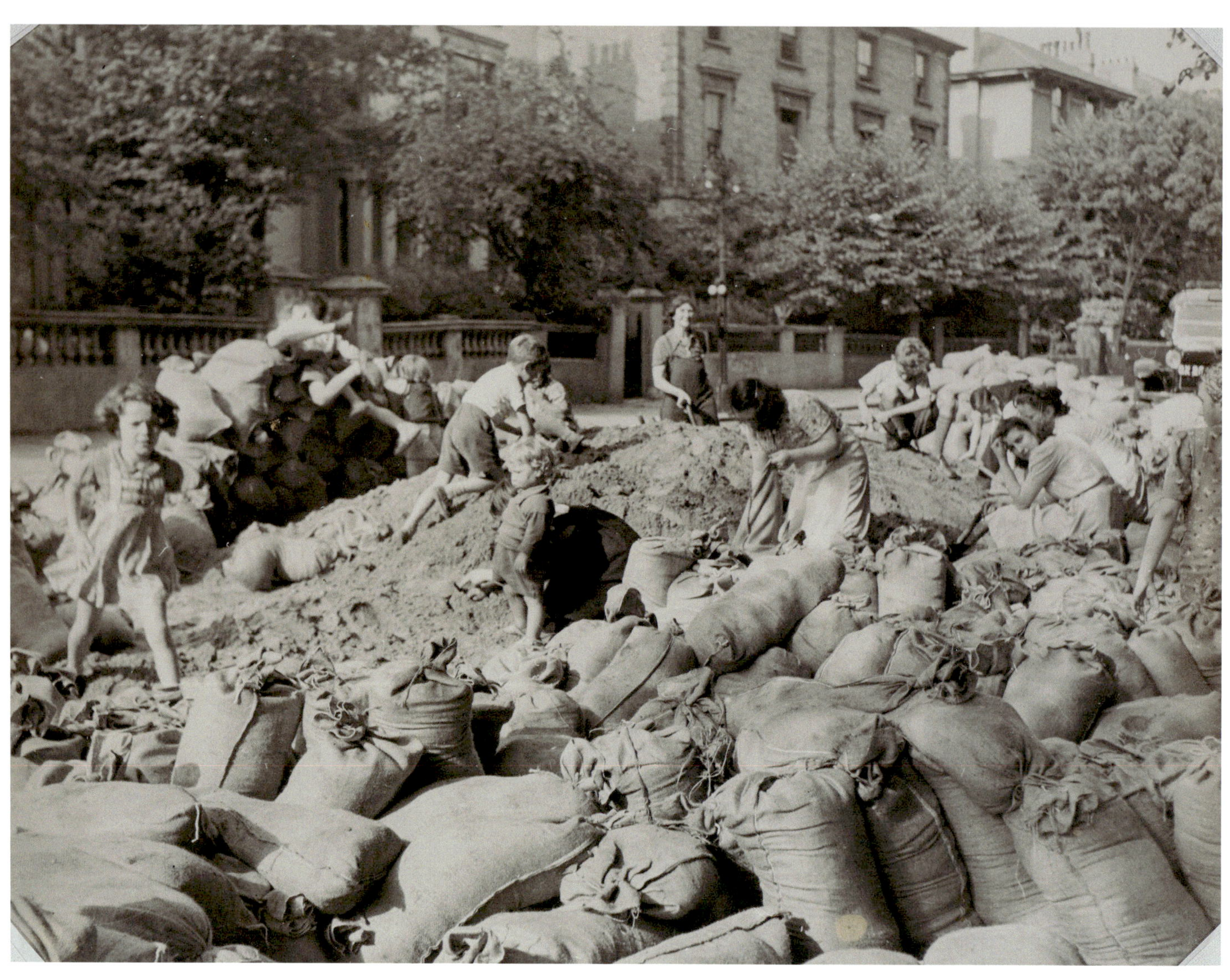

Cat. 34 **Edith Suschitzky Tudor-Hart**

Women making sandbags, London

Gelatin silver print, 1939
Gift from the Michael and Joyce Axelrod collection (Joyce Jacobson,
class of 1961) in memory of Cathy Picard Rosen

EDITH SUSCHITZKY TUDOR-HART

The Viennese documentary photographer Edith Suschitzky Tudor-Hart (1908–1973) interrupted a range of activities when she took the photograph *Women making sandbags, London* (cat. 34) on a street in 1939. In the harsh light, children play and gloveless women smile, stare, or work.[299] She made the photograph of Londoners preparing for war against Germany during the Popular Front campaign to oppose war and fascism.

Tudor-Hart came from a progressive social-democratic and Jewish working-class background. Having trained in photography at the Bauhaus in Dessau under Walter Peterhans, she would have found a deep correspondence with the school's utopian ideals. Tudor-Hart attended the Bauhaus from fall 1929 through spring 1930.[300] By summer semester 1929, the school had established a new photography department under Peterhans that fell within the advertising course.[301] He focused on amplifying texture by using bright light, which can be seen here in the strongly lighted cascades of bulging sacks, trampled sand, and ensemble of moving arms and legs.[302]

In her public life, Tudor-Hart contributed photographs to mainstream and leftist papers and magazines, including *The Listener*, *Lilliput*, *Design for Today*, *Picture Post*, and *Geographical Magazine*, as well as the TASS Soviet News agency.[303] She specialized in photographs of workers and children. Early in her career she had formally trained in London as a Montessori teacher.[304] In her personal life, she joined the Communist Party of Great Britain and acted as a key link connecting Communist members, activists, and operatives. Her photography has received prominent scholarly attention recently from Duncan Forbes through a series of writings and an exhibition shown at the Scottish National Portrait Gallery in Edinburgh and the Wien Museum Karlsplatz in Vienna. She married Alexander Tudor-Hart, a British doctor, in 1933. They moved to England soon after. [305]

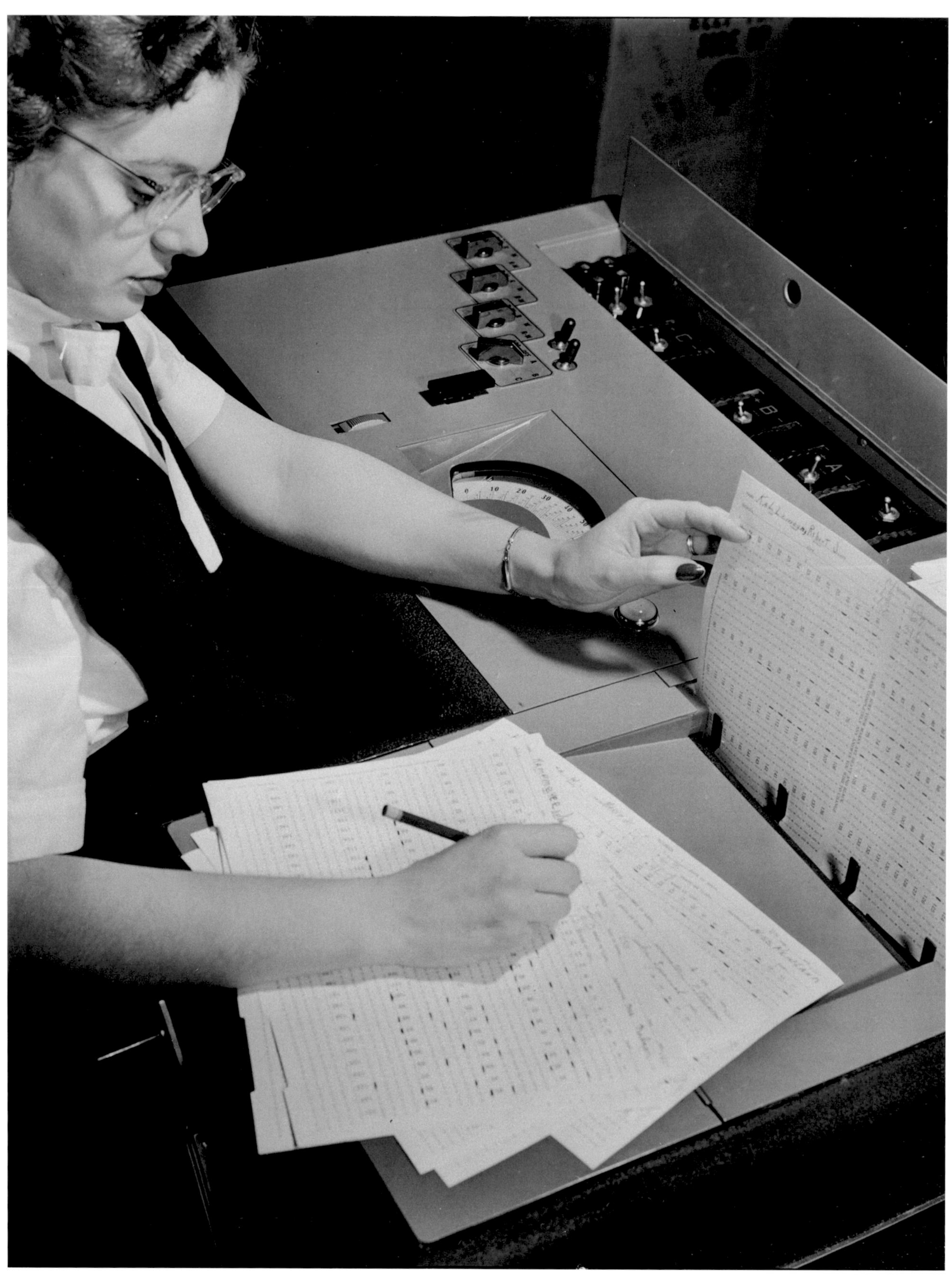

MARGARET BOURKE-WHITE

Looking down at an angle close enough to read the scores, Margaret Bourke-White (1904–1971) trained her camera on a woman grading exams at the State University of Iowa in Iowa City (cat. 35). Bourke-White took the photograph for an assignment at *Life* magazine in 1947 on the six thousand World War II veterans going to the university on the GI Bill of Rights. She photographed couples and babies in trailers; single veterans; and innovations for teachers, such as this machine for standardized testing on "most big examinations."[306] Working on sheets from students with various instructors, the business-like administrator or secretary in the photograph uses an IBM 805 Test Scoring Machine, which was invented in the mid-1930s to save time in grading exams.[307]

Born in New York City, Bourke-White grew up in New Jersey. Her father was an inventor and engineer focused on offset lithographic printing who had trained at Cooper Union. He occasionally took her on field and research trips, while her mother studied shorthand at Pratt Institute.[308] Bourke-White trained in photography with Clarence H. White at Columbia University in 1921–22, attracted by the promise of studying design and composition, as she confided in her autobiography.[309] She graduated from Cornell University with a B.S. degree in biology in 1927, making ends meet by taking up the camera her mother had given her years before and making "blurry" pictures, as she said of her pictorialist

landscape photographs, as well as taking pictures of buildings on campus.[310]

Encouraged to specialize in architectural photography by Cornell alumni, Bourke-White in the fall opened a photography studio in Cleveland, where she had also gone to school, winning appreciation for her breakthrough industrial photographs. She was allowed to photograph in the steel mills where women had been barred from entering, and she worked on the project there for five months.[311] In 1929, when the country was still in a period of economic prosperity for many, Henry Luce invited her to work for his new magazine *Fortune* in New York. She would undertake numerous projects with her 5x7 Corona view camera, tripod, and cumbersome strings of high-wattage light bulbs. Eventually she moved to New York and took up advertising photography.[312]

In summer 1930 Bourke-White went to Germany (sponsored by *Fortune*) and then Russia on her own. This was a breakthrough trip for a Western photographer, and her documenting of the rapid industrial changes taking place won her public adulation. She returned to Russia during the summers of 1931 and 1932 to research newspaper articles and make an industrial film. Alfred Eisenstaedt had written letters of introduction for her to artists in Moscow, Berlin, and Paris, and once there she concluded in her book, *Eyes on Russia*, "I had come to a country where an industrial photographer is accorded the rank of artist and prophet."[313]

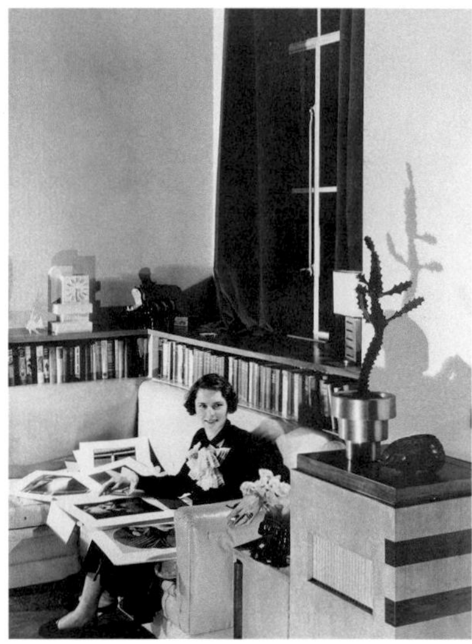

Figure 53. Margaret Bourke-White, *Self-Portrait*, ca. 1933. Gelatin silver print. 17 × 14 in. (43.2 × 35.6 cm). Frances Lehman Loeb Art Center, Vassar College, Purchase, Horace W. Goldsmith Foundation Fund, 2005.20

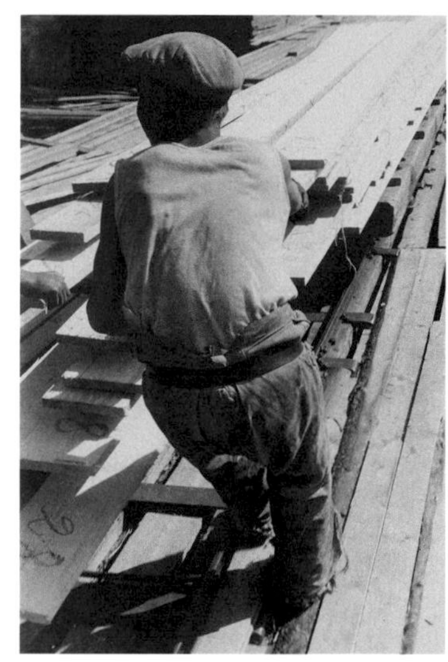

Figure 54. Alexander Rodchenko, *Vakhtan Timber Mill Worker*, 1931. Gelatin silver print. 9½ × 6¼ in. (24.1 × 15.9 cm). Frances Lehman Loeb Art Center, Vassar College, Gift from the Michael and Joyce Axelrod collection (Joyce Jacobson, class of 1961), 1999.6

She was drawn to seeing the country's industrial transformation —with substantial help from American business—and following the progress of its first Five Year Plan of new factories and industries.[314]

In New York in the 1930s, Bourke-White (fig. 53) channeled concerns for social issues of the Great Depression by supporting groups helping the country's youth, farmers, workers, unions, refugees, art students, and artists. She spoke in 1936 at the American Artists' Congress on the role of the artist in the Soviet Union and joined its executive committee.[315] She had acquired "a point of view," as she put it at mid-decade, developed in part from her work in the Soviet Union and in the poverty-stricken Dust Bowl and American South, the last with writer Erskine Caldwell, to whom she was briefly married.[316] Part of the Popular Front, the Congress brought a wide range of artists together to fight for social justice and the rights and economic welfare of artists. That year she also began working for *Life* as a photojournalist, having been invited by Luce.[317] Bourke-White returned to the Soviet Union in 1941, and in 1942 became a war correspondent for the U.S. Air Force and *Life*. She later worked for other military branches as well. In 1947 she made two trips to India, and it was about this time that *Life* sent her on the assignment to Iowa.[318]

In her photograph in *Life*, Bourke-White compressed the space by using the woman's arms to stretch across the tilting planes of the scorecards and the IBM machine, recalling Constructivist compositions (fig. 54). No doubt the IBM 805 brought Bourke-White back to her childhood and the mechanical world of her father, where she had grown up with his constant thinking, experimenting, designing, refining, and patenting with the offset press. As she wrote in her autobiography, "My love for industrial form and pattern was his unconscious gift."[319]

DOROTHY MEIGS EIDLITZ

An amateur photographer and art collector, Dorothy Meigs Eidlitz (1891–1976) took a photograph during the 1940s of a cautious, protective Muslim man escorting a woman, while another man runs in their direction (cat. 36). Hills, sand, and what appears to be the tip of a pyramid in the far left distance suggest a scene near Cairo, Egypt.

Eidlitz made at least thirty-six photographs in the 1940s, according to an exhibition checklist from 1975, and the Loeb has twenty-two of those prints in the collection, given by the artist in 1976.[320] Eidlitz, Vassar class of 1914, was experimenting with various styles in these prints, including the romantic pictorialist style of the turn of the century and a more straightforward photojournalistic approach of the decades afterward. Portraits, still lifes, landscapes, comical views with children and cats, and places ranging from Paris to Nazareth to Stockbridge, Massachusetts,

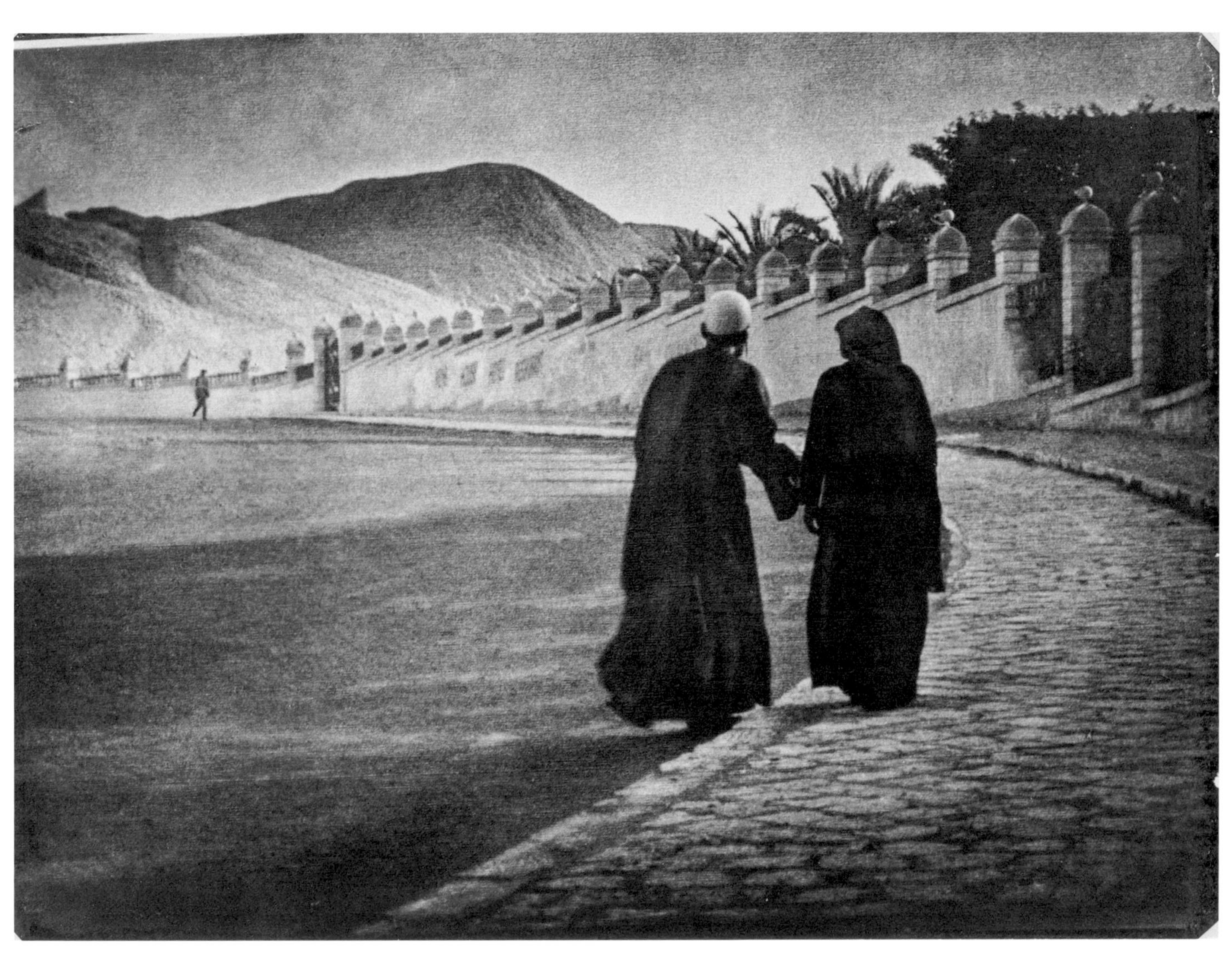

Cat. 36 **Dorothy Meigs Eidlitz**

Escort

Gelatin silver print, not later than 1947

Gift of the artist, class of 1914

are some of the subjects she covered. She apparently enjoyed traveling and exploring, as she was a member of the Society of Women Geographers, formed in 1925 as an organization for female scientists.[321]

Very little has been written on Eidlitz, and this brief sketch is compiled mostly from materials in the object files at the Loeb, her obituary in the *New York Times*, and the descriptions for her papers at the University of Wyoming. During the first half of the 1940s Eidlitz was a war-service photographer with the American Women's Voluntary Services.[322] She also joined the related postwar organization, the Volunteer Service Photographers, whose members taught therapeutic photography skills in veterans hospitals, later opening up its services to civilian hospitals and other medical facilities.[323]

Born in New Haven, Eidlitz earned a B.A. in 1914 from Vassar and did graduate work at the University of Pennsylvania and Columbia University. She became a social worker in Philadelphia and with the War Department of the federal government during World War I.[324] In 1920 the society page of the *New York Tribune* announced her marriage to research chemist Robert Stunzi of Zurich, Switzerland, and their plans to move to Kobe, Japan, for the next three years.[325] Her time there is documented in photographs of people and landscapes found in scrapbooks in her papers at the University of Wyoming. While in Japan, she was president of the Kobe Women's Club, a cultural group for English-speaking women, and a champion of women's rights.[326] In 1927 she remarried, to New York lawyer Ernest F. Eidlitz.[327]

Like Miss Bennett (cat. 12) and other upper-class women of late eighteenth-century England, Eidlitz did not turn professional, and she sometimes contributed photographs to church and charitable publications. One of the earliest recognitions for her photography was her inclusion in *Poet's Corner*, a collection of plates and verse by well-known photographers and poets, published in New York and London by American Studio Books in 1946. During this decade and the next she was living in Riverdale, the Bronx.[328] By the fifties she was collecting art, including photographs by Bill Brandt, Eugene Smith, Lisette Model, and Brassaï purchased from a Greenwich Village photography shop called Limelight. Said the gallery director, she was "a typical Westchester matron. Yet she had to be somewhat unusual. Photographs were a poor investment; it was not as it was in the art world, where if you bought a few paintings and called yourself a collector, you had dealers (and artists) eating out of your hand. Collecting photographs was an act of love."[329] Her photographs may also be found in the National Gallery of Canada and the Brooklyn Museum. In her later years, Eidlitz lived in Winter Park, Florida, and St. Andrews, New Brunswick, Canada, where she established an arts and nature center in 1964.[330]

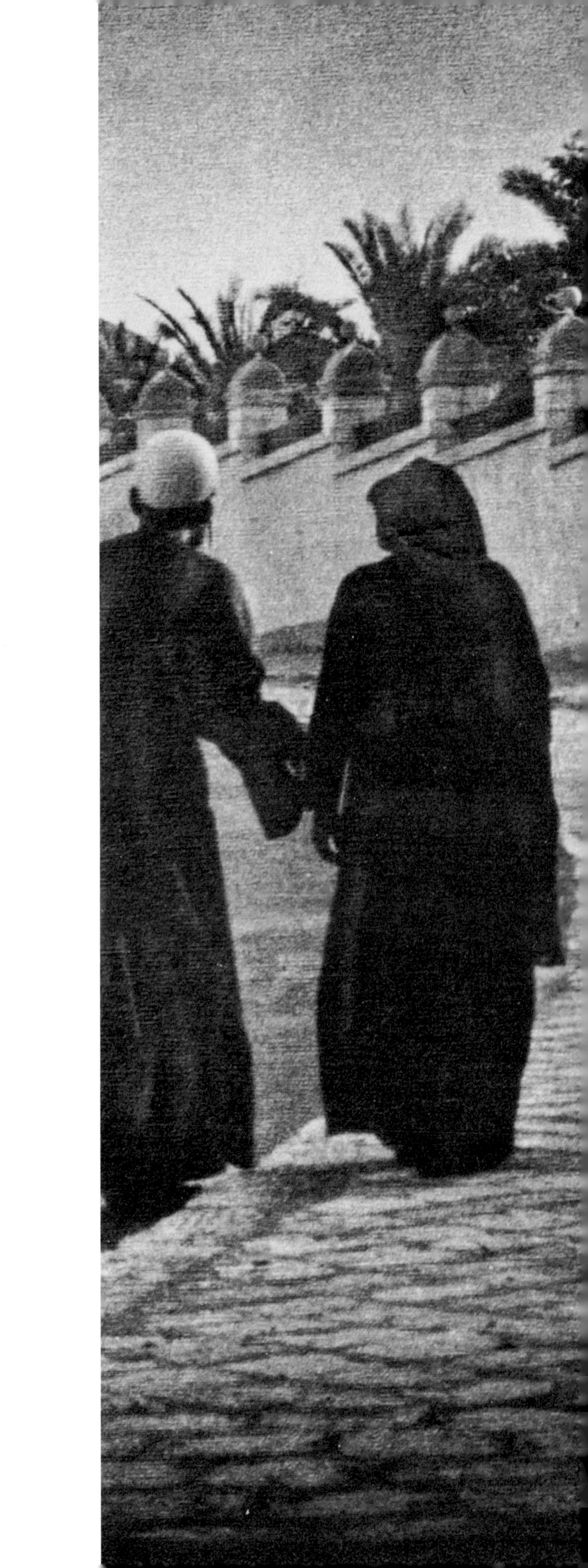

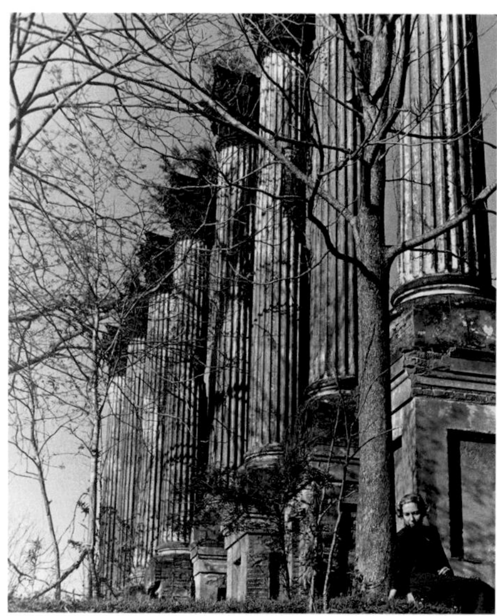

Figure 55. Rosalie McKenna, *Eudora Welty, "Windsor," Mississippi*, 1954. Gelatin silver print. 13⅛ × 10½ in. (33.3 × 26.7 cm). Frances Lehman Loeb Art Center, Vassar College, Gift of the artist, 1987.53.57

ROSALIE THORNE MCKENNA

The photographer Rosalie Thorne McKenna (1918–2003) was raised in coastal Mississippi and Alabama. In 1954 she was sent to Mississippi on assignment for *Mademoiselle*, and as she confided in her autobiography, *A Life in Photography*, "I was in my element: clay and sandy soil, gravel roads, slash and loblolly pines, Spanish moss, white mansions, wooden shacks, black faces and warmth."[331]

McKenna and influential poet John Malcolm Brinnin were working on an illustrated article about the Southern writer Eudora Welty and the kinds of places in and around Jackson that appeared in her stories.[332] Welty showed them typical locations but shied away when McKenna began aiming her camera toward her instead, writing to Mary Lou Aswell,

> *It was fun to have Rollie and John Brinnin—never was quite sure what they came to get, or knew what they aimed to do with it. I was glad to show them (as well as I could, but it wasn't easy) any scenes they could photograph typical of my stories. But I was uneasy when Rollie, without warning, began photographing me—in the grocery etc. I told her I wanted none of that,—but don't know if she understood my complete aversion to publicity-like stuff. (Being her hostess I may have not expressed myself as violently as I feel.)*[333]

McKenna was ultimately successful, however, and made a memorable view of the author sitting below the ruined Greek Revival plantation house "Windsor" (fig. 55). She also made a rich photographic record of vignettes in the countryside and city streets with views of African Americans, explaining later, "If I had an intent, it was to show their dignity and self-respect in the midst of poverty." They were "an integral part of my daily life" growing up, she added. A country store and a church, farm cabins, a bottle tree to warn off bad spirits, "Club Desire," and the "First and Last Colored Café" were some of the environments McKenna photographed.[334]

In one photograph, a circumspect, well-dressed older woman is crossing the street (cat. 37). She seems not to have taken notice of the white photographer and strides in the middle of the crosswalk, looking further off to our right while hugging her purse. Her face and hands are well worn, set off from the smooth heavy coat that drapes and almost encases her. At the time, the South was deeply segregated, with severe racial discrimination, heavy voter suppression, "separate, but equal" Jim Crow laws, and deadly violence against blacks.[335]

In a photograph taken a few years later, in rural Florida, McKenna was no longer capturing the familiar scenes of Welty's stories in conjunction with the author. Rather, she photographed a fraught situation with an unhappy young girl on a cabin porch

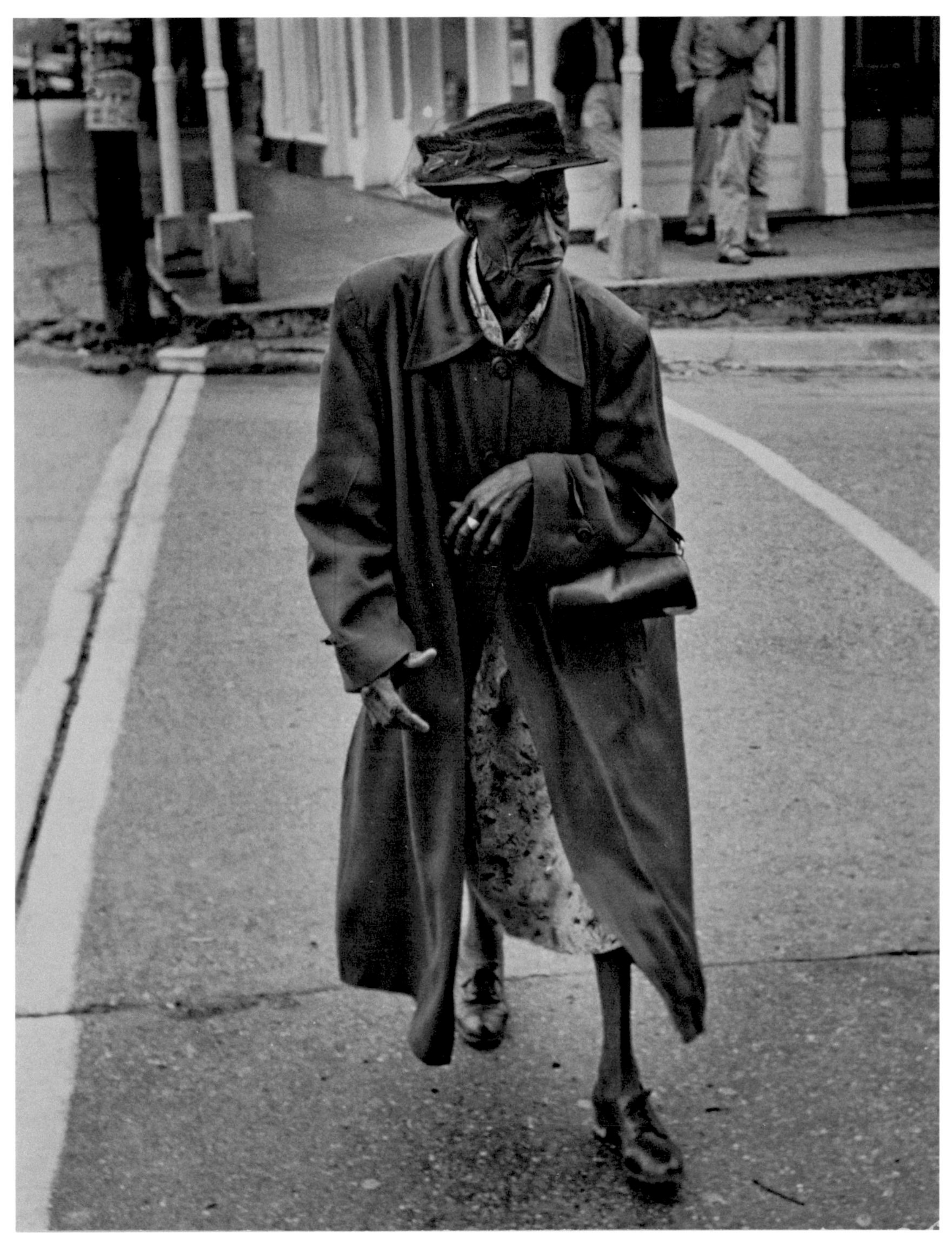

Cat. 37 **Rosalie Thorne McKenna**

Woman Crossing the Street, Mississippi

Gelatin silver print, 1954

Gift of the artist, class of 1940

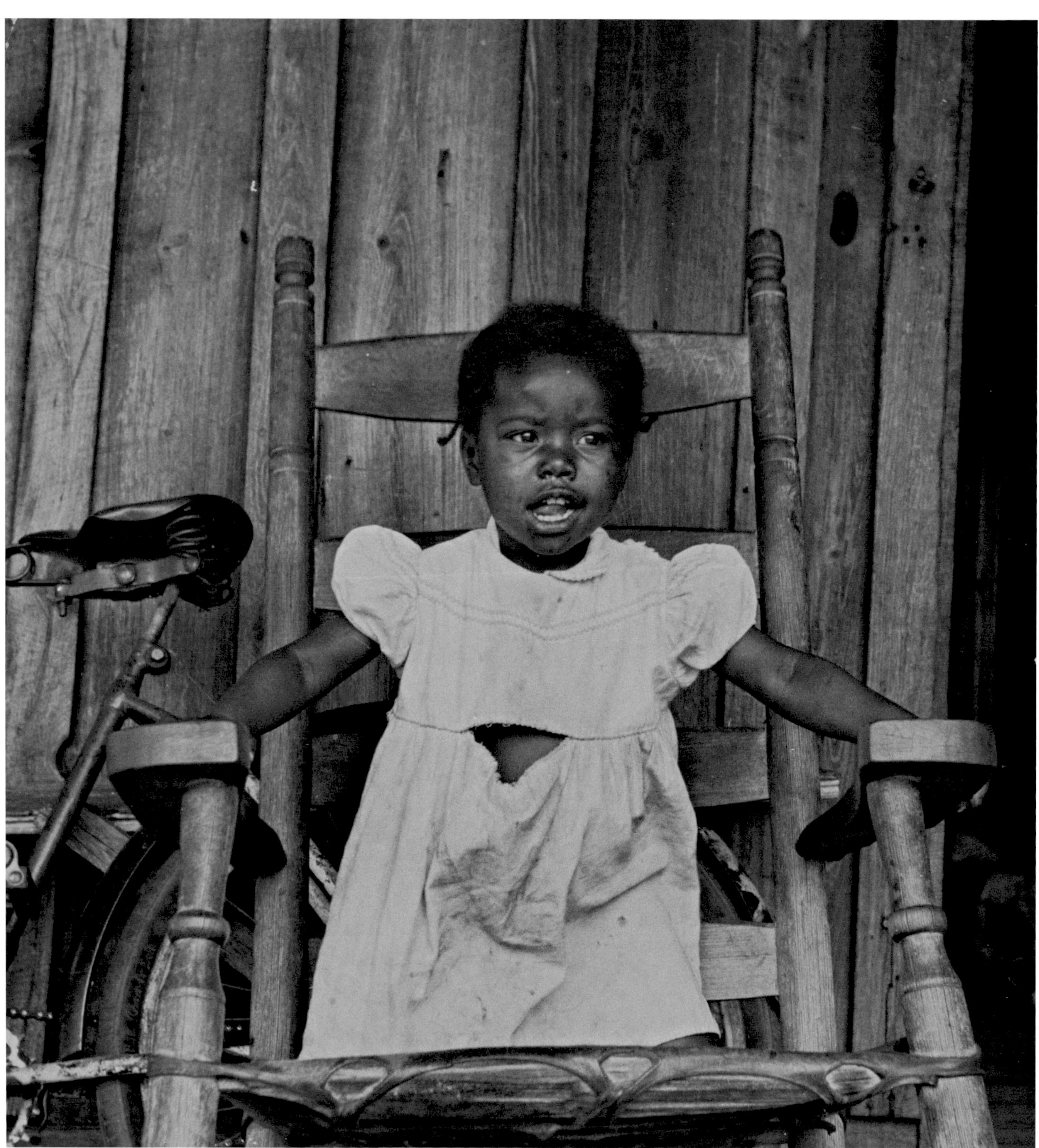

(cat. 38). The toddler looks fiercely in the distance and away from the photographer who, one surmises, may have been too close to her with her camera. With the poverty of Blacks across the South, McKenna's Florida photograph could have just as easily been taken in Mississippi. Though the southern terrain may have been familiar to her, she ventured directly into unpredictable, unstable circumstances.

Born in Houston, McKenna was exposed to an adventurous life early on. In Mississippi, she lived with extended family in a lively home at a Gulf Coast inn, with visitors coming and going constantly. After the economic crash of 1929, the family subsisted and traveled on a borrowed schooner, and then they renovated outbuildings at Fort Gaines on Dauphin Island, Alabama, turn-ing them into another inn.[336] In 1940 she graduated from Vassar, bought property in Millbrook, 15 miles east of Poughkeepsie, joined the Navy, and in 1945 married Yale graduate and fellow lieutenant Henry Dickson McKenna (they divorced in 1949). She began an M.A. in art history at Vassar, traveled to Europe as part of that work, and then graduated in 1949 with a two-volume thesis, "A Study of the Architecture of the Main Building and the Land-scaping of Vassar College, 1860–1870." McKenna bought her first camera in 1948 while on a study trip to Paris.[337] She would become widely known for her portrait photographs of writers and artists, and she would also contribute substantially to both architectural and landscape photography.

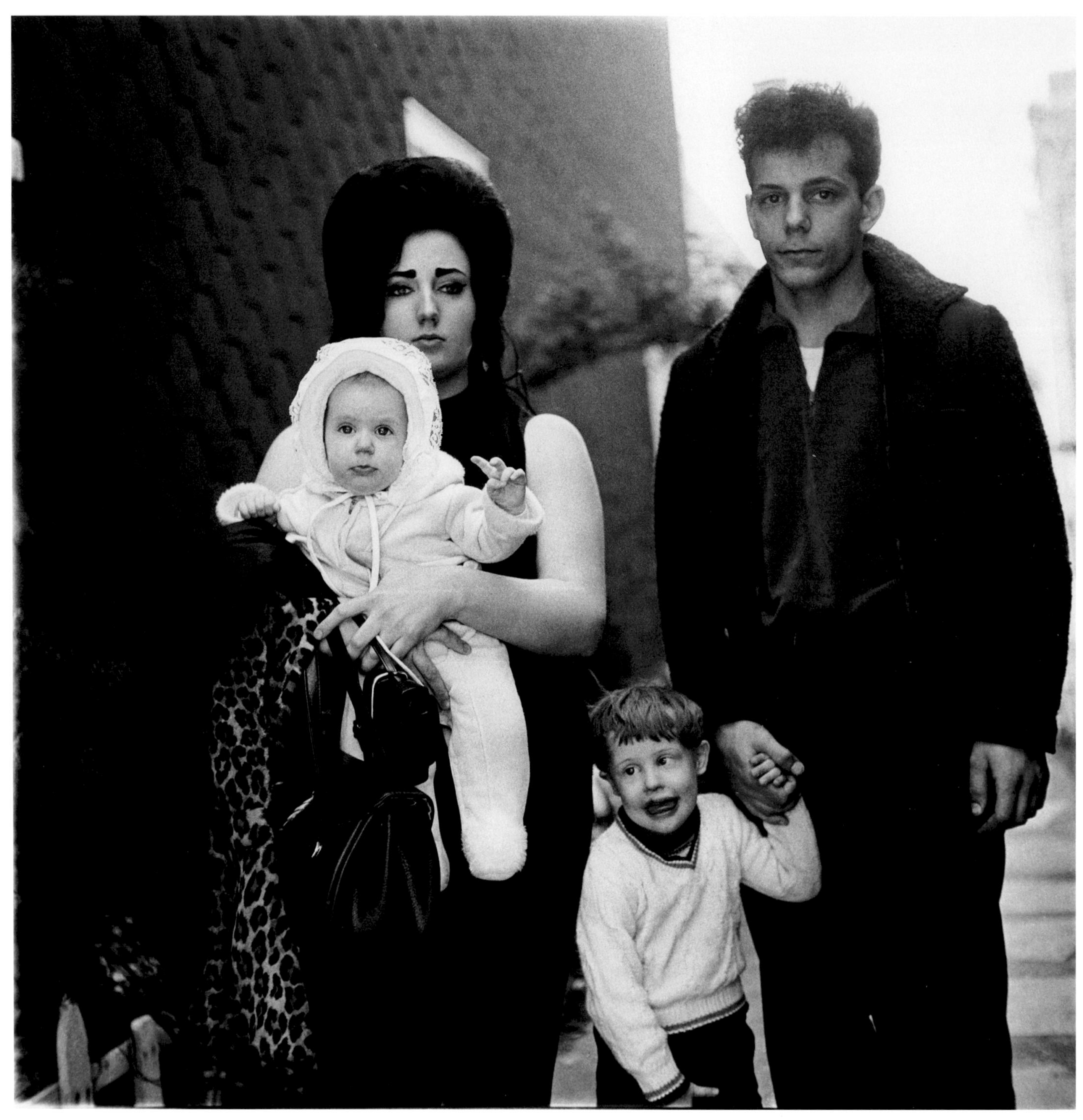

Cat. 39 **Diane Arbus**

A young Brooklyn family going for a Sunday outing, N.Y.C. 1966

Gelatin silver print
Purchase, Louise Woodruff Johnston, class of 1922, Fund

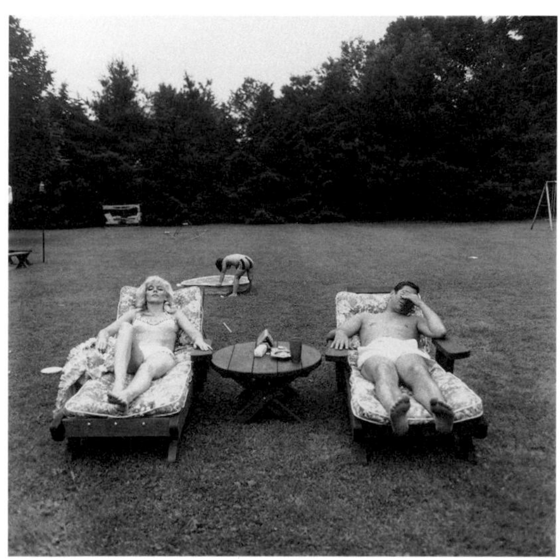

Figure 56. Diane Arbus, *A family on their lawn one Sunday in Westchester, N.Y. 1968*. Gelatin silver print. 19⅞ × 15⅞ in. (50.5 × 40.3 cm). Frances Lehman Loeb Art Center, Vassar College, Purchase, Louise Woodruff Johnston, class of 1922, Fund, 1974.21.5

DIANE ARBUS

In this intimate encounter (cat. 39), a young working-class family in Brooklyn poses for photographer Diane Arbus (1923–1971), while, ironically, exuding the styles of those magnetic Hollywood icons of the fifties and sixties, the actors Elizabeth Taylor and James Dean. The fabricated attributes of Taylor's "Cleopatra" eyes and puffy black hair, and Dean's turned-up collar and white T-shirt—telltale signs of the popular stars—overlap with all of those things that "un-match" in this personal documentary portrait, including a baby wearing a thick winter romper and a young boy with cognitive differences.

Arbus paired this photograph with *A family on their lawn one Sunday in Westchester, N.Y. 1968* (fig. 56) for a 1968 article in the *London Sunday Times Magazine*, with text crafted by editors from her notes. In the other family, the handsome upper-middle-class couple rest like islands in a bulldozed and seeded suburban lawn.[338]

In *A young Brooklyn family going for a Sunday outing, N.Y.C. 1966*, Arbus expertly binds the personal space of portraiture with the public arena of the street venture, presenting the family in a kind of shared, personal experience. Her opinion of the camera is as follows:

The process itself has a kind of exactitude, a kind of scrutiny that we're not normally subject to. I mean that we don't subject each other to. We're nicer to each other than the intervention of the camera is going to make us. It's a little bit cold, a little bit harsh.[339]

Arbus seems to intrude—the couple does not smile—though she had actually gotten to know the family a bit. The text in the *Times* article described Marylin and Richard Dauria: they lived in the Bronx and had met at school. Richard, an immigrant from Italy, worked as a car mechanic. Marylin was twenty-three and looked like Elizabeth Taylor, people said, and so she dyed her hair to look more like the actress. After the picture-taking was over, the family left in the car for a visit to see one of their parents.

In 1966, five years before her suicide, Arbus was a freelance photographer, teaching photography part time at Parsons School of Design. She won a Guggenheim Fellowship that year, her second, for her photography project "American Rites, Manners, and Customs," and undertook major magazine assignments involving portrait photography.[340] Born in New York, she grew up on the Upper East Side and Central Park West in a well-to-do family, with her father, David Nemerov, the fashion director and later president and chair of Russeks, a Fifth Avenue department store. Arbus attended the Ethical Culture School and the Fieldston School, where she majored in art, and in 1941 she married Allan Arbus, the future actor, and together they established a fashion photography firm. In the 1940s, she studied photography with Berenice Abbott and began photographing herself and her family and friends.

The collaboration dissolved in 1956, and she studied that year with photographer Lisette Model, whose advice strengthened Arbus's confidence in her own vision. She then went on to win numerous magazine assignments, her researches in these and in her more personal photographs taking in distinctive personalities.[341]

CONCLUSION

Female artists have achieved much, as witnessed by this survey, but there is also still a lack of equality in their status. When I began this study I was startled by the imbalance in the Loeb collection with the number of works made by women, which are roughly 6 percent of those made by men. A deep sadness accompanied my seeing the far fewer female names before the mid-nineteenth century in the collections database. I was alarmed to discover in the literature the powerful effects of social-conduct books and other didactic writings on women's place in society. Seventeenth-century voices such as Jacques du Bosc praising learned women were later crowded out by reformist voices steering women toward marriage and a separate domestic or private sphere. Discovering this scheme felt like a key opening a long-sealed door hiding how many women had been shepherded onto certain life paths. Finally, I was struck by extraordinary artists like Florine Stettheimer and how their enormous need for private spaces fueled their emotional lives and artistic visions.

The Loeb is committed to acquiring works by women, escalating the steady focus of efforts during the last century. The art museum strives to collect art by women of color. The past two decades have seen works by Elizabeth Catlett, Margaret Burroughs, Kara Walker, Wangechi Mutu, Inez Nathaniel Walker, Sabanita Lopez Ortiz, and others purchased or given to the collection. With our renewed commitment to representing diversity throughout all layers of the museum, the collecting of works by female artists, historical and contemporary, will increase, furnishing the potential for an even richer art collection in the future.

Notes

1. "Modernity and the Spaces of Femininity," in Griselda Pollock, *Vision and Difference: Femininity, Feminism, and the Histories of Art* (London: Routledge, 1988), 50–90.

2. Very few works of art by women before that time are in the collection, which includes almost 22,000 objects.

3. "Account of the Life and Works of Angelica Kauffman," *The Lady's Magazine* 39 (1808): 62.

4. Quoted in Linda Nochlin, "Some Women Realists: Part 2," *Arts Magazine* (May 1974), reprinted in Maura Reilly, ed., *Women Artists: The Linda Nochlin Reader* (New York: Thames and Hudson, 2015), 86.

5. Temma Balducci and Heather Belnap Jensen, eds., *Women, Femininity, and Public Space in European Visual Culture, 1789–1914* (London: Routledge, 2017), see esp. their introduction, 1–16.

6. Mary Busch, "Gallery Celebrates Agnes Rindge Claflin," *Vassar Quarterly* 74, no. 3 (1 March 1978): 37–40.

7. "A Transcript of a Recorded Conversation Between Linda Nochlin and Molly Nesbit in New York City, Jan. 28, 2011," *Vassar 150,* http://150.vassar.edu/histories/art/nochlin.html.

8. Linda Nochlin, "Starting from Scratch: Linda Nochlin Traces the Beginnings of Feminist Art History," *Women's Art Magazine* 61 (November–December 1994): 6–11.

9. The data gives a statistic of 40,080,000 never-married women out of a total of 135,550,000 women; data from http://www.statista.com.

10. Quoted in Margaret L. King, *Women of the Renaissance* (Chicago: The University of Chicago Press, 1991), 185. See also 164, 175.

11. Ibid., 175, 178–79, 207.

12. Michèle Cohen, "'To think, to compare, to combine, to methodise': Girls' Education in Enlightenment Britain," in *Women, Gender, and Enlightenment*, ed. Sarah Knott and Barbara Taylor (New York: Palgrave Macmillan, 2005), 227, 230–31, 237.

13. Linda L. Clark, *Women and Achievement in Nineteenth-Century Europe* (Cambridge: Cambridge University Press, 2008), 168.

14. Tiffany K. Wayne, *Women's Roles in Nineteenth-Century America* (Westport, Conn.: Greenwood Press, 2007), 72–75.

15. Betty Ring, *Girlhood Embroidery, American Samplers, and Pictorial Needlework, 1650–1850,* vol. 1 (New York: Alfred A. Knopf, 1993), xvii.

16. Ibid., xvii, 13–16.

17. Ann Sutherland Harris, "Sofonisba Anguissola," in Harris and Linda Nochlin, *Women Artists: 1550–1950* (Los Angeles: Los Angeles County Museum of Art, 1976), 106–8.

18. Ann Sutherland Harris, "Artemisia Gentileschi," in Harris and Nochlin, *Women Artists*, 118–23.

19. Kim Sloan, *"A Noble Art": Amateur Artists, and Drawing Masters, c. 1600–1800* (London: British Museum Press, 2000), 213–14.

20. Anonymous [Elba Huffman Bouslog], *Letters from Old-Time Vassar* (Poughkeepsie, N.Y.: Vassar College, 1915), 121–24.

21. Ibid., 78.

22. Judy Sund, "Columbus and Columbia, Man of Genius Meets Generic Woman, Chicago, 1893," in *Critical Issues in American Art: A Book*

of Readings, ed. Mary Ann Calo (Boulder, Colo.: WestviewPress, 1998), 223.

23. Schapiro quoted in Moira Roth, "Interview with Miriam Schapiro," in *Miriam Schapiro: The Shrine, The Computer, and The Dollhouse* (San Diego, Calif.: Mandeville Art Gallery, 1975), 9.

24. Ibid.

25. Sloan, *"Noble Art,"* 213; Whitney Chadwick, *Women, Art, and Society*, 5th ed. (London: Thames and Hudson, 2012), 7. See also Linda Nochlin's essay, "Women Artists after the French Revolution," in Harris and Nochlin, *Women Artists*, esp. 50–52.

26. Betsy Fahlman, "The Art Spirit in the Classroom, Educating the Modern Woman Artist," in *American Women Modernists: The Legacy of Robert Henri, 1910–1945*, ed. Marian Wardle (Provo, Utah: Brigham Young University Museum of Art, 2005), 103.

27. Paula J. Birnbaum, *Women Artists in Interwar France: Framing Femininities* (London: Routledge, 2016), 4.

28. Nancy Mowll Mathews, "Training and Professionalism, 19th and 20th Centuries:

North America, 19th century, USA," in *Dictionary of Women Artists*, ed. Delia Gaze, vol. 1 (London: Fitzroy Dearborn Publishers, 1997), 136. National Academy of Design, "Historical Overview," http://www.nationalacademy.org/historical-overview, gives a date of 1857.

29. Karin Althaus and Susanne Böller, "Florine Stettheimer, 1871–1944: A Chronology," in Matthias Mühling et al., *Florine Stettheimer* (Munich: Hirmer Verlag GmbH, 2014), 17.

30. Mathews, "Training," 136.

31. Henry Adams, *Eakins Revealed: The Secret Life of an American Artist* (Oxford: Oxford University Press, 2005), 50–51.

32. Margaret Bourke-White, *Portrait of Myself* (Boston: G. K. Hall and Co., 1985), 14–15.

33. Quoted in Linda Nochlin, *Realism Now* (Poughkeepsie, N.Y.: Vassar College Art Gallery, 1968), 41. My thanks to Andrew Hottle for his assistance in providing much helpful information on the artist and her painting in the exhibition.

34. Linda Nochlin, "Alice Neel," lecture, Victoria Miro Gallery, London, May 2004, printed

in Reilly, *Linda Nochlin Reader* (New York: Thames and Hudson, 2015), 283.

35. Ilya M. Veldman, *Crispijn de Passe and His Progeny (1564–1670): A Century of Print Production*, trans. Michael Hoyle (Rotterdam: Sound and Vision Publishers, 2001), 15. I have used Veldman's spelling of names and life dates for the De Passes. For the catalogue raisonné of their prints, see Daniel Franken, *L'Oeuvre gravé des van de Passe* (Paris: F. Muller et Cie, 1881; repr., Amsterdam: G. W. Hissink and Co., 1975).

36. Arthur M. Hind, *Engraving in England in the Sixteenth and Seventeenth Centuries*, vol. 2 (Cambridge: Cambridge University Press, 1955), 4. See 39–46, 245–302, plates 12–18, 144–88, on the De Passe workshop.

37. Nadine Orenstein, "Who Took the King of Sweden to Bed?," *Print Quarterly* 8, no. 1 (March 1991): 44, 46. See also Veldman, *Crispijn de Passe*, 200, 283–95, 315.

38. See the illustrations in *Hollstein's Dutch and Flemish Etchings, Engravings, and Woodcuts*, ed. K. G. Boon, comps. J. Verbeek and Ilja M. Veldman, vol. 16 (Amsterdam: Van Gendt and Co.), 211–220.

39. Franken, *L'Oeuvre gravé*, no. 1356; Velden, *Crispijn de Passe*, 247–48.

40. Antony Griffiths, *The Print in Stuart Britain, 1603–1689* (London: British Museum Press, 1998), 52, cat. 10; Velden, *Crispijn de Passe*, 248.

41. Veldman, *Crispijn de Passe*, 250, 284.

42. Griffiths, *Print in Stuart Britain*, 52.

43. Hind, *Engraving in England*, 302; Veldman, *Crispijn de Passe*, 284.

44. Roger Lockyer, "Villiers, George, first duke of Buckingham," *Oxford Dictionary of National Biography*, online version, 19 May 2011; Jane Ohlmeyer, "MacDonnell, Katherine, duchess of Buckingham and marchioness of Antrim," *Oxford Dictionary of National Biography*, online version, 3 January 2008. On the developments surrounding the marriage, see Philip Gibbs, *The Romance of George Villiers 1st Duke of Buckingham*, 2nd ed. (London: Methuen and Co., 1908), 86–90. See also the brief biography on Katherine Manners by Colleen E. Kennedy in *A Biographical Encyclopedia of Early Modern Englishwomen: Exemplary Lives and Memorable Acts, 1500–1650*, ed. Carol Levin, Anna Riehl Bertolet, and Jo Eldridge Carney (London: Routledge, 2016).

45. Edgar Williams, *Ostrich* (London: Reaktion Books Ltd, 2013), 74.

46. Alison Weir, *Henry VIII: The King and His Court* (New York: Ballantine Books, 2008), 118. For Villiers purchasing the property, see Roger Lockyer, *Buckingham: The Life and Career of George Villiers, First Duke of Buckingham 1592–1628* (London: Routledge, 2014), n.p.

47. See Mrs. A. T. Thomson, *The Life and Times of George Villiers, Duke of Buckingham*, vol. 1 (Frankfurt: Outlook Verlag GmbH, 2018), 113–14.

48. James Granger, *A Biographical History of England from Egbert the Great to the Revolution*, 5th ed., vol. 3 (London: William Baynes and Son, 1824), 199–200.

49. Horace Walpole, *The Works of Horatio Walpole, Earl of Orford*, vol. 4 (London: G. G. and J. Robinson, 1798), 21.

50. See the impression, National Portrait Gallery, London, NPG D16671 (from William Fleming Collection), with the handwritten inscription on the border of the mount below, "This sho d have a border round upon a separate plate." I am thankful to master printer Felix Harlan for looking at the image of the print from the Loeb collection and surmising that the paper may have suffered from too much printing pressure, "possibly due to the blankets having absorbed moisture," or that the paper suffered from shifting while being run though the press. Felix Harlan, email message to author, 3 April 2020.

51. Velden, *Crispijn de Passe*, 315.

52. Catherine Lafarge, "The Seventeenth and Eighteenth Centuries from Madeleine de Scudéry to Marie-Madeleine Joliveau de Segrais: Introduction," in *French Women Poets of Nine Centuries*, comp. Norman R. Shapiro (Baltimore: Johns Hopkins University Press, 2008), 262. On Scudéry, see 274–85; on Chéron, see 357–65.

53. A. J. Dézallier d'Argenville, "Elizabeth-Sophie Chéron," in *Abrégé de la vie des plus fameux peintres*, vol. 4 (Paris: De Bure l'Aîné, 1762), trans. in Julia K. Dabbs, *Life Stories of Women Artists, 1550–1800* (Farnham, England: Ashgate, 2009), 354.

54. Léon Gréder, *Elisabeth-Sophie Chéron* (Paris: Henri Jouve, 1909), 21–22, 56. Clara Erskine Clement, *Women in the Fine Arts* (Boston: Houghton, Mifflin and Company, 1905), 83.

55. Charles Le Blanc, *Catalogue de l'œuvre de Jean Georges Wille, Graveur* (Leipzig: Rudolphe Weigel, 1847), x, 113–14, cat. 144.

56. For court fashions of that decade, see, for instance, Gerard van Honthorst, *Portrait of Friedrich Wilhelm, Elector of Brandenburg, and His Wife, Louise Henriette, Countess of Orange-Nassau*, 1647, Rijksmuseum; and Circle of Sir Anthony van Dyck, *Portrait of Lady Mary Villiers as Saint Agnes*, 1640, private collection. Mary Villiers was the daughter of Katherine Manners (see cat. 1) and Georges Villiers. I am grateful for these images being made available on the website http://fashionhistory.fitnyc.edu.

57. Le Blanc (Wille) 144, but see also his cat. 118, note, p. 92, where the author believes that all plates published by Odieuvre have an early state before letters were engraved on the plate.

58. Véronique Meyer, "Elisabeth-Sophie Chéron," http://www.siefar.org/dictionnaire.

59. Georges Duplessis, *Mémoires et Journal de J.-G. Wille, Graveur du Roi*, vol. 1 (Paris: Jules Renouard, 1857), 68–69.

60. Gréder, *Elisabeth-Sophie Chéron*, 20.

61. Germaine Greer, *The Obstacle Race* (New York: Farrar Straus Giroux, 1979), 259.

62. Ferme L'huis, *Éloge Funebre de Madame Le Hay* (Paris: François Fournier, 1712), 27, 35–36.

63. Margaret Moore Booker, *Nantucket Spirit: The Art and Life of Elizabeth Rebecca Coffin* (Nantucket, Mass.: Mill Hill Press, 2001).

64. Nantucket Historical Association, 1998.0065.001.

65. Booker, *Nantucket Spirit*, 16–17.

66. Mary A. Mineah, in "Contemporary Notes, The Classes: 1870," *Vassar Quarterly* 15, no. 4 (1 November 1930): 264.

67. Quoted in "Alumnae Lunch," *Vassar Miscellany* 24, no. 9 (1 June 1895): 444–45.

68. Elizabeth R. Coffin, [Artist Statement], in *Exhibition of Work by Elizabeth R. Coffin*, Vassar College, May 15–June 8, 1920, exhibition brochure, object file, X.16, Frances Lehman Loeb Art Center.

69. "Personals, '70," *Vassar Miscellany* 21, no. 8 (1 May 1892): 438.

70. See Coffin, [Artist Statement]. For property information, see Edouard A. Stackpole

Collection, 1750–1990, Nantucket Historical Association, folder 807.

71. Coffin, [Artist Statement].

72. *Brooklyn Daily Eagle*, 19 November 1893, 13, quoted in Booker, *Nantucket Spirit*, 81.

73. Arthur Hoeber, "The New York Water-Color Club," *International Studio* 33, no. 131 (January 1908): cv–cvii (ill. cvi).

74. On the construction of the watercolor, see Hilda Belcher, New York, letter to Martha Wood Belcher, postmarked November 1907; letter in the possession of the Belcher family. I wish to thank Stephen Belcher for his generosity and foresightedness in sharing this and other letters with the Loeb staff. For Belcher and O'Keeffe rooming together, see Janie Cohen, "Hilda Belcher, A Realist Rediscovered," *American Art Review* 6, no. 4 (August–September 1994): 97n5, where the information is from Stephen Paterson Belcher III, in conversation with Cohen.

75. On Belcher, see esp. Cohen, "Hilda Belcher," 90–97; Carol Lowrey, *A Legacy of Art* (New York: National Arts Club, 2007), 48–49; and Wardle, *American Women Modernists*. See also *Woman's Who's Who of America, 1914–1915*, ed. John William Leonard (New York: American Commonwealth Company, 1914), 91.

76. See Chase's *The Song*, 1907, Crystal Bridges Museum of American Art, Promised Gift.

77. The Loeb Art Center has dozens of studies and artifacts related to the decoration of the Alumnae House living room and the painting *The Donors* that were gifts in 1982 and 1983 from the Violet Oakley Memorial Foundation.

78. See Patricia Phagan, *A Taste for the Modern: Gifts from Blanchette Hooker Rockefeller, Edna Bryner Schwab, and Virginia Herrick Deknatel* (Poughkeepsie, N.Y.: Frances Lehman Loeb Art Center, Vassar College, 2011).

79. See Sally Mills, "What the Triptych Means: The Vassar Art of Violet Oakley," *Vassar Quarterly* 80, no. 3 (1 March 1984): 23–25;

and the series of articles on the dedication of the house, in *Vassar Quarterly* 9, no. 4 (1 August 1924): 259–63. See also Bailey Van Hook, *Violet Oakley: An Artist's Life* (Newark: University of Delaware Press, 2016), 247–48, 267–70, 283–84; and Sally Mills, *Violet Oakley: The Decoration of the Alumnae House Living Room* (Poughkeepsie, N.Y.: Vassar College Art Gallery, Vassar College, 1984).

80. For a preliminary study showing the triptych as it would look when completed, see Violet Oakley, *Study for End of Room, Vassar College Alumnae House with Triptych*, watercolor on paper, Frances Lehman Loeb Art Center, Vassar College, Gift of Celia Faulkner Clevenger, class of 1958, 1987.24.1.

81. Mary Baker Eddy, *Science and Health with Key to the Scriptures* (Boston: The Christian Science Board of Directors, 1875), chap. 16, lines 561:11 and 545:6–7.

82. Van Hook, *Violet Oakley*, 248, 267.

83. Ibid., 268–69.

84. Ibid., 10, 84, 91–122, 143–44, 196–97, 273–75, 295–97, 325, 355–57.

85. Bailey Van Hook, "The Early Career of Violet Oakley, Illustrator," *Woman's Art Journal* 30, no. 1 (Spring–Summer 2009): 29–38, 37n16.

86. Van Hook, *Violet Oakley*, 128–39, 383–86.

87. See the rich array of portrait images on the website of the Woodmere Art Museum, "The Violet Oakley Experience," http://www .woodmereartmuseum.org/the-violet-oakley -experience.

88. The print is undated. Max Lehrs, who wrote the first catalogue raisonné of Kollwitz's prints, gives "1893?" for the work. See Lehrs, "Käthe Kollwitz," *Die Graphischen Künste* 26 (1903): 61, no. 11.

89. See Elizabeth Prelinger, *Käthe Kollwitz* (Washington, D.C.: National Gallery of Art, 1992), 16, cat. 3; and Rosemary Betterton, "Mother Figures, The Maternal Nude in the Work of Käthe Kollwitz and Paula

Modersohn-Becker," *An Intimate Distance: Women, Artists and the Body* (London and New York: Routledge, 1996), 35; http:// kollwitz.de/en/Kollwitz-timeline.

90. See J. Diane Radycki, "The Life of Lady Art Students: Changing Art Education at the Turn of the Century," *Art Journal* 42, no. 1 (Spring 1982): 11.

91. Käthe Kollwitz, letter to Paul Hey, 26 February 1891, from Käthe Kollwitz, *Briefe der Freundschaft und Begegnungen*, ed. Hans Kollwitz (Munich: List, 1966), quoted in http://kollwitz.de/en/Kollwitz-timeline; and Kollwitz, letter to Max Lehrs, 1901, in Kollwitz, *Briefe*, 23, quoted in Elizabeth Prelinger, "Kollwitz Reconsidered," in Prelinger, *Käthe Kollwitz*, 21.

92. Käthe Kollwitz, "In Retrospect, 1941," in *The Diary and Letters of Kaethe Kollwitz*, ed. Hans Kollwitz, trans. Richard and Clara Winston (Evanston, Ill.: Northwestern University Press, 1955), 42.

93. See the painting by Morisot, *Paule Gobillard Painting*, 1886, Musée Marmottan, Paris; and Morisot, *Paule Gobillard Drawing*, 1886, pastel on canvas, private collection (http:// www.artsviewer.com/morisot-182.html).

94. On Morisot, see esp. Anne Higonnet, *Berthe Morisot* (Berkeley: University of California Press, 1995); Higonnet, *Berthe Morisot's Images of Women* (Cambridge, Mass.: Harvard University Press, 1994); Kathleen Adler and Tamar Garb, *Berthe Morisot* (Ithaca, N.Y.: Cornell University Press, 1987); Sylvie Patry et al., *Berthe Morisot: Woman Impressionist* (New York: Rizzoli Electa, 2018); and Linda Nochlin, "Morisot's *Wet Nurse*: The Construction of Work and Leisure in Impressionist Painting," in Reilly, *Linda Nochlin Reader*, 161–73, originally published in Nochlin, *Women, Art, and Power, and Other Essays* (New York: Harper and Row, 1988).

95. Higonnet, *Berthe Morisot*, 18–19.

96. Leila W. Kinney, "Morisot," *Art Journal* 47, no. 3 (Fall 1988): 236; Higonnet, *Berthe Morisot*, 13.

97. Higonnet, *Berthe Morisot*, 17, 18, 41. On Guichard, see René Chazelle, *Joseph Guichard, Peintre lyonnais (1806–1880), Disciple d'Ingres et de Delacroix* (Lyon: Presses universitaires de Lyon, 1992).

98. Higonnet, *Berthe Morisot*, 5, 9, 10, quote on p. 19.

99. Quoted in ibid., 196. On Morisot and Paule Gobillard, see Bill Scott, "A Painter's Painter," in Patry et al., *Berthe Morisot: Woman Impressionist*, 176–78, 182.

100. H. von Wedderkop perceived a possible Egyptian spirit in her work; Von Wedderkop, *Marie Laurencin* (Leipzig: Verlag von Klinkhardt and Biermann, 1921), 9. For a general overview on the Egyptian Revival, see James Stevens Curl, *The Egyptian Revival: Ancient Egypt as the Inspiration for Design Motifs in the West* (London: Routledge, 2013). For a color image of the design of the Chambre de Madame at the Exposition Internationale, see *Exposition des Arts décoratifs, Paris, 1925, Intérieurs en couleurs* (Paris: édition Albert Lévy, 1926.)

101. Louis Vauxelles, from his *L'Histoire générale de l'art français*, vol. 2 (1922), quoted in Christopher Green, *Art in France: 1900–1940* (New Haven: Yale University Press, 2000), 67. Gill Perry, *Women Artists and the Parisian Avant-garde: Modernism and "Feminine" Art, 1900 to the Late 1920s* (Manchester: Manchester University Press, 1995), 17, 110.

102. Elizabeth Louise Kahn, *Marie Laurencin* (Aldershot, England: Ashgate, 2003), 162.

103. Recorded by René Gimpel in a diary entry dated 20 December 1934, from Gimpel, *Diary of an Art Dealer*, trans. John Rosenberg (New York: Universe Books, 1987), 420; quoted in Bridget Elliott, "Arabesque: Marie Laurencin, Decadence and Decorative Excess," in *Modern Sexualities*, ed. Hugh Stevens and Caroline Howlett (Manchester: Manchester University Press, 2000), 96.

104. Birnbaum, *Women Artists*, 100.

105. Daniel Marchesseau, *Marie Laurencin: 1883–1956; Catalogue Raisonné de l'Oeuvre Peint* (Tokyo: Musée Marie Laurencin, 1986), 535; and Douglas Hyland and Heather McPherson, *Marie Laurencin: Artist and Muse* (Seattle: University of Washington Press, 1989), 82.

106. Birnbaum, *Women Artists*, 4, 117 (where the author discusses Laurencin's strong feminine themes as an ambitious response, or masquerade, to her marginalization).

107. Birnbaum, *Women Artists*, 103.

108. Melanie Herzog, "Art and Identity: Elizabeth Catlett," *School Arts* 92, no. 4 (December 1992): 23–26.

109. See Lisa E. Farrington, *Creating Their Own Image: The History of African-American Women Artists* (New York: Oxford University Press, 2005), 120–22.

110. Herzog, "Art and Identity"; Mey-Yen Moriuchi, "Transnationalism in the Art of Elizabeth Catlett," in *Elizabeth Catlett: Art for Social Justice*, ed. Klare Scarborough (Philadelphia: La Salle University Art Museum, 2015), 16.

111. Herzog, "Art and Identity"; Rebecca VanDiver, "Art Matters: Howard University's Department of Art from 1921 to 1971," *Callaloo* 39, no. 5 (2016): 1199–1218.

112. Herzog, "Art and Identity."

113. See James Allen et al., *Without Sanctuary: Lynching Photography in the United States* (Santa Fe: Twin Palms Publishers, 2000); Marlene Park, "Lynching and Antilynching: Art and Politics in the 1930s," *Prospects* 18 (1993): 311–65; and Patricia Phagan, "Critical Views of the South by Northern Artists," in *The American Scene and the South: Paintings and Works on Paper, 1930–1946*, ed. Phagan (Athens: Georgia Museum of Art, University of Georgia, 1996), 227–41.

114. Robert Berlind, "Elizabeth Catlett," *Art Journal* 53, no. 1 (Spring 1994): 28–30.

115. Farrington, *Creating Their Own Image*, 120; and Mary Ann Cain, *South Side Venus: The Legacy of Margaret Burroughs* (Evanston, Ill.: Northwestern University Press, 2018), 48–49. MH [Melanie Herzog], "Margaret Taylor Goss Burroughs," in *Paths to the Press: Printmaking and American Women Artists, 1910–1960*, ed. Elizabeth G. Seaton (Seattle: University of Washington Press, 2006), 105.

116. Leslie King-Hammond, *Black Printmakers and the WPA* (New York: Lehman College Art Gallery, 1989).

117. Melanie Anne Herzog, *Elizabeth Catlett: In the Image of the People* (Chicago: Art Institute of Chicago, 2005), 6.

118. On Maselli, see Sabina de Gregori, *Titina Maselli* (Venice: Fondazione Querini Stampalia, 2016). Earlier publications include *Titina Maselli* (Lisbon: Fundação Calouste Gulbenkian, Centro de Arte Moderna, 1988); and *Titina Maselli, opere recenti* (Rome: Galleria Giulia, 1983).

119. See, for instance, the photograph of Maselli by Rosalie McKenna, in Rosalie Thorne McKenna, *Rollie McKenna: A Life in Photography* (New York: Alfred A. Knopf, 1991), 210.

120. Anita Moreno, "Titina Maselli intervista ne Il Complesso di Michelangelo di Simona Weller," 3, http://www.academia.edu/35211146/Titina_Maselli_intervista_ne_Il_Complesso_di_Michelangelo_di_Simona_Weller. I am thankful to my 2020 Pindyck Fellow Gillian Redstone for her translations of several passages.

121. Daniela Tanzj and Andrea Bentivegna, "Titina Maselli and Her 'Urban' Art between Rome and New York" (17 March 2015), trans. Christine Djerrahian, *La Voce di New York*, http://www.lavocedinewyork.com/en/2015/03/17/titina-maselli-and-her-urban-art-between-rome-and-new-york/.

122. Howard Devree, "Across Centuries," *New York Times*, 10 May 1953, X 13.

123. Maselli is quoted in Moreno, "Titina Maselli," on the debate in Italian art in 1949–50 between realism and abstraction.

124. "R. Kirk Askew Jr. of Durlacher, 70," *New York Times*, 1 April 1974, 34; and Sybil Kantor, *Alfred H. Barr, Jr. and the Intellectual Origins of the Museum of Modern Art* (Cambridge, Mass.: MIT Press, 2003), 227.

125. George Dix Papers, Durlacher Bros. Files, Yale University, New Haven, Connecticut.

126. Sylvia May Stern, "Maselli Art Exhibit Shows Urban Life," *Vassar Miscellany News* 39, no. 18 (9 March 1955): 2.

127. Quoted in Nochlin, *Realism Now*, 41.

128. Nigel Whiteley, *Art and Pluralism: Lawrence Alloway's Cultural Criticism* (Liverpool: Liverpool University Press, 2012).

129. Robert Rauschenberg Oral History Project, "The Reminiscences of Sylvia Palacios Whitman," Columbia Center for Oral History Research, Columbia University, 2015, http://www.rauschenbergfoundation.org/sites/default/files/WHITMAN_Sylvia_FINAL.pdf. My many thanks go to Andrew Hottle for informing me about this source.

130. Marcela Guerrero, "Marilú Marini," Hammer Museum, http://www.hammer.ucla.edu/radical-women/artists/marilu-marini. My thanks again to Andrew Hottle for this information.

131. Andrew Hottle, email to author, 21 May 2020.

132. Quoted in Barbara J. Bloemink, "Visualizing Sight, Florine Stettheimer, and Temporal Modernism," in Elisabeth Sussman with Bloemink, *Florine Stettheimer: Manhattan Fantastica* (New York: Whitney Museum of American Art, 1995), 81, from Florine Stettheimer, *Crystal Flowers* (New York: private edition, 1949), 71.

133. Sloan, "Noble Art," 78.

134. Ibid., 148. See, for instance, Sloan's discussion on Lady Elizabeth Harcourt, p. 157, no. 109.

135. See Stephen Bending, *Green Retreats: Women, Gardens, and Eighteenth-Century Culture* (Cambridge: Cambridge University Press, 2013); Briony McDonagh, *Elite Women and the Agricultural Landscape, 1700–1830* (London: Routledge, 2018).

136. Lucien Monod, *Le prix des estampes anciennes et modernes*, vol. 1 (Paris: Éditions Albert Morancé, 1920), 57, where the print is listed as *While, Celia, from the hand . . .* and dated 1785, with the artist's last name as Bennet. Monod gave sale prices: 815 fr. in 1911 for a color impression, and 105 fr. in May 1913 for a bistre impression. In another example, it is given as *"While Celia from thy hand"* in the Edwin Truman sale at Sotheby, Wilkinson, & Hodge in London on 20 March 1906, lot 224, and was paired with *"Go, Happy Flowers"* and an amount noted in handwriting as 10 pounds, in *Catalogue of the Valuable Collection of Engravings of the Late Edwin Truman, Esq. M.R.C.S.*, Sotheby, Wilkinson, & Hodge, London, 1906, p. 16. *Two Girls with Doves* by Bennett after C. White was a color print that sold at Christie, Manson and Woods on 7 April 1906, for 3 pounds, see *Auction Sale Prices* 8, no. 51 (30 June 1906): 220. See also "Our Plates," *The Connoisseur* 22 (September–December 1908): 60, ill. [p. 22] (color), where it is entitled *"While Celia from Thy Hand." The Dove* may be yet another title for this work; see Julia Frankau, *Eighteenth Century Colour Prints* (London: Macmillan and Co., Limited, 1906), 245.

137. Charles White, *Untitled*, 1785, stipple and etching on silk, 5⅞ × 5⅛ in. (15 × 13 cm), Cooper Hewitt, Smithsonian Design Museum, Bequest of Elinor Merrell, 1995-50-7.

138. John Watkins, *Memoirs of Her Most Excellent Majesty Sophia-Charlotte, Queen of Great Britain* (London: Henry Colburn, 1819), 180, 320. Henry B. Wheatley, *London, Past and Present*, vol. 3 (London: John Murray, 1891), 299. With architect John Nash, George IV would later expand The Queen's House, converting it into Buckingham Palace.

139. David Alexander, "The Evolution of the Print Market and Its Impact on the Art Market, 1780–1820," in *London and the Emergence of a European Art Market, 1780–1820*, ed. Susanna Avery-Quash and Christian Huemer (Los Angeles: Getty Research Institute, 2019), 121–22. David Alexander, "Printmakers," in *Concise Dictionary of Women Artists*, ed. Delia Gaze (New York: Routledge, Taylor and Francis Group, 2001), 46.

140. On stipple, see Antony Griffiths, *Prints and Printmaking* (Berkeley: University of California Press, 1996), 81–83.

141. See Sloan, *"Noble Art,"* esp. 8; and David Alexander, *Caroline Watson and Female Printmaking in Late Georgian England* (Cambridge: Fitzwilliam Museum, 2014), 16, 21.

142. For a brief biography and review of his printing career, see Frankau, *Eighteenth Century Colour Prints*, 109–10, available for viewing on http://www.forgottenbooks.com, though illustrations by White were unavailable. I found the British Museum's website to be the most helpful in finding works printed by White.

143. See, for instance, the portrait by Richard Cosway in the Castle Howard Collection, reproduced in Amanda Foreman, *Georgiana, Duchess of Devonshire* (New York: Random House, 1998), following p. 236.

144. See, for example, works by Thomas Rowlandson, including the watercolor *Vauxhall Gardens* and the etching *The Syrens*, in Patricia Phagan, *Thomas Rowlandson: Pleasures and Pursuits in Georgian England* (Poughkeepsie, N.Y.: Frances Lehman Loeb Art Center, Vassar College, 2011), nos. 1, 8, pp. 58–59, 70.

145. W. Winters, *Our Parish Registers* (Waltham Abbey, Essex: W. Winters, 1885), 58–59, 234–35.

146. Ethel Stanwood Bolton and Eva Johnston Coe, *American Samplers* (Boston: The Massachusetts Society of the Colonial Dames of America, 1921), 1–2, 10; Ring, *Girlhood Embroidery*, xvii; and Joanne Lukacher, *Thanks Be*

To My Friends (Poughkeepsie, N.Y.: Frances Lehman Loeb Art Center, 2004), 5. See also the very helpful "Embroidery, a history of needlework samplers," http://vam.ac .uk/articles/embroidery-a-history-of -needlework-samplers.

147. Lukacher, *Thanks Be To My Friends*, 3.

148. "Embroidery, a history of needlework samplers."

149. It was catalogued as such by textile historian Marianne Huebner; Lukacher, *Thanks Be To My Friends*, 7.

150. Bolton and Coe, *American Samplers*, 3–5, 11–12, 14; see Ring, *Girlhood Embroidery*, 1:36–44.

151. See the "Fashion History Timeline" on the website of Fashion Institute of Technology, State University of New York at http:// fashionhistory.fitnyc.edu.

152. See photography curator Joel Smith's comments on this photograph, in the review by Bonnie Langston, "Through the Eyes of Women," *Daily Freeman* (17 February 2002), http://www.dailyfreeman.com/news/through -the-eyes-of-women/article_0f68a296 -5bca-52b9-b434-10fd10945a5d.html.

153. *Naturalist Photography, 1880 to 1920* (Winchester, Mass.: Lee Gallery, 1998), 1857.

154. Henry McBride, *Florine Stettheimer* (New York: Museum of Modern Art, 1946), 40.

155. On this, see Linda Nochlin, "Florine Stettheimer: Rococo Subversive," *Art in America* (September 1980), reprinted in Reilly, *Linda Nochlin Reader*, 140.

156. Advertisement, *The Athenaeum*, 24 July 1886, 98. For information on Stettheimer's early years in Germany, see Althaus and Böller, "Florine Stettheimer, 1871–1944," 14.

157. Althaus and Böller, "Florine Stettheimer, 1871–1944," 14–23. For the name of the building at 80 West 40th Street (Beaux Arts Studios), see Norval White, Elliot Willensky, and Fran Leadon, *AIA Guide to New York City* (Oxford: Oxford University Press, 2010).

158. Quoted in Georgiana Uhlyarik, "4 St.s Seen by Florine: A Case Study," in Stephen Brown and Uhlyarik, *Florine Stettheimer: Painting Poetry* (New York: The Jewish Museum, 2017), 47.

159. Quoted in Nochlin, "Florine Stettheimer," 138; the poem is from Florine Stettheimer, *Crystal Flowers* (New York: Private Edition, 1949), 78.

160. Nochlin, "Florine Stettheimer," 152n40.

161. Amy Hartman, "Rosella Hartman: Biography," http://www.askart.com/artist/Rosella _Fiene_Hartman/100946/Rosella_Fiene _Hartman.aspx.

162. *World Biography*, vol. 1 (New York: Institute for Research in Biography, 1948), 1772.

163. For information on her Guggenheim awards, see http://www.gf.org/fellows/all -fellows/rosella-hartman/. See *First Biennial Exhibition of Contemporary American Sculpture, Watercolors, and Prints* (New York: Whitney Museum of American Art, 1933), 6, where a drawing titled *Bathers* is no. 188. I have been unable to see correspondence or other information on the drawing *Bathers* in the exhibition files of the Whitney Museum of American Art. While I surmise it is the same drawing as the Vassar work, I cannot know for certain at this writing. Hartman made several lithographs printed by Grant Arnold in Woodstock at the Woodstock Artist Association; for this, see Patricia Phagan, *Made in Woodstock: Printmaking from 1903 to 1945* (Poughkeepsie, N.Y.: Frances Lehman Loeb Art Center, Vassar College, 2002), esp. 45.

164. Stuart Preston, "Woodstock Summer," *New York Times*, 4 September 1949, 8X.

165. Doris Lee and Faith Baldwin, "Why Art and Writing Are Ideal Professions for Women: One of the World's Most Famous Women Painters . . . ," *Chatelaine* 40, no. 1 (January 1967): 8.

166. Helen Knox Spain, "Two Renowned Artists to Pick Show's Best," *The Atlanta Journal and The Atlanta Constitution*, 24 August 1952, 12E.

167. Mary Jane Appel, "Doris and Russell Lee: A Marriage of Art," *Journal of the Illinois State Historical Society* 111, no. 4 (Winter 2018): 82–121. "Doris Lee," in Karal Ann Marling and Helen A. Harrison, *7 American Women: The Depression Decade* (Poughkeepsie, N.Y.: Vassar College Art Gallery, 1976), 31. PP [Patricia Phagan], "Doris Emrick Lee," in Seaton, *Paths to the Press*, 180.

168. Elizabeth G. Seaton, Jane Myers, and Gail Windisch, *Art for Every Home: Associated American Artists, 1934–2000* (Manhattan, Kans.: Marianna Kistler Beach Museum of Art, Kansas State University, 2015), 26, 60, 132, 140, 142, 144–45, 180, 198–199, 229, 255, 268, 272, and numerous other references within the text.

169. Karen Tsujimoto, "Painting as a Visual Diary, The Art of Joan Brown," in Tsujimoto and Jacquelynn Baas, *The Art of Joan Brown* (Berkeley, Calif.: Berkeley Art Museum, 1998), 174–75; Baas, "To Know This Place for the First Time, Interpreting Joan Brown," in ibid., 189.

170. Schapiro quoted in Roth, "Interview with Miriam Schapiro," 14.

171. See the discussion on the term *private plate* in David Alexander, *Caroline Watson and Female Printmaking in Late Georgian England* (Cambridge: Fitzwilliam Museum, 2014), 15.

172. Nicholas Russell, "Nicholas Toke and Godinton Park," *History Today* 42 (September 1992): 62.

173. Francesca Consagra, "The 'Ever Growing ELM' . . . ," in *Landscapes of Retrospection: The Magoon Collection of British Drawings and Prints, 1739–1860* (Poughkeepsie, N.Y.: Frances Lehman Loeb Art Center, Vassar College, 1999), 87.

174. See Lisa Heer, "Amateur Artists: 18th and 19th Centuries," in *Dictionary of Women Artists*, ed. Delia Gaze, vol. 1 (London: Fitzroy Dearborn Publishers, 1997), 70–79.

175. Robert Furley, *A History of the Weald of Kent*, vol. 2, part 2 (London: John Russell Smith, 1874), 688, 744; "Obituary: Earl Cornwallis," *Gentleman's Magazine*, n.s. 38 (July–December 1852): 90. See also http://godintonhouse.co.uk. A photograph of her is in the collection of the National Portrait Gallery, London: Camille Silvy, *Julia (née Cornwallis), Viscountess Holmesdale*, 1861, albumen print, National Portrait Gallery, London, NPG Ax52845.

176. It is unclear if Lady Filmer made her own prints, states Tirza Latimer and Harriet Riches, "Women and Photography," 11 February 2013, Oxford Art Online. See also Mary Warner Marien, *Photography: A Cultural History*, 2nd ed. (London: Laurence King Publishing, 2006), 94–95; and the album with albumen silver photographs, with watercolor and gold paint, in "My Book," of Mary Georgiana Caroline Cecil Filmer, 1862, Harvard University Art Museums, P1982.359.

177. Harry W. Russell, "Notes on the Ancient Stained Glass, Memorial Brasses, and an Altar-Slab in the Church of St. Mary, Great Chart," *Archaeologia Cantiana* 26 (1906): 97n1.

178. Russell, "Nicholas Toke," 62.

179. John Julian, *A Dictionary of Hymnology* (New York: Charles Scribner's Sons, 1892), 1181, see also 840–41, 852, 1168; Charles Seymour Robinson, *Annotations Upon Popular Hymns* (New York: Hunt and Eaton, 1893), 199. John Bernard Burke, *A Genealogical and Heraldic History of the Landed Gentry of Great Britain and Ireland*, 5th ed., vol. 2 (London: Harrison, 1871), 1388.

180. "Country Homes, Gardens Old and New: Godinton, Kent, The Seat of Mr. G. Ashley Dodd," *Country Life* 14, no. 341 (18 July 1903): 94, 93 (illustration of the Great Hall).

181. "In Focus: Last Days in the Old Home," godintonhouse.co.uk, added 1 May 2020.

182. See Lilly Martin Spencer, letter to National Academy of Design(?), 1897(?), Lilly Martin Spencer Papers, Archives of American Art, Smithsonian Institution, cited in Robin Bolton-Smith and William H. Truettner, *Lilly Martin Spencer, 1822–1902: The Joys of Sentiment* (Washington, D.C.: National Collection of Fine Arts, 1973), 215, 225.

183. For interpretations of Spencer's relationship with middle-class audiences and the ideals of domesticity, see Elizabeth Johns, *American Genre Painting: The Politics of Everyday Life* (New Haven: Yale University Press, 1991), esp. 162; and David M. Lubin, *Picturing a Nation: Art and Social Change in Nineteenth-Century America* (New Haven: Yale University Press, 1994), esp. 161–62, 165, 203.

184. Bolton-Smith and Truettner, *Lilly Martin Spencer*, 16; Henry T. Tuckerman, *Book of the Artists* (New York: G. P. Putnam and Son, 1867), 436–37.

185. Laura Groves Napolitano, "Nurturing Change: Lilly Martin Spencer's Images of Children" (PhD diss., University of Maryland, College Park, 2008), 8, 12.

186. Lubin, *Picturing a Nation*, 173–74, 203.

187. Lilly Martin Spencer, letter to Angelique Martin, 20 April 1854, Spencer Papers, Archives of American Art, Smithsonian Institution, quoted in Sarah Burns and John Davis, *American Art to 1900: A Documentary History* (Berkeley: University of California Press, 2009), 326.

188. Johns, *American Genre Painting*, 162; April F. Masten, "Shake Hands? Lilly Martin Spencer and the Politics of Art," *American Quarterly* 56, no. 2 (June 2004): 378.

189. Aimee E. Newell, *A Stitch in Time: The Needlework of Aging Women in Antebellum America* (Athens: The Ohio University Press, 2014), 14.

190. Mrs. Trollope, *Domestic Manners of the Americans* (London: Whittaker, Treacher, and Co., 1832), 59; Bolton-Smith and Truettner, *Lilly Martin Spencer*, 172.

191. "Mrs. Lilly M. Spencer," *Poughkeepsie Eagle-News*, 23 December 1898, 8.

192. Malaria had been a persistent disease in the Hudson River port for several years. According to a New York State health study from 1904, malarial and typhoid fevers marked Poughkeepsie's health statistics and poor water conditions from 1893 on, with more deaths from these illnesses than in any other location in the state. Frederick J. Mann, "Sand Filters and Typhoid Fever in Poughkeepsie," *American Medicine* 8, no. 12 (17 September 1904): 514.

193. On Cassatt's imagery of children and mothers, see Griselda Pollock, *Mary Cassatt: Painter of Modern Women* (London: Thames and Hudson, 1998), 186–98.

194. Achille Ségard, *Mary Cassatt, un Peintre des Enfants et des Mères* (Paris: Librairie Paul Ollendorff, 1913), 108.

195. Nancy Mowll Mathews, "Maternité," in Mathews and Pierre Curie, *Mary Cassatt: An American Impressionist in Paris* (Brussels: Mercatorfonds, 2018), 76–95.

196. Mary Cassatt, letter to Paul Durand-Ruel, 10 November [1903], Nancy Mowll Mathews, *Cassatt and Her Circle: Selected Letters* (New York: Abbeville Press Publishers, 1984), 287.

197. Nancy Mowll Mathews, "An American in Paris," in Mathews and Curie, *Mary Cassatt*, 30.

198. Nancy Mowll Mathews, "The Making of an Impressionist," in Mathews and Curie, *Mary Cassatt*, 49; Nancy Mowll Mathews, "Cassatt, Mary (Stevenson)," Oxford Art Online.

199. Mathews and Curie, *Mary Cassatt*, 14–18.

200. Mathews, "An American in Paris," 37, and Mathews, "Maternité," in Mathews and Curie, *Mary Cassatt*, 37, 78–95; Mathews, "Cassatt, Mary (Stevenson)," Oxford Art Online.

201. Phoebe Hoban, *Alice Neel: The Art of Not Sitting Pretty* (New York: St. Martin's Press, 2010), 48, 57–62.

202. Ibid., 4.

203. Nochlin, "Alice Neel," in Reilly, *Linda Nochlin Reader*, 284; Denise Bauer, "Alice Neel's Portraits of Mother Work," *NWSA Journal* 14, no. 2 (Summer 2002): 102–20.

204. Hoban, *Alice Neel*, 21.

205. Quoted in Patricia Hills, *Alice Neel* (New York: H. N. Abrams, 1983), 29; see also Hoban, *Alice Neel*, 38–39.

206. Hoban, *Alice Neel*, 40–61.

207. See esp. Nochlin, "Alice Neel," in Reilly, *Linda Nochlin Reader*; Ann Sutherland Harris, "Neel, Alice (Hartley)," Oxford Art Online; and Wayne Koestenbaum, *Alice Neel: Paintings from the 1930s* (New York: Robert Miller Gallery, 1997).

208. "Academy Picks 15 for Fellowships," *New York Times*, 21 July 1947, 15L; and Kathleen Weil Garris, "Sculptress Indicates Influences and Life," *Vassar Miscellany News* 37, no. 7 (12 November 1952): 2, 6.

209. Carol Scarvalone Kushner, "Concetta Scaravaglione: Italian American Sculptor," *Italian Americana* 11, no. 2 (Spring–Summer 1993): 180; Norman L. Kleeblatt and Susan Chevlowe, *Painting a Place in America: Jewish Artists in New York 1900–1945* (New York: The Jewish Museum, 1991), 189–90, 194.

210. Rosa Scaravaglione, letter to Concetta Scaravaglione, July 1925, The Concetta Scaravaglione Trust Collection, quoted in Kushner, "Concetta Scaravaglione," 181, 190n5.

211. "Concetta Scaravaglione," in Marling and Harrison, *7 American Women*, 37–39.

212. See "Joan Brown: Keeping a Diary," in Caroline A. Jones, *Bay Area Figurative Art, 1950–1965* (San Francisco: San Francisco Museum of Modern Art, 1989), 145–55, quoted on p. 153.

213. Karen Tsujimoto, "Painting as a Visual Diary: The Art of Joan Brown," in Tsujimoto and Jacquelynn Baas, *The Art of Joan Brown* (Berkeley, Calif.: Berkeley Art Museum, 1998), 11–13.

214. Sharon E. Bliss, "Chronology," in ibid., 232–34.

215. Joan Brown, interview with Lynn Gumpert, from "Joan Brown," in Gumpert, Ned Rifkin, and Marcia Tucker, *Early Work: Lynda Benglis, Joan Brown, Luis Jimenez, Gary Stephan, Lawrence Weiner* (New York: The New Museum, 1982), 20.

216. Tsujimoto, "Painting as a Visual Diary," 52–62.

217. *The Ford Foundation Annual Report 1965*, 129. See the photograph of the workshop, 23.

218. Paul Brach, "Schapiro's Shrines," in *Miriam Schapiro: The Shrine*, 17. See also the "Biography and Chronology," 25.

219. Schapiro quoted in Roth, "Interview with Miriam Schapiro," 12.

220. "Biography and Chronology," 23.

221. Thalia Gouma-Peterson, *Miriam Schapiro: Shaping the Fragments of Art and Life* (Lakeland, Fla.: Polk Museum of Art, 1999), 25–26. On the Shrine paintings, see 56–61.

222. Ibid., 22; Barbara Delatiner, "Feminist Art, Traditional Forms," *New York Times*, 16 July 1989, 8.

223. "Biography and Chronology," 21.

224. On *L'Estampe originale*, see Patricia Eckert Boyer and Phillip Dennis Cate, *L'Estampe originale: Artistic Printmaking in France, 1893–1895* (New Brunswick, N.J.: Jane Voorhees Zimmerli Art Museum, 1991).

225. Caroline Watson, letter to William Hayley, 19 July 1805, in Alexander, *Caroline Watson*, 106.

226. Elba Huffman, letter to her mother, 19 December 1869, in [Bouslog], *Letters*, 37.

227. Elba Huffman, letter to her mother, 30 January 1870, in ibid., 61–62. She is referring to the art professor Henry Van Ingen and the English professor Truman J. Backus.

228. See *Angelika Kauffmann Retrospektive*, ed. Bettina Baumgärtel (Düsseldorf: Kunstmuseum, 1998), 360, ill. 202.

229. See David Alexander, "Kauffman and the Print Market in Eighteenth-century England," 141–78, and his "Chronological Checklist of Singly Issued English Prints after Angelica Kauffman," 179–89, in *Angelica Kauffman: A Continental Artist in Georgian England*, ed. Wendy Wassyng Roworth (Brighton: The Royal Pavilion, Art Gallery and Museums, 1992).

230. See the inscription in the bottom border of the print. For Vernon, see J. K. Laughton, revised by Nicholas Tracy, "Vernon, Sir Edward," *Oxford Dictionary of National Biography*.

231. Angelica Goodden, *Miss Angel: The Art and World of Angelica Kauffman, Eighteenth-Century Icon* (Pimlico, 2005; repr., New York: Random House, 2011).

232. See, for instance, the series of reviews in *London Weekly Magazine* 1 (15 July 1780): 190–92, 274–75, 316–17.

233. On Kauffman, see esp. Roworth, *Angelica Kauffman*; Victoria Manners and G. C. Williamson, *Angelica Kauffmann, R.A.: Her Life and Her Works* (New York: Hacker Art Books, 1976); Angela Rosenthal, *Angelica Kauffman: Art and Sensibility* (London: Paul Mellon Centre for Studies in British Art, 2006); and Peter Walch and Lin Barton, "Kauffman, (Maria Anna) Angelica," Oxford Art Online.

234. Alexander, *Caroline Watson*, 16.

235. Raffaella Sarti, *Europe at Home: Family and Material Culture, 1500–1800*, trans. Allan Cameron (New Haven: Yale University Press, 2002), 118–19; Lucy Inglis, *Georgian London, Into the Streets* (London: Penguin Books, 2013), 89–90.

236. Mary Robinson, Maria Cosway, and Caroline Watson, *The Winter Day* (London: R. Ackermann's Repository of Arts, 1804), twelve sepia aquatint plates.

237. For images and verses, see Alexander, *Caroline Watson*, 53, 83, 88, 90–91. See the complete folio of prints at the Yale Center for British Art.

238. "The Winter's Day," *The Literary Magazine, and American Register* 2, no. 12 (September 1804): 416.

239. Alexander, *Caroline Watson*, 13, 17, 20, 31. See Alexander's "Chronological Checklist of Prints by Caroline Watson," 74–103.

240. For this brief biographical sketch, I drew upon Diane Boucher, "Maria Cosway (1760–1838): A Commentator on Modern Life," *British Art Journal* 18, no. 3 (Winter 2017): 78ff.

241. Maria Hadfield Cosway, *Progress of Female Dissipation*, engraved by A. Cardon from the original drawings by Mrs. Cosway (London: R. Ackermann's Repository of Arts, 1800), with eight aquatints. Maria Hadfield Cosway, *A Progress of Female Virtue*, engraved by A. Cardon from original drawings by Mrs. Cosway (London: R. Ackermann's Repository of Arts, 1800), with eight aquatints. See the copies at the Yale Center for British Art.

242. On Church, see Jacqueline Marie Musacchio, "Infesting the Galleries of Europe: The Copyist Emma Conant Church in Paris and Rome," in *Nineteenth-Century Art Worldwide* 10, no. 2 (Autumn 2011), http://www.19thc-artworldwide.org/autumn11/infesting-the-galleries-of-europe-the-copyist-emma-conant-church-in-paris-and-rome. Much of the factual information in my text is based on Musacchio's groundbreaking article.

243. See the brief biography in *Third General Catalogue of Colby College, Waterville, Maine* (Waterville, Maine: Colby College, 1909), 163.

244. "Art and Artists," *New York Times*, 29 November 1860, 2.

245. "Books, Authors and Art," *Springfield Weekly Republican*, 30 March 1867, 6.

246. Musacchio, "Emma Conant Chuch," note 66.

247. Ibid., esp. notes 5 and 6.

248. Emma Conant Church, letter to Matthew Vassar, 1 January 1863, Vassar College Archives and Special Collections Library, cited in Musacchio, "Emma Conant Church," note 76.

249. Musacchio, "Emma Conant Church."

250. Matthew Vassar, letter to Miss Church, 15 December 1863, transcribed in Elizabeth Hazelton Haight, *The Autobiography and Letters of Matthew Vassar* (New York: Oxford University Press, 1916), 119–20.

251. Musacchio, "Emma Conant Church."

252. *Fifth Annual Catalogue of the Officers and Students of Vassar College, Poughkeepsie, N.Y., 1869–70* (New York: S. W. Green, Printer, 1870), 14, 20. See [Bouslog], *Letters*, 104–5, 110–11.

253. Henry Lyman, "Obituaries, Miss Hannah W. Lyman, Lady Principal of Vassar College, Poughkeepsie, N.Y.," in *Lyman Anniversary, Proceedings at the Reunion of the Lyman Family* (Albany, N.Y.: Joel Munsell, 1871), 30–31.

254. [Bouslog], *Letters*, 10–11, 16–17, 29, and 47.

255. Ibid., 8, 16–17, 29, 32, 35, 36, 47, 48, 66, 89, 100, 102, 111–12, 114–19.

256. Ibid., 18.

257. Ibid., 65, 131, 136, 140–42.

258. Ibid., 67–68.

259. Clipping, "Mrs. Elba H. Bouslog, Outstanding Resident, Called Away by Death" (newspaper unknown, probably in Bay St. Louis, Mississippi), 27 July 1933, courtesy of the family. Clipping, "The Vassar Girl That Was—and Still Is," *Ladies Home Journal* (October 1925), courtesy of the family. My sincere thanks go to Jim Corbett for his generous assistance. "Associate Alumnae of Vassar College, 1938 Biographical Register Questionnaire," Alumnae and Alumni of Vassar College, Biographical File, Vassar College Archives and Special Collections Library. Courtesy of Dean Rogers, Vassar College Archives and Special Collections Library.

260. Malvina Hoffman Inventory Records. I am enormously grateful to Joel Rosenkranz, Mark Ostrander, and Janis Conner of Conner-Rosenkranz Gallery in New York for researching their files for the correct title of this work.

261. Malvina Hoffman, *Heads and Tales* (New York: Charles Scribner's Sons, 1936), 57, 58, 67; Hoffman, *Yesterday Is Tomorrow, A Personal History* (New York: Crown Publishers, Inc., 1965), 157, 161, 192.

262. Hoffman, *Heads and Tales*, 117, 129.

263. Anna Coleman Ladd, *Women's Overseas Service League*, 1921, American Numismatic Society, N.Y., 0000.999.40668. Discussed and illustrated in Patricia Phagan and Peter van Alfen, eds., *The Art of Devastation: Medals and Posters of the Great War* (Poughkeepsie, N.Y.: Frances Lehman Loeb Art Center, 2017), 338.

264. Marianne Kinkel, *Races of Mankind: The Sculptures of Malvina Hoffman* (Springfield: University of Illinois Press, 2011), 42–43.

265. Hoffman, *Yesterday*, 56–58, 67–68, 116.

266. Janis C. Conner, *A Dancer in Relief: Works by Malvina Hoffman* (Yonkers, N.Y.: Hudson River Museum, 1984), [8, 10].

267. Jennifer Schuessler, "Exiled Sculptures Return," *New York Times*, 21 January 2016, C1.

268. See, for instance, Andrew Hemingway, *Artists on the Left* (New Haven: Yale University Press, 2002), 20–24; Patricia Phagan, "William Gropper and *Freiheit*: A Study of His Political Cartoons, 1924–1935" (PhD diss., City University of New York Graduate Center, 2000), 182, 382, 393–94n6.

269. Oral history interview with Marion Greenwood, 31 January 1964, Archives of American Art, Smithsonian Institution.

270. Pablo O'Higgins, letter to Marion and Grace Greenwood, 12 June 1934, quoted in James Oles, *South of the Border* (New Haven: Yale University Art Gallery, 1993), 187, 291n 134. See 186–87, 190–93, for discussion and illustrations of the drawing and mural.

271. Stephen Haber, Armando Razo, and Noel Maurer, *The Politics of Property Rights: Political Instability, Credible Commitments, and Economic Growth in Mexico, 1876–1929* (Cambridge: Cambridge University Press, 2003), 216–17.

272. "Fight Mexican Wage Law," *New York Times*, 7 January 1934, 3; and "Tampico, City of 36,000 Is Important Gulf Oil Port, *New York Times*, 26 September 1933, 16.

273. "To March on Mexico City," *New York Times*, 10 August 1932, 8; and "March of Jobless Thousands Halted by Mexican Troops," *New York Times*, 27 August 1932, 1.

274. Oles, *South of the Border*, 185–87, 191–93; Oral history interview, Archives of American Art; *Vida Americana*: *Mexican Muralists Remake American Art, 1925–1945*, ed. Barbara Haskell (New York: Whitney Museum of American Art, 2020), 32.

275. Marling and Harrison, *7 American Women*, 28–29; see also http://www.mbamericana.com/marion-greenwood-archive.

276. Karen Arnett Chachere, "Burroughs, Margaret Taylor Goss," in *Writing African American Women: An Encyclopedia of Literature by and About Women of Color*, ed. Elizabeth Ann Beaulieu, vol. 1 (Westport, Conn.: Greenwood Press, 2006), 135.

277. MH [Melanie Herzog], "Margaret Taylor Goss Burroughs," in Seaton, *Paths to the Press*, 104; and Timothy J. Gilfoyle, "Culture Makers: Making History Interviews with Timuel Black and Margaret Burroughs," *Chicago History* 36, no. 3 (Winter 2010): 52–64.

278. Gilfoyle, "Culture Makers"; and John E. Fleming and Margaret T. Burroughs, "Dr. Margaret T. Burroughs: Artist, Teacher, Administrator, Writer, Political Activist, and Museum Founder," *The Public Historian* 21, no. 1 (Winter 1999): 31–55.

279. Chachere, "Burroughs," 135; Cain, *South Side Venus*, 19–20.

280. Cain, *South Side Venus*, 18, 20–21.

281. Ibid., 31; Bill V. Mullen, *Popular Fronts: Chicago and African-American Cultural Politics, 1935–46* (1999; repr. ed., Springfield: University of Illinois Press, 2015), 75–105.

282. Chachere, "Burroughs," 135.

283. Robert Bone and Richard A. Courage, *The Muse in Bronzeville: African American Creative Expression in Chicago, 1932–1950* (New Brunswick, N.J.: Rutgers University Press, 2011), 146; Brian Dolinar, *The Black Cultural Front: Black Writers and Artists of the Depression Generation* (Jackson: University Press of Mississippi, 2012), 23–34, 76–77.

284. Cain, *South Side Venus*, 28, 39–54; Gilfoyle, "Culture Makers."

285. Cain, *South Side Venus*, 49, 54, 62–63; Mullen, *Popular Fronts*, 2–5.

286. Margaret Taylor Goss, "A Negro Mother Looks at War," *Chicago Defender*, 31 August 1940, 24, quoted in Mullen, *Popular Fronts*, 87.

287. Cain, *South Side Venus*, 106.

288. Ibid., 107.

289. Ibid., 105–6; Gilfoyle, "Culture Makers: Interviews."

290. Margaret G. Burroughs, "Woman's Viewpoint," for the Associated Negro Press (ANP), Summer 1951, DuSable Museum, Margaret Burroughs Papers, Series II, box 46, folder 376, quoted in Cain, *South Side Venus*, 104.

291. Alexander Alland, Sr., *Jessie Tarbox Beals: First Woman News Photographer* (New York: Camera/Graphic Press Ltd., 1978), 45.

292. Bourke-White, *Portrait of Myself*, 42.

293. Alland, *Jessie Tarbox Beals*, 11–26.

294. Ibid., 39, 56.

295. Her poetry was collected in Jesse Tarbox Beals, *Songs of a Wanderer* (privately published, 1928).

296. Alland, *Jessie Tarbox Beals*, 62–63.

297. Ibid., 65–67.

298. For other documentary photographs by her from this period in her life, see the Community Service Society website, http://css.cul.columbia.edu/catalog/.

299. Tudor-Hart used a Rolleiflex camera. Peter Stephan Jungk, "Lives of the Artists, Edith Tudor-Hart: My Great-Aunt, the Spy," 27 May 2019, http://www.tate.org.uk/tate-etc/issue-46-summer-2019/lives-artists-edith-tudor-hart-great-aunt-spy-peter-stephan-jungk.

300. Elizabeth Otto and Patrick Rössler, *Bauhaus Women: A Global Perspective* (London: Herbert Press, Bloomsbury Publishing, 2019), 130–33.

301. Adrian Sudhalter, "14 Years Bauhaus," in Barry Bergdoll and Leah Dickerman, *Bauhaus, 1919–1933: Workshops for Modernity* (New York: Museum of Modern Art, 2009), 333. Summer semester of 1929 included 122 male students and 51 female students.

302. Leah Dickerman, "Bauhaus Fundaments," in Bergdoll and Dickerman, *Bauhaus*, 34.

303. Jungk, "Lives of the Artists"; Otto and Rössler, *Bauhaus Women*.

304. Otto and Rössler, *Bauhaus Women*.

305. Duncan Forbes, "Politics, Photography, and Exile in the Life of Edith Tudor-Hart," in Shulamith Behr and Marian Malet, *Arts in Exile in Britain 1933–1945: Politics and Cultural Identity* (Amsterdam: Rodopi, 2005), 73–74. See also Duncan Forbes, "'Tracking' Edith Tudor-Hart," *History Workshop Journal* 84 (Autumn 2017): 238–39; and *Edith Tudor-Hart: In the Shadow of Tyranny*, ed. Duncan Forbes (Edinburgh: National Galleries of Scotland, 2013).

306. "Veterans at College," *Life*, 21 April 1947, 105–13, cat. 35 is reproduced on p. 111.

307. See http://www.ibm.com/ibm/history/ibm100/us/en/icons/testscore/.

308. Bourke-White, *Portrait of Myself*, 14–15, 18.

309. Ibid., vii, 29.

310. Gretchen Ritter, "A Legacy of Firsts: Women at Cornell," in *The Inauguration of Elizabeth Garrett* ([Ithaca, N.Y.: Cornell University], 2015); and Bourke-White, *Portrait of Myself*, 29–32.

311. Bourke-White, *Portrait of Myself*, 48–50.

312. Ibid., 62–68, 80.

313. Margaret Bourke-White, *Eyes on Russia* (New York: Simon and Schuster, 1931), 26, 42.

314. Bourke-White, *Portrait of Myself*, 90–104; and Vicki Goldberg, *Margaret Bourke-White: A Biography* (New York: Harper and Row Publishers, 1986), 136–38.

315. Bourke-White, *Portrait of Myself*, vii; Goldberg, *Margaret Bourke-White*, 157; and Melissa A. McEuen, *Seeing America: Women Photographers Between the Wars* (2000; repr. ed., Lexington: University Press of Kentucky, 2004), 232.

316. Goldberg, *Margaret Bourke-White*, 149.

317. Bourke-White, *Portrait of Myself*, 141.

318. Ibid., vii–viii, 197.

319. Ibid., 65.

320. *Exhibition of Black and White Photographs by Dorothy Meigs Eidlitz* (Winter Park, Fla.: All Saints' Episcopal Church, 1975), exhibition brochure with checklist and brief biography, Eidlitz object files, Frances Lehman Loeb Art Center, Vassar College.

321. "Biographical Sketch" in *Exhibition of Black and White Photographs*. John Hessler, "For Women Who Know No Boundaries," blogs.loc.gov/maps/2019/04/for-women-who-know-no-boundaries/.

322. "Biographical Sketch"; Doris Weatherford, *American Women During World War II: An Encyclopedia* (New York: Routledge, 2010), 21–23.

323. "Biographical Sketch"; http://www.jhproject.org/history/.

324. "Biographical Sketch"; *Who's Who in American Art* (New York: Jaques Cattell Press, R. R. Bowker, 1973), 207; and George Dugan, "Dorothy Eidlitz, 85, Patron of Arts and Champion of Women's Rights," *New York Times*, 1 November 1976, 42.

325. "Dorothy Meigs Becomes Bride of Dr. Robert Stunzi," *New York Tribune*, 21 March 1920, 5; "Contemporary Notes: 1914," *Vassar Quarterly* 5, no. 4 (1 July 1920): 298.

326. Scrapbooks, Dorothy Eidlitz Papers, American Heritage Center, University of Wyoming; http://www.wyomingpublicmedia.org/post/archives-air-65-flowers-japan-dorothy-eidlitz-papers; Dugan, "Dorothy Eidlitz."

327. "Contemporary Notes: 14," *Vassar Quarterly* 12, no. 4 (1 September 1927): 265.

328. "Ernest F. Eidlitz, Lawyer 60 Years," *New York Times*, 23 March 1959, 31.

329. Helen Gee, *Limelight: A Greenwich Village Photography Gallery and Coffeehouse in the Fifties; A Memoir* (Albuquerque: University of New Mexico Press, 1997), 89–90.

330. "Biographical Sketch."

331. Rosalie Thorne McKenna, *A Life in Photography* (New York: Alfred A. Knopf, 1991), 11.

332. Ibid., 11–12.

333. Eudora Welty, letter to Mary Lou Aswell, n.d. [spring 1954], Eudora Welty Collection, Mississippi Department of Archives and History, Jackson, Mississippi, quoted in Suzanne Marrs, *Eudora Welty: A Biography* (Orlando: Harcourt, Inc., 2005), 233. I have been unable to locate an article on Welty by Brinnin and McKenna that appeared in *Mademoiselle*.

334. McKenna, *Life in Photography*, 11–21.

335. In 1955, only 21,502 Blacks were registered to vote in Mississippi, as against 423,456 registered whites. See Neil R. McMillen, *Dark Journey: Black Mississippians in the Age of Jim Crow* (Urbana: University of Illinois Press, 1990), table, 36. Lynchings in Mississippi from 1877 to 1950 were the highest in the country, at 654. See also http://lynchinginamerica.eji.org/report/.

336. McKenna, *Life in Photography*, 3–9.

337. Ibid., 41–91.

338. Diane Arbus, "Two American Families," *London Sunday Times Magazine*, 10 November 1968, 56. See Elisabeth Sussman and Doon Arbus, *Diane Arbus: A Chronology* (New York: Aperture, 2011), 76. See also Anthony W. Lee and John Pultz, *Diane Arbus: Family Albums* (New Haven: Yale University Press, 2003), 22–23.

339. Diane Arbus, Marvin Israel, and Doon Arbus, *Diane Arbus: An Aperture Monograph* (New York: Aperture, 1972), 2, quoted in Sandra Phillips et al., *Diane Arbus: Revelations* (New York: Random House, 2003), 59.

340. Sussman and Arbus, *Diane Arbus*, 51, 54.

341. Ibid., 1–2, 4, 8–11, 18–19. See also Gerry Badger, "Arbus, Diane," Oxford Art Online, for a helpful review of her life and major literature.

Checklist

All works are from the collection of the Frances Lehman Loeb Art Center, Vassar College, Poughkeepsie, New York; height precedes width.

PORTRAITS: INTIMATE APPRAISALS

1. **Magdalena de Passe** (Dutch, 1600–1638)
The lively portraicture of the most noble and right honourable Lady The Lady Katherin Marchionesse of Buckingham. &c., ca. 1620–23
Engraving with burnishing on cream laid paper
Sheet (trimmed within platemark): 4⅝ × 3 in. (11.8 × 7.6 cm)
Franken 507, Hollstein Dutch 22, O'Donoghue 2, Hind II 302 1, Granger II 169
Gift of Mrs. William Reed Thompson (Mary Thaw, class of 1877)
1938.1.110

2. **Johann Georg Wille** (German, 1715–1808)
After Elisabeth Sophie Chéron (French, 1648–1711)
Mlle. de Scudéry, 1739
Etching and engraving on cream laid paper
Unrecorded proof, Le Blanc (Wille) 144, Firmin-Didot 2449
Platemark: 6 × 4¼ in. (15.2 × 10.8 cm)
Sheet: 17½ × 13 in. (44.5 × 33 cm)
Gift of Mrs. William Reed Thompson (Mary Thaw, class of 1877)
1938.1.134.a

3. **Elizabeth Rebecca Coffin** (American, 1850–1930)
Study of a Head, ca. 1893
Oil on canvas
Unframed: 22¼ × 16⅛ in. (56.5 × 41 cm)
Gift of the artist, class of 1870
X.16

4. **Hilda Belcher** (American, 1881–1963)
The Checkered Dress (Portrait of O'Keeffe), 1907
Watercolor and gouache on cream laid paper, with JW watermark, mounted on paperboard
Sheet and mount: 21¾ × 15¾ in. (55.3 × 40 cm)
Bequest of Mary S. Bedell, class of 1873
1932.1.5

5. **Violet Oakley** (American, 1874–1961)
Blanchette Hooker and Helen Hooker as Torchbearers, 1924
Red chalk with traces of graphite on beige laid paper
Sheet: 18⅞ × 13⅝ in. (47.9 × 34.6 cm)
Gift of the Violet Oakley Memorial Foundation
1983.29.12

6. **Käthe Kollwitz** (German, 1867–1945)
Self-Portrait at the Table, ca. 1893
Etching and aquatint on cream wove paper
Platemark: 7¹⁄₁₆ × 5⅛ in. (18 × 13 cm)
Sheet: 13¾ × 9⅛ in. (34.9 × 23.2 cm)
Gift of Emily Brown
1961.3.1

7. **Berthe Morisot** (French, 1841–1895)
Profile Portrait of Paule Gobillard, 1886
Pastel on faded blue laid paper mounted on paperboard
Sight: 25½ × 19¾ in. (64.8 × 50.2 cm)
Gift of Jane Crowley Koven in memory of her daughter Constance
Henriette Koven Stransky, class of 1960
2004.31

8. **Marie Laurencin** (French, 1883–1956)
Three Women, 1935
Oil on canvas
Unframed: 15 × 18⅛ in. (38.1 × 46 cm)
Bequest of June Bingham Birge, class of 1940
2009.6

9. **Elizabeth Catlett** (American, 1915–2012)
Negro Woman, 1945
Lithograph on cream wove paper
Image: 12 × 8⅝ in. (30.5 × 22 cm)
Sheet: 15 × 11 in. (38.1 × 27.9 cm)
Purchase with funds given by Arthur A. Anderson, Edward J.
Guarino, Marcia Widenor, Africana Studies, and various donors
2008.10

10. **Titina Maselli** (Italian, 1924–2005)
Woman Resting Her Head on Her Hands, ca. 1955
Pen and ink, brush and wash, and graphite on cream wove paper
Sheet: 18¹³⁄₁₆ × 23⅞ in. (47.8 × 60.6 cm)
Gift of Mrs. R. Kirk Askew, Jr.
1983.40.2

11. **Sylvia Sleigh** (Welsh, 1916–2010)
The Willows: Sylvia Castro, 1967
Oil on canvas
Unframed: 48 × 72 in. (121.9 × 182.9 cm)
Gift of the estate of Sylvia Sleigh
2017.31.2

IDYLLIC LANDSCAPES: COMFORT AND SECURITY

12. **Charles White** (English, 1751–1785)
After Miss T. Bennett (English, late 18th century)
While, Celia, from the hand . . . (also called *Two Girls with Doves* and perhaps *The Dove*), 1785
Color stipple engraving on cream laid paper
Image: 7¾ in. (19.7 cm), diameter
X.301

13. **Eliza Phipps** (English, 19th century)
Sampler ("Small is my skill, and tender are my years . . ."), 1828 or 1818
Silk threads on wool ground
Sight: 15 × 18⅜ in. (38.1 × 46.7 cm)
Transfer from Vassar College Libraries, Special Collections, Martha Clawson Reed Collection
1997.7.89

14. **Unknown maker** (American, early 19th century)
Sampler (Adam and Eve in the Garden of Eden), ca. 1808
Silk threads on linen/wool ground
Sight: 15⅜ × 18⅜ in. (39.1 × 46.7 cm)
Gift of Mrs. James W. Packard (Elizabeth Gillmer, class of 1894)
1960.9.112

15. **Florence Maria Cushing** (American, 1853–1927)
Untitled (Man and woman at a stream), ca. 1886
Albumen print
Image: 7⁵⁄₁₆ × 4⁷⁄₁₆ in. (18.6 × 11.3 cm)
Sheet: 14 × 11⅛ in. (35.5 × 28.1 cm)
Anonymous gift
1998.26

16. **Florine Stettheimer** (American, 1871–1944)
Natatorium Undine, 1927
Oil and encaustic on canvas
Unframed: 50½ × 60 in. (128.3 × 152.4 cm)
Gift of Ettie Stettheimer
1949.5

17. **Rosella Hartman** (American, 1894–1993)
Untitled, 1933
Brush and black ink on paper
Image: 21½ × 17½ in. (54.6 × 44.5 cm)
Sheet: 24³⁄₁₆ × 19⅜ in. (61.4 × 49.2 cm)
Gift of Susan and Steven Hirsch, class of 1971
1995.12

18. **Doris Lee** (American, 1905–1983)
Garden at Night, ca. 1950
Oil on canvas
Unframed: 41⅞ × 24¼ in. (106.4 × 61.6 cm)
Bequest of the artist
1984.44

DOMESTIC SCENES: PRIVATE AND PERSONAL

19. **John Henry Le Keux** (English, 1812–1896)
After Miss Cornwallis, perhaps Lady Julia Mann Cornwallis, later Viscountess Holmesdale (English, 1844–1883)
Godington Hall, Kent (Private Plate), probably mid-1850s
Etching on chine collé on cream wove paper (a page from an album)
Platemark: 6 × 8½ in. (15.2 × 21.6 cm)
Sheet (album page): 11⅝ × 18 in. (29.5 × 45.7 cm)
Gift of Matthew Vassar
1864.2.1096

20. **Lilly Martin Spencer** (American, b. England 1822–1902)
The Spinner, 1894
Oil on canvas
Unframed: 27⅛ × 17⅜ in. (68.9 × 44.1 cm)
Gift of Mr. and Mrs. Herbert L. Shultz (Barbara H. Rodie, class of 1942)
1982.8

21. **Mary Cassatt** (American, 1844–1926)
Denise Holding Her Child, ca. 1905
Drypoint with surface tone on beige laid paper
Platemark: 8¼ × 5⅞ in. (21 × 14.9 cm)
Sheet: 13¼ × 9⅜ in. (33.7 × 23.8 cm)
Breeskin 204
Gift of Alicia Craig Faxon, class of 1952
1990.20.1

22. **Alice Neel** (American, 1900–1984)
Mother and Child, 1927
Brush and watercolor over graphite on cream wove paper
Sheet: 11¾ × 8¾ in. (29.9 × 22.2 cm)
Gift of Mrs. John Benson Brooks (Frances K. B. Jones,
class of 1940)
1990.19.5

23. **Concetta Scaravaglione** (American, 1900–1975)
Girl with Cocks, 1947–48
Italian walnut
44½ × 7 × 8½ in. (113 × 17.8 × 21.6 cm)
Gift of Mr. John M. Stratton, in honor of his daughter
Mrs. Tuxton B. Pratt, Jr. (Elizabeth Stratton, class of 1950)
1966.17

24. **Joan Brown** (American, 1938–1990)
Getting Ready for the Bath, 1961
Oil on canvas
64 × 64 in. (162.6 × 162.6 cm)
Gift of Mary Coxe Schlosser, class of 1951
2009.20

25. **Miriam Schapiro** (American, b. Canada 1923–2015)
Published by Tamarind Lithography Workshop
Shrine, 1964
Four-part color lithograph on cream wove Rives BFK paper
Overall: 50³⁄₁₆ × 12 in. (127.5 × 30.5 cm)
Gift of Dorothy Seiberling Steinberg, class of 1943,
and Leo Steinberg
1982.1

NARRATIVES: THE STIMULUS OF IDEAS

26. **Angelica Kauffman** (Swiss, 1741–1807)
Chrysothemis, ca. 1778
Black chalk, heightened with white chalk, on prepared paper
Sheet: 16 × 9 in. (40.6 × 22.9 cm)
Purchase, Suzette Morton Davidson, class of 1934,
Fund 1968.24

27. **Caroline Watson** (English, 1760/61–1814)
After Maria Cosway (English, b. Italy, 1759–1838)
Published by Rudolph Ackermann, Repository of Arts, London
Mis'ry's Victims, 1803, eighth of twelve plates from the folio *The
Winter Day*, with verse by Mary Darby Robinson, 1804
Etching with aquatint on brown laid paper
Platemark: 9³⁄₁₆ × 11⅝ in. (23.3 × 29.5 cm)
Sheet: 10⅞ × 12¾ in. (27.6 × 32.4 cm)
Alexander 69
Purchase, Suzette Morton Davidson, class of 1934,
Fund 1972.12

28. **Emma Conant Church** (American, 1831–1893)
After Carlo Dolci (Italian, 1616–1687)
Madonna and Child, 1862
Oil on canvas with original frame
Unframed: 35½ × 28¼ in. (90.2 × 71.8 cm)
Gift of Matthew Vassar
1864.1.13

29. **Elba Huffman Bouslog** (American, 1850–1933)
Diana, ca. 1869–70
Charcoal with stumping on beige wove paper
Sheet: 25 × 19 in. (63.5 × 48.3 cm)
Gift in memory of the artist Elba Huffman Bouslog,
by Patsy Denton Corbett, granddaughter of the artist
2020.7

30. **Malvina Cornell Hoffman** (American, 1885–1966)
Pax, 1923, cast in 1924
Bronze on wooden base; cast at Roman Bronze Works, Brooklyn,
New York, 1924
With base: 11⅜ × 5½ in. × 5¾ (28.6 × 14 × 14.6 cm)
Without base: 7⅜ × 5½ × 5¾ in. (18.7 × 14 × 14.6 cm)
Gift of Mrs. Hobart Cale (Marion L. Davis, class of 1929)
1977.63.1

31. **Marion Greenwood** (American, 1909–1970)
Mexican Workers, early preliminary drawing for a section of
her fresco *The Industrialization of the Countryside*, Mercado
Abelardo L. Rodríguez Civic Center, Mexico City, 1934
Black conté crayon on two joined sheets of kraft paper
Sheet: 27½ × 32 in. (69.9 × 81.3 cm)
Gift of Mrs. Patricia Ashley
1976.44.2

32. **Margaret Taylor Goss Burroughs** (American, 1917–2010)
Black Venus, 1957
Linoleum cut on Japanese paper
Block: 14 × 11 in. (35.5 × 28 cm)
Sheet: 18½ × 12½ in. (47 × 31.5 cm)
Purchase, Betsy Mudge Wilson, class of 1956, Memorial Fund
2020.11

DOCUMENTARY PHOTOGRAPHS: INTO THE STREETS
33. **Jessie Tarbox Beals** (American, b. Canada 1871–1942)
Nurse Attending to Ill Women at Home, ca. 1914
Gelatin silver print
Sheet: 7⅝ × 9¹³⁄₁₆ in. (19.4 × 24.9 cm)
Mount: 10⁹⁄₁₆ × 13¾ in. (26.9 × 34.9 cm)
Gift from the Michael and Joyce Axelrod collection (Joyce
Jacobson, class of 1961)
2011.29.3

34. **Edith Suschitzky Tudor-Hart** (Austrian, 1908–1973, active in
Great Britain)
Women making sandbags, London, 1939
Gelatin silver print
Sheet: 7⁷⁄₁₆ × 9½ in. (18.9 × 24.1 cm)
Gift from the Michael and Joyce Axelrod collection (Joyce
Jacobson, class of 1961) in memory of Cathy Picard Rosen
2010.16.8

35. **Margaret Bourke-White** (American, 1904–1971)
Mechanical Grading of Exams, 1947
Gelatin silver print
Sheet: 13⅝ × 10⅜ in. (34.5 × 26.4 cm)
Gift from the Michael and Joyce Axelrod collection (Joyce
Jacobson, class of 1961) in honor of Howard Greenberg
2003.49.5

36. **Dorothy Meigs Eidlitz** (American, 1891–1976)
Escort, not later than 1947
Gelatin silver print
Sheet: 14 × 18¾ in. (35.5 × 47.7 cm)
Gift of the artist, class of 1914
1976.16.2

37. **Rosalie Thorne McKenna** (American, 1918–2003)
Woman Crossing the Street, Mississippi, 1954
Gelatin silver print
Image: 13¼ × 10⅞ in. (33.7 × 27.6 cm)
Sheet: 14⁵⁄₁₆ × 18⅞ in. (36.3 × 48 cm)
Gift of the artist, class of 1940
1987.53.86

38. **Rosalie Thorne McKenna** (American, 1918–2003)
Black Girl on Chair, Florida, 1957
Gelatin silver print
Image: 10½ × 9⅝ in. (26.7 × 24.5 cm)
Sheet: 13¼ × 10⅛ in. (33.7 × 25.7 cm)
Gift of the artist, class of 1940
1987.53.83

39. **Diane Arbus** (American, 1923–1971)

A young Brooklyn family going for a Sunday outing, N.Y.C. 1966

Gelatin silver print

Image: 15⁵⁄₁₆ × 15⁵⁄₁₆ in. (38.9 × 38.9 cm)

Sheet: 20 × 16⅛ in. (50.9 × 41 cm)

Purchase, Louise Woodruff Johnston, class of 1922, Fund

1974.21.7

Selected Bibliography

Compiled by Anna Molloy, class of 2023, and Breanna Piercy, class of 2021

Balducci, Temma, and Heather Belnap Jensen, eds. *Women, Femininity, and Public Space in European Visual Culture, 1789–1914*. London: Routledge, 2017.

Beaulieu, Elizabeth Ann. *Writing African American Women*. 2 vols. Westport, Conn.: Greenwood Press, 2006.

Bigwood, Carol. *Earth Muse: Feminism, Nature, and Art*. Philadelphia: Temple University Press, 1993.

Birnbaum, Paula J., ed. *Women Artists in Interwar France: Framing Femininities*. London: Routledge, 2016.

Booker, Margaret Moore. *Among the Stars: The Life of Maria Mitchell*. Nantucket, Mass.: Mill Hill Press, 2007.

Borzello, Frances. *Seeing Ourselves*. London: Thames and Hudson, 1998.

———. *A World of Our Own*. New York: Watson-Guptill Publications, 2000.

Broude, Norma, and Mary D. Garrard, eds. *The Expanding Discourse: Feminism and Art History*. New York: Icon Editions, 1992.

———, eds. *Reclaiming Female Agency: Feminist Art History after Postmodernism*. Berkeley: University of California Press, 2005.

Cahill, Thomas. *Mysteries of the Middle Ages: The Rise of Feminism, Science, and Art from the Cults of Catholic Europe*. New York: N. A. Talese, 2006.

Chadwick, Whitney. *Women, Art, and Society*. London: Thames and Hudson, 2012.

Cheney, Liana de Girolami, Alicia Craig Faxon, and Kathleen Lucey Russo. *Self-Portraits by Women Painters*. Aldershot, England: Ashgate, 2000.

Clark, Linda L. *Women and Achievement in Nineteenth-Century Europe*. Cambridge: Cambridge University Press, 2008.

Cohen, Michèle. "'To think, to compare, to combine, to methodise': Girls' Education in Enlightenment Britain." In *Women, Gender, and Enlightenment*, edited by Sarah Knott and Barbara Taylor, 224–42. New York: Palgrave Macmillan, 2005.

Dabbs, Julia K. *Life Stories of Women Artists, 1550–1800: An Anthology*. Farnham, Surrey, and Burlington, Vt.: Ashgate Publishing, 2009.

Fahlman, Betsy. "The Art Spirit in the Classroom, Educating the Modern Woman Artist." In Wardle, *American Women Modernists*, 93–115.

Farrington, Lisa E. *Creating Their Own Image: The History of African-American Women Artists*. New York: Oxford University Press, 2005.

Fine, Elsa Honig. *Women and Art*. Montclair, N.J.: Allanheld and Schram/Prior, 1978.

The Frances Lehman Loeb Art Center, Vassar College: The History and the Collection. Munich: Prestel, 2007.

Frederickson, Kristen, and Sarah E. Webb, eds. *Singular Women: Writing the Artist*. Berkeley: University of California Press, 2003.

Gómez, Leticia Ruiz. *A Tale of Two Women Painters: Sofonisba Anguissola and Lavinia Fontana*. Translated by Jenny Dodman. Madrid: Museo del Prado Ediciones, 2019.

Greer, Germaine. *The Obstacle Race*. New York: Farrar, Straus, and Giroux, 1979.

Harris, Ann Sutherland, and Linda Nochlin. *Women Artists: 1550–1950*. Los Angeles: Los Angeles County Museum of Art, 1976.

Hemingway, Andrew. *Artists on the Left*. New Haven: Yale University Press, 2002.

King, Margaret L. *Women of the Renaissance*. Chicago: The University of Chicago Press, 1991.

Kitch, Carolyn. *The Girl on the Magazine Cover*. Chapel Hill: The University of North Carolina Press, 2001.

Kleeblatt, Norman L., and Susan Chevlowe, eds. *Painting a Place in America: Jewish Artists in New York 1900–1945*. New York: The Jewish Museum, 1991.

Langa, Helen. "Bold Gazes, Lively Differences: Women Printmakers' Images of Women." In Seaton, *Paths to the Press*, 50–63.

Marling, Karal Ann, and Helen A. Harrison. *7 American Women: The Depression Decade*. Poughkeepsie, N.Y.: Vassar College Art Gallery, 1976.

Mathews, Nancy Mowll. "Training and Professionalism, 19th and 20th Centuries: North America, 19th century, USA." In *Dictionary of Women Artists*, vol. 1, edited by Delia Gaze, 132–36. London: Fitzroy Dearborn Publishers, 1997.

McCusker, Carol, ed. *Breaking the Frame: Pioneering Women in Photojournalism*. San Diego, Calif.: Museum of Photographic Arts, 2006.

Miglietti, Francesca Alfano, ed. *Through Women's Eyes: From Diane Arbus to Letizia Battaglia; Passion and Courage*. Translated by Jeffrey Jennings. Venice: Tre Oci, 2015.

Munro, Eleanor. *Originals: American Women Artists*. New York: Simon and Schuster, 1979.

Newell, Aimee E. *A Stitch in Time: The Needlework of Aging Women in Antebellum America*. Athens: The Ohio University Press, 2014.

Nochlin, Linda. *Realism Now*. Poughkeepsie, N.Y.: Vassar College Art Gallery, 1968.

———. "Starting from Scratch: Linda Nochlin Traces the Beginnings of Feminist Art History." *Women's Art Magazine* 61 (November–December 1994): 6–11.

Park, Marlene. "Lynching and Antilynching: Art and Politics in the 1930s." *Prospects* 18 (1993): 311–65.

Patterson, Martha H., ed. *The American New Woman Revisited*. New Brunswick, N.J.: Rutgers University Press, 2008.

Peintres femmes, 1780–1830: Naissance d'un combat. Paris: Musée du Luxembourg, 2021.

Phagan, Patricia, ed. *The American Scene and the South: Paintings and Works on Paper, 1930–1946*. Athens: Georgia Museum of Art, University of Georgia, 1996.

Phagan, Patricia, and Peter van Alfen, eds. *The Art of Devastation: Medals and Posters of the Great War*. Poughkeepsie, N.Y.: Frances Lehman Loeb Art Center, 2017.

Piland, Sherry. *Women Artists: An Historical, Contemporary, and Feminist Bibliography*. 2nd ed. Metuchen, N.J., and London: The Scarecrow Press, Inc., 1994.

Pollock, Griselda. *Vision and Difference: Femininity, Feminism, and the Histories of Art*. London: Routledge, 1988.

Reckitt, Helena, ed. *Art and Feminism*. London: Phaidon, 2001.

———, ed. *The Art of Feminism: Images that Shaped the Fight for Equality, 1857–2017*. San Francisco: Chronicle Books, 2018.

Reilly, Maura, ed. *Women Artists: The Linda Nochlin Reader*. New York: Thames and Hudson, 2015.

Ring, Betty. *Girlhood Embroidery: American Samplers and Pictorial Needlework, 1650–1850*. 2 vols. New York: Alfred A. Knopf, 1993.

Seaton, Elizabeth G., ed. *Paths to the Press: Printmaking and American Women Artists, 1910–1960*. Manhattan, Kans.: Marianna Kistler Beach Museum of Art, Kansas State University, 2006.

Slatkin, Wendy. *Women Artists in History*. 4th ed. Upper Saddle River, N.J.: Prentice Hall, 2001.

Sloan, Kim. *"A Noble Art": Amateur Artists and Drawing Masters, c. 1600–1800*. London: British Museum Press, 2000.

Sund, Judy. "Columbus and Columbia, Man of Genius Meets Generic Woman, Chicago, 1893." In *Critical Issues in American Art: A Book of Readings*, edited by Mary Ann Calo, 221–42. Boulder: Westview Press, 1998.

Tague, Ingrid H. *Women of Quality: Accepting and Contesting Ideals of Femininity in England, 1690–1760*. Woodbridge, Suffolk: The Boydell Press, 2002.

Tinagli, Paola, and Mary Rogers, eds. *Women and the Visual Arts in Italy, c. 1400–1650*. Manchester: Manchester University Press, 2012.

Todd, Ellen Wiley. *The "New Woman" Revised*. Berkeley: University of California Press, 1993.

"A Transcript of a Recorded Conversation Between Linda Nochlin and Molly Nesbit in New York City, Jan. 28, 2011." *Vassar 150*. http://150.vassar.edu/histories/art/nochlin.html.

Treves, Letizia, ed. *Artemisia*. London: National Gallery, 2020.

Wardle, Marian, ed. *American Women Modernists: The Legacy of Robert Henri, 1910–1945*. Provo, Utah: Brigham Young University Museum of Art, 2003.

Wayne, Tiffany K. *Women's Roles in Nineteenth-Century America*. Westport, Conn.: Greenwood Press, 2007.

Witzling, Mara R., ed. *Voicing Our Visions*. New York: Universe, 1991.

This publication accompanies the exhibition *Women Picturing Women: From Personal Spaces to Public Ventures* at the Frances Lehman Loeb Art Center, Vassar College, Poughkeepsie, New York, from February 6 to June 13, 2021. The exhibition is organized by the Frances Lehman Loeb Art Center.

All works in the exhibition are in the collection of the Frances Lehman Loeb Art Center.

The publication and exhibition benefit from the generous support of donors to the Friends of the Frances Lehman Loeb Art Center Exhibition Fund.

Library of Congress Cataloging-in-Publication Data
Names: Phagan, Patricia (Patricia Elaine), author. | Vassar College. Frances Lehman Loeb Art Center, organizer, host institution.
Title: Women picturing women : from personal spaces to public ventures / Patricia Phagan.
Description: Poughkeepsie, New York : The Frances Lehman Loeb Art Center, Vassar College, [2021] | "This publication accompanies the exhibition Women Picturing Women: From Personal Spaces to Public Ventures at the Frances Lehman Loeb Art Center, Vassar College, Poughkeepsie, New York, from February 6 to June 13, 2021"—Colophon. | Includes bibliographical references.
Identifiers: LCCN 2021007456 | ISBN 9781646570218 (hardcover)
Subjects: LCSH: Women in art—Exhibitions. | Women artists—Exhibitions. | Vassar College—Art patronage—Exhibitions.
Classification: LCC N7629.P68 F737 2021 | DDC 700.82—dc23
LC record available at https://lccn.loc.gov/2021007456

Published by the Frances Lehman Loeb Art Center, Vassar College
www.fllac.vassar.edu

For the Frances Lehman Loeb Art Center:
Project Manager: Patricia Phagan

Distributed by ARTBOOK | D.A.P.
75 Broad Street, Suite 630
New York, NY 10004
www.artbook.com

Produced by Lucia | Marquand, Seattle
www.luciamarquand.com

For Lucia | Marquand:
Copy edited by Susan Higman Larsen
Designed by Meghann Ney
Rights permissions acquired by Gina Broze
Typeset in Karmina Sans by Maggie Lee
Proofread by Ivy Long
Color management by iocolor, Seattle
Printed and bound in China by Artron Art Group
All measurements are in inches and centimeters, height precedes width.

Front cover: cat. 4
Back cover, inside: cat. 10 (detail)
Frontispiece: cat. 3 (detail)
P. 4: cat. 9 (detail); p. 7: cat. 6 (detail); p. 11: cat. 35 (detail); p. 18: cat. 10 (detail); p. 28: cat. 1 (detail); p. 56: cat. 12 (detail); p. 73: cat. 18 (detail); p. 75: cat. 19 (detail); p. 81: cat. 20 (detail); p. 91: cat. 25 (detail); p. 92: cat. 26 (detail); p. 114: cat. 33 (detail); p. 125: cat. 36 (detail)